MURDER
—— AT ——
TEAL'S
POND

OTHER TITLES BY DAVID BUSHMAN

Conversations with Mark Frost: Twin Peaks, Hill Street Blues, and the Education of a Writer

Twin Peaks FAQ: All That's Left to Know About a Place Both Wonderful and Strange

Buffy the Vampire Slayer FAQ: All That's Left to Know About Sunnydale's Slayer of Vampires, Demons, and Other Forces of Darkness

MURDER
—— AT ——
TEAL'S
POND

DAVID BUSHMAN
& MARK T. GIVENS

FOREWORD BY **MARK FROST**, CO-CREATOR OF **TWIN PEAKS**

Published by Thomas & Mercer, Seattle

www.apub.com

Amazon, the Amazon logo, and Thomas & Mercer are trademarks of Amazon.com, Inc., or its affiliates.

ISBN-13: 9781542026437 (hardcover)
ISBN-10: 1542026431 (hardcover)
ISBN-13: 9781542026420 (paperback)
ISBN-10: 1542026423 (paperback)

Cover design by Faceout Studio, Jeff Miller

Printed in the United States of America

First edition

For Betty Calhoun, storyteller.

Contents

FOREWORD

What's the first "ghost story" you remember? One that left marks, if not scars. That gripped you with the singular chill of mortality introducing itself.

Mine came by way of my maternal grandmother—one for whom the words *colorful* and *strange* don't begin to do justice—a more than apt stand-in for the archetype of the crone, one of mythology's eternal guides to the underworld. The former head of the WPA's music division and a charter member of the OSS in London during WWII, Betty Lawson Calhoun was brilliant, complicated, and an inveterate fabulist.

Her family were city folks, her father an accomplished engineer and professor at Rensselaer Polytechnic Institute in Troy, New York, a then-thriving industrial hub just upriver from Albany. When the Spanish flu pandemic devastated the country in 1918, Thomas Lawson decided to move his wife and two young daughters to the country. On a rustic, rugged, heavily wooded plateau twenty miles to the southeast, near the shores of an idyllic, arrowheaded alpine lake, he bought a decaying eighteenth-century farmhouse. He transformed it into a substantial ten-room home, bought up most of the raw acreage around the shoreline, built roads and a windmill, selling lots or cabins to friends and colleagues, soon creating a lively, upper-middle-class summer retreat community.

Life for the fortunate families on the shores of that lake changed forever and for good. For the mountain folk surrounding them, who'd been living in isolation on that plateau for seven generations, little changed. They worked for the newcomers but kept their distance, eking out a hardscrabble living from the land, logging, making charcoal and, during Prohibition, moonshine. Two different worlds.

Legends abounded. These mountain families, nine of them in particular, were said to be descendants of Hessian mercenaries, deserters from the British Army during the American Revolution, drawn to this area for its resemblance to their ancestral Black Forest. The one the Brothers Grimm made famous as the source of all that's sinister. A more local talent, Washington Irving, captured the same eerie mood of these Upstate woods, hills, and ponds, where the indifferent savagery of nature infected those who dared intrude and try to tame it. Whenever thunder rattled the panes, Betty always referenced the local lore; it was the sound of Rip van Winkle's eerie Dutchmen, bowling ninepins in their mountain lair.

When we were youngsters, the locals were presented to us as peasants out of Russian literature: colorful, dim, loyal, with an edge of uncivilized danger. A more prosaic explanation, learned later, is that two centuries of deprivation, ignorance, intermarriage, alcoholism, madness, and incest yielded little but pain and tragedy. We heard constant whispers of terrible things that happened "up the mountain" and met many of these folks throughout childhood. A few chilled me to the bone; let's just say, when I later saw the movie, the locals in *Deliverance* seemed familiar to me.

So, to Betty's ghost story: two local laborers, hill folk, staggering back up the mountain after a payday pub crawl in town—a weekly ritual—encounter something uncanny.

Full moon. Clear, still night, early fall, with a whisper of winter in the air. As the men approach a small cow pond on the right, a desperate, loud, lowing moan fills them with fear. And then, hovering above the water in the moonlight, a glowing apparition that in their pickled minds assumes the shape of a struggling human form. The two drunks sprint home in terror, instantly sober, pledging to reform their ways.

Our eyes were like saucers. We drove by that cow pond every day on our way up and down the mountain. Haunted? Damn.

And then, with a cackle, Betty revealed that the next day a nearby farmer discovered one of his Guernseys had wandered off and gotten stuck in the shallows.

So I ask, innocently, why did they think it was a ghost in the first place?

Oh. Ten years earlier the body of a young woman, a murder victim, had been found floating in that pond. Betty offers this as a throwaway, a punch line, the end.

I didn't take it that way. A real person died in that water. She never mentioned a name and, when pressed, remembered no details. As time passed, without knowing a single fact about this young woman—or if this story was entirely invented—the image of that poor, forgotten soul lodged in a corner of my mind.

Two years later in California, that feeling hit much closer to my life. While away at boarding school in Canada, a girl I knew well—Susan Freschi, fourteen, daughter of my father's boss and sister to one of my best friends—was assaulted and killed by a deranged young man. As time passed, and I learned more about the pervasive threat of sexual violence that women face on an everyday basis, these two dreadful events coalesced in my mind.

Twenty-five years later these conflated memories found fictional life as Laura Palmer. Or rather, Laura Palmer became a way to explore and explain what might have happened to that lost girl in the pond.

After *Twin Peaks* went off the air, I bought a place on that lake myself and began spending summers there for the first time in decades. It turned out a fellow I'd known since childhood, John Walsh, a local jack-of-all-trades and one of the hill folk—his grandfather had worked for my great-grandfather and Betty—had been equally obsessed with this story and for years had been digging to learn more.

She was real. She had a name. Twenty-year-old Hazel Drew—beautiful, blonde, and connected to a number of powerful men—died in that pond one hot July night in 1908. She was a local girl who'd moved to the city, encountered a new way of life, and got caught up in the fast lane. Her story became a regional and then a national scandal. Even Betty's tall tale of the two drunks, ten years later, mistaking a lost calf for Hazel's ghost, turned out to be true.

David Bushman, a *Variety* editor when we first met in the nineties, emailed me a few years ago. He'd caught wind of this story—I'd made a passing reference to it in an interview—and he and his writing partner, Mark Givens, wanted to dig in and investigate. I offered my blessings and a few leads to follow, including my old childhood friend from up the mountain.

What they've produced here is a meticulous reconstruction of a sensational, forgotten crime, the investigation that followed, and its aftermath on the Capital region—over a century later—all rendered as gripping and immediate as an episode of *Law and Order: SVU*. It is also a relentless search for answers and justice, not only for Hazel Drew but for all the women who continue to fall victim to this monstrous plague of violence. It is, we now know, a crime as old as time.

I think of her whenever I pass Teal's Pond. The ripples this murder created in that still water have continued to radiate around the world for a hundred years. For all of our Hazels and Susans and Lauras, this book is a monument of remembrance to their lost and stolen lives.

Mark Frost, cocreator of *Twin Peaks*

DRAMATIS PERSONAE

The Victim

Hazel Irene Drew: twenty-year-old Troy woman whose body is found floating in Teal's Pond on July 11, 1908

The Detectives

Duncan C. Kaye: Rensselaer County detective and the district attorney's right-hand man; Republican foot soldier and alleged sympathizer of the anti-Catholic American Protective Association

John W. Lawrenson: Troy police detective assigned to the case

John H. Murnane: Rensselaer County detective who was partnered with Lawrenson and focused on Troy

Jarvis P. O'Brien: Rensselaer County district attorney, in charge of the investigation; Republican Party stalwart

William P. Powers: Rensselaer County detective who focused on Sand Lake; also active in the Republican Party

Louis Unser: Troy police detective who worked the countryside with Powers

The Doctors

Dr. Elias B. Boyce: Sand Lake local who was first doctor on the scene; helped with the autopsy, and insisted Hazel was strangled

Dr. Harry O. Fairweather: Troy doctor who assisted in autopsy; vocal opponent of strangulation theory

Dr. Elmer E. Reichard: Sand Lake physician who assisted in autopsy

Morris H. Strope: Rensselaer County coroner

The Family

John Drew: Hazel's father; heavy drinker who couldn't hold a steady job

Joseph H. Drew: Hazel's older brother

Julia A. Drew: Hazel's mother, disabled by a childhood bout with polio; reporters remarked on her cold demeanor and strange behavior, including consulting a psychic during the investigation

William "Willie" M. Drew: Hazel's younger brother

Eva Lapp Drew: Hazel's sister-in-law (married to Joseph Drew) and confidant

Minnie Taylor: Hazel's maternal aunt and possibly her closest confidant; a quirky woman who, detectives were convinced, knew more than she was sharing

William Taylor: Hazel's maternal uncle and owner of a farm near Teal's Pond; a sullen man whose eccentricities and apparent indifference to his niece's death befuddled investigators

The Employers

Edward R. and Mary L. Cary: Rensselaer Polytechnic Institute professor and Troy city engineer, and his wife; Hazel's final employers

Thomas W. and Nellie M. Hislop: former city treasurer of Troy and his wife—Hazel's first employers; Thomas's political career was tarnished by a financial scandal that was brewing while Hazel worked for him

John H. and Adelaide Tupper: wealthy coal merchant and his wife; Hazel's second employers

The Friends

Amelia Huntley: Hazel's Watervliet friend who, according to one report, claimed to have seen her on July 6

Mina and Frank Jones: Mina was one of Hazel's closest friends; the Joneses moved from Troy to Providence and then to Maine

Sarah Moran: a Watervliet friend who said she did not see Hazel on July 6

Ida Rowe: another Watervliet friend who said she did not see Hazel on July 6

Carrie A. Weaver: one of Hazel's closest friends, who worked as a domestic servant for the Greenes, friends of the Carys

The Country

John Abel: liveryman who claimed to have driven Hazel to William Taylor's farm in the spring, despite Taylor's denial

Mabel Brown: Crooked Lake hotelier who told of being visited by women from the Alps camp

Peter Cipperly: farmer who reported seeing a woman resembling Hazel on an Averill Park–bound trolley on July 7

Minnie Clifford: former caretaker at Alps camp who reported hearing a scream coming from the camp on either the night of the murder or the night before

Christopher Crape: Averill Park hotelier who reported a strange automobile in the vicinity of Teal's Pond on what may have been the night of the murder

Lawrence Gruber: teenage camper who discovered Hazel's body

Rudolph Gundrum: Taborton charcoal burner who was one of the last people to see Hazel Drew alive on Taborton Road the evening of July 7

William and Elizabeth Hoffay: Taborton farmers who reported seeing two men and a wagon on Taborton Road on July 7

Aurilla E. Horton: Averill Park woman who believed she saw Hazel walking at the bottom of Taborton Mountain on evening of July 6

Alexander and Henry E. Kramrath: Albany brothers who owned the Alps camp, reportedly the site of wild sex parties

Willis D. Larkin: proprietor of Larkin Brothers Funeral Home in Sand Lake, where Hazel's autopsy was conducted

Ebenezer Martin: Sand Lake justice of the peace who was one of the first officials at the scene of the crime

Gilbert Miller: Taborton resident who notified authorities of the body's discovery

Charles Rankie: Taborton farmer who claimed to have seen a man at the pond on recent Sundays matching description provided by the Hoffays

Frank and Frederika Richmond: William Taylor's farmhands, who lived at the Taylor farm but could not provide him with an alibi. Note: Frederika's name was spelled various ways in contemporaneous newspaper reports.

Henry and Charlotte Rollman: Taborton residents who reported seeing Hazel Drew on Taborton Road on July 7

Julia and Henry Rymiller: Taborton residents who drove on Taborton Road on July 7 but didn't see Hazel

Frank Smith: young Taborton farmhand said to be infatuated with Hazel; dismissed by neighbors as a "half-wit," he was one of the last people to see Hazel alive; his antics and inconsistent testimony during the investigation infuriated detectives

John Smith: Frank Smith's father, who informed William Taylor that the body in the pond was likely Hazel

Libbie Sowalskie: Taborton farmer with whom Willie Drew was boarding at the time of the murder

Tom Sowalskie: Libbie's hulking son, rumored to have violent tendencies that included torturing animals

Conrad "Coon" Teal: Taborton farmer who owned the pond in which Hazel's body was found

George White: camper from Averill Park who helped retrieve the body from the pond

Marie Yeabauer: Taborton resident who drove on Taborton Road on July 7 but didn't see Hazel. Note: Yeabauer was spelled various ways in contemporaneous newspaper reports.

The City

Adelbert Atwood: parcel clerk at Union Station in Troy who would play an innocent but crucial role in the investigation

William and Florence Barker: cuff-and-collar manufacturer and his wife who lived across from the Carys on Whitman Court

Thomas Carey: Troy fireman who saw Hazel walking on the street on July 7

William Cushing: Troy bartender and Republican county committee-man who admitted to driving a rig out to Sand Lake on July 7 but claimed he wasn't near Teal's Pond

Lawrence Eagan: grocery store employee who first said he saw Hazel on July 6, then said he wasn't sure

Arthur and Mary Greene: Rensselaer Polytechnic Institute professor and his wife; employers of Hazel's friend Carrie Weaver

George B. Harrison: wealthy businessman and employer of Hazel's aunt Minnie Taylor

Edward J. Knauff: Hazel's onetime dentist

Anna LaBelle: sales clerk at Frear's department store who knew Hazel— exactly how well became a matter of some dispute

Samuel LeRoy: Troy train conductor suspected of involvement in the murder

John E. Magner: train conductor suspected of meeting with Hazel at Union Station

Jeanette Marcellus: Hazel's friend who saw her at Union Station on July 6

Henrietta Robertson: mother of Hazel's friend Lillian; saw Hazel at Union Station on July 6

Fred W. Schatzle: Troy embalmer who helped his friend William Cushing rent a rig on July 7

Mary Schumaker: Hazel's seamstress

William Shyne: proprietor of Shyne's Horse Mart, a Troy livery that played a key role in the investigation into Hazel's death

The Admirers

Harry (last name unknown): author of a letter to Hazel signed "Knight of the Napp Kinn and Your Artist Friend," in which he apologized for possibly bruising her wrists

William C. Hogardt: Dedham, Massachusetts, man who called Hazel "one of his most intimate friends"

Edward Lavoie: former sweetheart of Hazel; detectives found a news clipping about him in Hazel's possessions

F. W. Schlafflin: meat-packer who met Hazel three years earlier and whose photo was found among her possessions

The Press

William M. Clemens: reporter/"criminologist" who covered the investigation into Hazel's murder for the *World*, annoying detectives and his peers in the press with his unsubstantiated and sensational reports

Louis H. Howe and John Kelly: reporters who found Hazel's glasses

Harold D. Neach: *Troy Standard* journalist who was said to be a passenger in a car that zoomed past Crape's Hotel on its way up Taborton Mountain

INTRODUCTION

So death, the most terrifying of ills, is nothing to us, since
so long as we exist, death is not with us; but when death comes,
then we do not exist.

—Epicurus

Welcome to the town of Sand Lake, New York, population 8,425: a
beatific, pastoral town nestled in the south-central corner of Rensselaer
County, about thirteen miles east of Albany, the state capital. On the
town's outskirts, deep within the woody terrain, lies the neighborhood
of Taborton, named after Mount Tabor in Lower Galilee, Israel, which
is where, according to the New Testament, the transfiguration of Jesus
occurred; he radiated with light and conversed with the great prophets
Moses and Elijah.

Taborton Road, the main route in and out, twists and turns for
eight and a half miles from the bottom of Taborton Mountain, at the
so-called Four Corners of Sand Lake, up past the Kipple (a variation
of the German word *gipfel*, meaning "summit," about 1,850 feet above
sea level), past Big and Little Bowman Ponds, and, finally, on to the
eastern tip of the mountain, where you arrive at a crossroads: turn left
and you're bound for East Poestenkill or Berlin; turn right and your
destination is Cherry Plain.

It's a lonely stretch of woods with acres and acres of trees, vegetation, and wildlife—you can walk for miles without ever encountering another person.

A lonely stretch of *haunted* woods, some might say. Folklorist Harold W. Thompson wrote in *Body, Boots & Britches: Folktales, Ballads and Speech from Country New York* of a Taborton farmer who had encountered a series of curious incidents in his barn: the tail and mane of one of his horses had been inexplicably braided; and the animal was so fatigued that the farmer was convinced someone had taken it out driving all night. Late at night, he checked in on the horse and discovered a strange black cat perched upon its back. Determined to frighten the cat away, he stabbed the feline in the back with a three-tined pitchfork. The following morning, the farmer's mother—rumored by many in the woods to be a witch—was so ill that she was unable to rise from bed, but then the horse's braiding abruptly unraveled, and the animal regained its vigor. Three days later, a doctor, examining the farmer's mother, discovered three deep wounds in her back.

This sometimes charming, sometimes eerie little town is where Hazel Drew perished, and where our journey began.

Technically, our journey began in 2013 at a retrospective tribute to the television series *Twin Peaks* at the University of Southern California in Los Angeles. Mark Frost, who cocreated the show with David Lynch, commented that his own inspiration for the series—although not Lynch's—was an unsolved murder from the early 1900s in Upstate New York, where he and his family would spend summers at the home of his maternal grandmother, Betty Calhoun. Betty would regale Mark and his brother, Scott (who also wrote for *Twin Peaks* and is the author of the companion book *The Autobiography of F.B.I. Special Agent Dale Cooper: My Life, My Tapes*), with stories, many of them embellished—if not outright fabricated—including one about the murder of a young woman in the woods around the turn of the twentieth century that had never been solved. According to Betty, the ghost of the victim, whose body was discovered in a pond, still lingered in the woods, waiting for her slayer to be publicly exposed.

As Mark would later recall: "She would tell us all sorts of fantastic stories about life on the mountain, and one that really caught my ear was when she was a young girl she'd been told a story, something along the lines of a guy who had gone down to a tavern, kind of gotten a toot on, and was walking his way back up the mountain late at night, and he heard what he thought were the moans of a ghost. He saw something white flashing in the moonlight and scuttled home in terror."

Mark couldn't be sure, but he believed the woman's name was Hazel Grey.

We have both long been obsessed with *Twin Peaks*. One of us (Mark) hosts a podcast about it, titled *Deer Meadow Radio* (https:// deermeadowradio.libsyn.com); the other (David) has authored articles, essays, and books about it. We both also love a good mystery.

We were going to solve the murder of Hazel Grey!

Except there was no Hazel Grey. And "Upstate New York" wasn't much of a clue (or *clew*, as it was spelled back then).

There was, however, a Hazel *Drew*, slain in the woods of Sand Lake, New York, in the summer of 1908. Her murderer was never identified or apprehended.

We were on our way.

⌒

We first visited Sand Lake in 2016 after connecting with town historian Bob Moore, a friendly, snowy-haired man with spectacles who looks exactly like the middle school history and social studies teacher he used to be. Bob showed us vintage postcards, guided us on tours, answered countless emails and phone calls, even fed us seafood chowder and offered up a spare bedroom.

On our behalf, Bob consulted a psychic, who told him maybe he was so obsessed with the case because he was a reincarnated iteration of the murderer. (We kept our eye on Bob for a while after that and made a note never to have him return to that psychic.)

Most importantly, he organized a community: a group of people—some lifelong residents of Taborton, others descendants of people involved in the case, still others simply interested locals—who, over the course of the next four-plus years, would become our Baker Street Irregulars. They shared their knowledge of, and insights into, the region and assisted us as we tracked down clues. (We even roped in a former FBI agent—not Dale Cooper—to help with the probe, but he disappeared somewhere along the way; we still don't know what happened to him.)

Chills crawled down our spines as descendants and family members of crucial figures in the case shared firsthand recollections of their ancestors, such as the grandchildren of Hazel's cousin Etta Becker, who spent the July Fourth weekend with her in 1908, less than forty-eight hours before her death. Unfortunately, whatever they talked about during those final conversations never shook that far down the family tree.

We learned, among other things, that the Taborton woods may or may not be haunted by otherworldly spirits, but they almost certainly hosted feverish anti-Catholic meetings of the Ku Klux Klan–like American Protective Association inside their caves, not far from where local youngsters erected treehouses and teenagers trysted away from the eyes of their parents.

We heard a long-standing rumor among locals that three influential townspeople—a doctor, a lawyer, and an undertaker—had played a role in Hazel's death and the ensuing cover-up, though none of the three has ever been definitively identified. In Sand Lake rumors were easier to track down than actual names.

We hit roadblocks—plenty of them. There's nothing easy about investigating a 113-year-old cold case. Bob Moore tried valiantly to pry records from the Larkin Brothers Funeral Home, where Hazel's autopsy was performed, but all we wound up with was an entry in a logbook. We located a photo of a very young Hazel Drew with her mother but couldn't persuade the family to share it. We searched high and low for the county's investigative records; turns out they were likely shipped off for storage and destroyed in a flood. Nothing remains—no paper records, no physical artifacts, no physical evidence whatsoever. One afternoon, the Rensselaer County clerk dropped a huge box of coroner reports on our laps, including parchments from as far back as the 1870s. Anything from 1908? Of course not.

Most devastatingly, we lost one of our "amateur sleuths," lifelong Taborton resident John Walsh, who passed away on October 11, 2019, at the age of fifty-five. It was Walsh who had first helped Mark Frost research the case, decades earlier, while Mark was developing *Twin Peaks*.

We came *very* close—we briefly thought—to blowing the case wide open with the discovery that Anna LaBelle, who worked at Frear's department store in Troy and knew Hazel Drew (the extent of their friendship remains a mystery), shared a name with a small-time madam in Troy (alias: Alice Davis) who was active in the city's red-light district, known as the Line. This Anna LaBelle, the madam, left her estate, valued at about twenty-six thousand dollars, to Abbott Jones, a powerful Troy lawyer who defended gangster Jack "Legs" Diamond in 1931 against charges of kidnapping and assault (never mind that he was gunned down the day after his acquittal following a romp in the sack with his mistress). Jones was elected district attorney of Rensselaer County shortly after the Hazel Drew murder, defeating Jarvis O'Brien, who had led the investigation.

Were the two Anna LaBelles one and the same? If so, did it have any bearing on the Hazel Drew investigation?

Question two became irrelevant once we discovered the answer to question one: there was no connection between the two Anna LaBelles.

So *that's* what it felt like for the detectives trying to crack the case in 1908.

That lead came courtesy of Mark Marshall, a retired Averill Park school messenger who ran point for us on the ground in Sand Lake and is responsible for many of the ideas and revelations that follow. Mark grew up in Griswold Heights, a housing project on the east side of Troy, about six blocks from where Hazel Drew last lived; his current neighborhood, in East Poestenkill, still houses the remains of the church that the Drew family attended. Soon we were calling him "the Detective."

If Mark Marshall and Bob Moore had been around in 1908, the murder of Hazel Drew would have been solved.

⁓

Hazel Drew was killed in Taborton but lived in Troy, about ten and a half miles northwest of Sand Lake. We soon discovered this was really a tale of two cities (technically one town and one city). Six years ago we hardly knew anything about Troy; now we could write a book, except it's already been done, many times, usually by local historian Don Rittner. Who knew that Uncle Sam was the namesake of Samuel Wilson, a Troy butcher who supplied meat to the troops during the War of 1812? That "'Twas the Night Before Christmas" was first published in the *Troy Sentinel*, submitted by the daughter of a Trojan rector? President Chester Arthur grew up in Troy; Herman Melville wrote *Typee* and *Omoo* there. George Washington Gale Ferris Jr., inventor of the Ferris wheel, graduated from Troy's Rensselaer Polytechnic Institute.

There are scoundrels and ignominy, too: Mary Alice Fahey (Mame Faye) ran her ridiculously profitable prostitution business on the streets of downtown Troy (with protection from police). Jack "Legs" Diamond was acquitted in the courthouse there, and it was Troy hatter Thomas P. "Boston" Corbett who put a bullet in the head of John Wilkes Booth in a Virginia barn in 1865.

⁓

Twin Peaks brought us here, and it is to *Twin Peaks* that we now return.

Similarities between the Hazel Drew murder and the TV series poked at us, relentlessly. Sand Lake, we found out, has twin peaks of its own: Perigo Hill, in the northeast corner of the town, and Oak Hill, near the center, each rising to an elevation of nine hundred feet. The eastern part of the town, including Taborton, is rich with woods, evoking the anagogic Ghostwood of *Twin Peaks*. Laura Palmer's body was discovered on the bank of a lake by lumberjack Pete Martell as he went out fishing early one morning; Hazel's in a mill pond by two young men on a weekend camping and fishing outing. Back in the day—before the denuding of the forests—lumbering was big business in Sand Lake; the mills, powered first by water and then by steam, employed over two hundred people, enriching their owners, just like Twin Peaks' Packard Mill. When the mills shut down in Sand Lake and Troy, industry moved on, and those jobs were lost for good, evoking the third season of *Twin Peaks*.

Colorful characters like Hazel's erratic parents, charcoal burner Rudolph Gundrum, "half-witted" farmhand Frank Smith, belligerent Aunt Minnie Taylor, and recalcitrant Uncle William Taylor seemed like real-life counterparts to the Log Lady, Dr. Jacoby, Major Briggs, and Sarah Palmer.

Finally, during one particularly exhilarating moment, we came across the name Thomas Lawson, who one day, many years hence, would become the maternal great-grandfather of Mark Frost, the man who had sent us on this journey in the first place. Lawson, a highly respected professor at Rensselaer Polytechnic Institute in Troy at the time, was a minor player in the story of Hazel Drew—a colleague and friend of her last employer, fellow RPI professor Edward Cary, who doubled as city engineer for a time—but even still! We admit to momentary anxiety over the discovery—neither one of us wanted to be responsible for discovering that Frost's great-grandfather was somehow implicated in the death of the woman who inspired his great-grandson's most acclaimed and enduring creation. Thankfully, neither of us had to make that phone call.

The deeper we probed, the more striking the similarities between the two women at the center of these stories—Hazel Drew and Laura Palmer—became. Both were beautiful and beguiling young women who inspired male obsession. Laura, as her psychiatrist, Dr. Jacoby, famously said, built fortresses around her secrets; Hazel, too, had secrets, and those around her either failed to penetrate them or went to their graves protecting them. In Laura's case, clues were everywhere, yet everyone in her orbit ignored them, resulting in her death. Might Hazel, too, have been saved if people had been paying closer attention?

True, Laura came from a wealthy family—her father was a successful attorney employed by the wealthiest man in town—while Hazel was of modest means at best; her father was a rapscallion who loved booze and couldn't seem to hold a job. But Hazel did leave home at an early age and would go on to interact with some of the most influential, politically wired families in town, exposing her to a lifestyle foreign from her own.

Both Laura and Hazel dreamed of escape and reinvention; in the end, fate determined otherwise.

If Hazel had been a man, or a person of wealth, might her murderer have been apprehended?

Perhaps.

Still, Hazel's murder and the ensuing investigation didn't lack for attention; rather, it became front-page fodder for newspapers across the country. Why? A working-class girl from a poor family is murdered in a remote section of woods that most people had never even heard of. *Something* about this story was obsessively compelling, drawing the attention even of famous journalists like Elizabeth Meriwether Gilmer (pen name: Dorothy Dix) and William M. Clemens.

As we continued to investigate, reasons started to suggest themselves. First, there was the political angle. Hazel's employers were powerful people. District Attorney Jarvis O'Brien was up for reelection. Rumors of wild sex parties and young women held captive against their will at a camp (or summer home) not far from the scene of her death surfaced. Allegations of secret affairs and possibly even an unwanted pregnancy were tossed around daily in newspaper articles. We started out wondering who *killed* Hazel Drew; we wound up just as immersed in another, even more rudimentary mystery: Who *was* Hazel Drew? Because almost all of the people who controlled the narrative contemporaneously—chiefly investigators and reporters—were men, the story was filtered through the male gaze, and Hazel—like Laura Palmer and her antecedent, the eponymous protagonist of the 1944 Otto Preminger film noir *Laura*—became a projection on a screen, absorbing whatever qualities or shortcomings these unreliable narrators assigned to her: woman as defined by male obsession.

As we said earlier, investigating a 113-year-old cold case wasn't easy. We do, however, believe we've uncovered the murderer, and we make a pretty strong case for the prosecution. The solution is explosive. Read on to find out who—and why.

Hazel Drew has been dead for 113 years.

Epicurus notwithstanding, Hazel is still here.

Chapter 1

MURDER AT THE POND

Dusk descends on the mountains of Taborton, though inside the woods it is already darkening. Listen and you can hear the humming of insects. The cricket frogs call to her, like marbles clicking. The night is frightfully hot and still, though she shivers as an invisible gust of heat brushes past her, bending the patchy grass on the roadside as it sputters along and dies. Watch out for water snakes, she remembers; she has seen them here before: scaly, greenish-brown serpents with round heads, button-like eyes, and slender, banded bodies—three or four feet long when fully stretched.

Am I doing the right thing? a voice in the back of her head tugs, but she manages to quash it.

The morning before last, she had woken up in the same bed as she had almost every morning for the past five months, rising to the same melodies of chirping birds and the same view of the handsome homes across Whitman Court in fashionable East Troy.

Now, all that seems a distant memory.

My peace I give unto you: not as the world giveth, give I unto you. Let not your heart be troubled, neither let it be afraid. It was a favorite verse of hers from Sunday School—so long ago now, she recalls with an odd smile as she continues up the road.

She had left her parents as a teenager and, over the past five years, lived with and worked for three different families, but she wasn't going to be a domestic servant toiling away for the elite of Troy forever, washing clothes and dishes and picking up after others' children.

She had overcome her share of obstacles in life already. She had made plans and would see them through—whatever lay ahead, she was ready for it. She was fearless. Hadn't a fortune-teller just warned her she would die a sudden death before year's end? Hadn't she simply laughed the dire prediction off?

Just then she hears a sound, a rustling in the trees. Campers? A drunken lumberjack? Probably just a deer or rabbit. She squints, peering deeper into the woods, but it is getting darker by the minute and she can't make anything out. As long as it isn't that Smith boy following her. He's a nice enough fella, but she isn't sure about the man who was with him in the buggy. She doesn't need to be dealing with that sort of thing tonight.

Many women her age would have been spooked by Taborton this time of evening. Stories abounded of the dangers in these woods. She remembers one in particular: on a cold winter night some fifty years ago, a farmer had killed his hired hand and dumped the body in that pond behind the field, where it lay hidden by dead leaves and rubbish. The following spring, when the snow had melted, a passerby had discovered it. Nobody was ever arrested for the crime, but the farmer was driven so mad by guilt that he committed suicide.

Some time back, she remembers, Bertha Nennisteil, a local girl, had been accosted on this very road by two hooligans, but she fought them off and returned home safely.

Still, Hazel isn't afraid. She knows these woods intimately, every twist and turn. Although she's been in Troy for many years now, she grew up in woods like these, not far from here, and visited often when her family lived nearby, as a refuge from all the pressures of her life.

The air smells of damp grass and rich dirt, and she inhales slowly, savoring it. What does it remind her of? Home.

She looks down at her feet with mild disgust: her beautiful Cuban heels, once a shiny patent leather, are coated now with dust and mud. She pauses to remove her black straw hat and stares briefly at the ostrich plumes. A hat, she once heard someone say, was more than an article of clothing; it was an extension of the wearer's personality. *And what does that say about me?* she wonders. She wipes at her brow with her sleeve. Her hair has dampened and matted in the heat. How many men had complimented her on her radiant blonde hair and glittering blue eyes?

The young woman chuckles to herself. "If they could see me now."

As the moon continues its ascent into the sky, she is suddenly overcome with weariness, no doubt a reaction to the hectic events of the past few days. She collects herself, clearing those thoughts from her mind, and continues to trudge up the hill. Destiny awaits her, just around the corner.

She hears the screeching of an owl, and then another rustling sound. Someone is here.

~

Saturday, July 11, 1908: It was a day like so many other days that summer in the sleepy town of Sand Lake, New York: oppressively hot. Across the state people slept in parks or on rooftops, or even on open streets, to escape the sweltering heat and humidity as temperatures soared above ninety. Reports of deaths, prostrations, and "sudden insanity" poured into police stations. In Brooklyn, New York, two men—judged to have been driven crazy by the excessive heat—tried to kill their wives with carving knives.

Situated in the middle of Rensselaer County, the little town of Sand Lake is more or less equidistant from two major Upstate New York cities, Troy and Albany, about eleven miles southeast of the former and thirteen miles east of the latter. Though small in both area (thirty-five square miles) and population (2,128), the town of Sand Lake comprised three official hamlets—Averill Park, West Sand Lake, and Sand Lake, which shared its name with the town—each with its own culture and identity.

The hamlet of Averill Park—named after wealthy lawyer and landowner Horatio F. Averill, who notoriously was run out of Troy after orchestrating the arrest of escaped Virginia slave Charles Nalle in 1860—was the hub of activity in Sand Lake. Over two hundred people—including women and children—were employed there at various water-powered mills, churning out everything from paper to woolen long johns to hosiery (Kane Mill alone produced thirty thousand pairs of hosiery a year). Other locals farmed their land, hunted, forged iron, sapped maple trees, or cut wood to earn their livelihoods.

Averill Park was known to locals as "the village" and served as the de facto center of town. The streets were dotted with mom-and-pop shops, including an ice cream parlor, pharmacy, grocery store, bakery, shoe-maker, and tailor, and hot summer nights would find residents convening with neighbors on the steps of the post office or the porches of hotels and country stores, hoping to conjure up a breeze. On Sundays, bells clanged throughout town as churches—mostly Protestant—beckoned worshippers to their spires, including the Sand Lake Baptist Church, whose Troy-manufactured bell bore the Latin inscription *Defunctos ploro* ("I mourn the dead").

Averill Park was the last stop on the Troy and New England Railway trolley line, which was the sole means of public transportation into the village. It ran eight miles between the Troy neighborhood of Albia and Averill Park and, despite the grandest of intentions, never did reach downtown Troy or New England, due to evaporating funds. During the summer, visitors from points north and south—especially Troy, Albany, and even New York City, one hundred and fifty miles to the south— poured into Averill Park for day or weekend outings, some for the entire summer. Liverymen lined up at the trolley station on Orient Avenue, waiting to drive them to their hotels or summer homes. Hotels sprouted up like trees in a forest, and demand was so great during July and August that the establishments were often booked to capacity. They'd host nightly dances, concerts, card games, and other social gatherings for guests. The Maple Grove Hotel even had its own regional baseball team, made up solely of hotel guests.

Nearby Crooked Lake had been a favorite haunt of President Theodore Roosevelt when he was governor of New York State; he enjoyed hunting in the nearby woods and gazing out at the town's vista from Bears Head Rock. But it was triangular Crystal Lake, about a mile south of the trolley terminus, that was especially popular, offering swimming, boating, picnicking, fishing, and even an amusement park. Boasting a Ferris wheel, carousel, dance hall, concession stands, and beach, it was known as the Upstate Coney Island.

It was the high life, but not for everyone. There was an unspoken but very real barrier between the wealthy visitors and the townies, who generally kept their distance, wary of the interlopers, except to earn a living or make a fast buck chauffeuring them around the area, pointing out the best hunting and fishing sites or where to find live bait.

To the east of Averill Park is the hamlet of Sand Lake; to Averill Park's west is the appropriately named West Sand Lake. Like Averill Park, each of these communities contained its own huddled collection of homes, churches, hotels, shops, and mills. The populations of the hamlets of Sand Lake and West Sand Lake were much smaller than Averill Park's, and they lacked the recreational attractions that drew the summer tourists.

Taborton was an unofficial hamlet of sorts in the easternmost corner of town, stretching over hilly, heavily wooded terrain. It was home to the "mountain people," known for their earthiness and practicality—and innate distrust of outsiders. Life in Taborton was different from that in other Sand Lake neighborhoods. Those from Taborton were more likely to be self-sufficient farmers, lumberjacks, or charcoal burners, rather than factory or mill workers. Their sprawling rural properties gave them more space than their neighbors in town, breeding a strong sense of individuality and a wide variety of eccentric characters. Nighttime on lonely Taborton Mountain could be eerily silent, except for the random sounds of wildlife and the sporadic rifle shots that echoed through the region as farmers, stretched out in their lawn chairs with jugs of hard cider by their side, blasted away at beavers that had wandered down the creeks to graze on their crops.

Insulated and remote, the hills of Taborton were just the place for a group of restless young boys looking to escape their daily, humdrum lives.

Lawrence Gruber, a teenager from Averill Park, worked full-time at the Faith Knitting Company on Burden Lake Road, not far from the village center, spinning and cutting raw wool and cotton into finished garments ("Have faith, Will, have faith," friends and family counseled cofounder William D. Mahony). But the weekends were his to spend any way he wanted, and he wasn't about to let the heat wave interfere with his routine: he and six of his friends regularly camped out in the Taborton woods, without any meddlesome adult supervision. They'd fish and squirrel hunt during the day; at night, as the darkness deepened and the stars glittered, they'd huddle around a crackling campfire, chowing down on fresh fish and guzzling the liquid refreshments of their choice, gazing at the shadows of the dancing flames into the late hours.

On the evening of Friday, July 10, the boys pitched their tents in their usual spot, about a hundred feet from a pool of water in the shape of a warped figure eight, known by the locals as Teal's Pond, after the farmer who owned the property, Conrad "Coon" Teal. Years earlier, Teal had dammed Horse Heaven Brook, which ran down Taborton

Mountain, with a large barrier of boulders piled high upon one another, creating a pond to power his sawmill, though he had since converted the mill to steam. The secluded pond was small but deep toward the middle, much of its water hidden by the wild undergrowth on its shores. The boys' chosen spot was thick with majestic pine, maple, and oak trees, all the better to shield them from the ferocious sun that greeted them in the mornings and lingered deep into the summer days.

At 9:30 a.m. on Saturday, Gruber, on his way to run some errands, spotted an object floating in the dense, stagnant pond, about a hundred feet south of the boys' campsite. Convinced it was a discarded article of clothing or errant piece of trash, he paid it no mind.

About five hours later, Gruber happened upon the pond again, crossing the dam on his way to the main road. The object was still visible—closer now, about sixteen feet from the southern shore, slowly floating in water three to four feet deep. This time, Gruber paid attention, and in a matter of seconds he came to the horrifying realization that what he was staring at was neither clothing nor trash, but a lifeless human body.

⁓

His first instinct was to call for help. One of his camping buddies, George White, had just set out for a dinner appointment at the home of Gilbert Miller, a Taborton farmer. Luckily, White was still within earshot.

"George, come back!" Gruber yelled, his cries piercing the stillness of the woods. "I think there's a body in the pond!"

The panic in his friend's voice startled White before he fully grasped the meaning of the words. He scampered back along the shoreline to Gruber, who pointed to the corpse lazily floating toward them, face-down, arms outstretched, only its head and shoulders visible above the surface of the water. The body was close enough now for them to see the drenched frock clinging to it. Large black crescent-shaped hair combs with rhinestones and a "rat"—a half-moon-shaped accessory used to plump up pompadours, often made of human hair—remained clasped firmly in place on her matted mane.

It was a harrowing sight, yet mesmerizing: somehow, they couldn't look away. Gruber, already knowing the answer to his own question, nervously asked, "You think she's dead?"

"Must be," replied White solemnly, after a beat.

"Should we try to haul her in? Or fetch someone?"

For a moment, they were silent, pondering their predicament.

"Wait here," White finally said. "I'll get help."

He dashed off in search of Gilbert Miller, who, at fifty-four, had decades of life experience on the two boys. Gruber remained at the pond, standing silent vigil over the drifting body, wishing he were some-place else.

A longtime Taborton resident who knew the area inside and out, Miller immediately appreciated the gravity of the situation. The afternoon before, he, too, had caught sight of an object floating in Teal's Pond, while on his way down the mountain to deliver milk to Crape's Hotel, which sat just beyond the Taborton border, on the outskirts of the neighboring hamlet of Sand Lake. He had continued along his way, thinking it was merely some empty bag or a bundle of clothes.

Miller and White hurried through the soggy marshlands back to the pond. Along the way, Miller spotted an object out of the corner of his eye, stopping him in his tracks, about twenty feet from the edge of the pond: a woman's stylish black straw hat, high crowned and adorned with three large black ostrich plumes. Upon closer examination, he noticed that the milliner's mark had been ripped out. Pinned to the hat was a pair of badly soiled black, wrist-length kidskin gloves. Miller stopped to collect them, believing they might have belonged to the girl who had been discovered floating in the pond. Hurriedly picking them up, he noticed a four-leaf-clover-shaped hatpin monogrammed with the letter *H*.

Gruber greeted White and Miller near the edge of the pond with obvious relief. Miller removed his hat, wiped the sweat from his brow, and squinted into the water. He noted that the body had drifted eastward, about five or six feet nearer the shore from where he had seen it the day before. The three of them stared at the partially submerged corpse in silence, wondering what to do next. Miller, sensing he should take charge, finally snapped out of his stupor.

"We better bring her in," he said.

They waded into the murky water, dragging the body into the shallows nearer to the dam.

"I wonder who it is," said Gruber, breaking the quiet tension. "Someone from around here?"

"Can't say," grunted Miller, "and I guess we won't know till we get her out and she's been flipped over—but we'd best leave that to the authorities."

He looked around, buying time to think.

"You fellas stay with her," he told the boys. "I'll see if I can go fetch somebody in town."

Then he turned and quickly disappeared down the mountain.

∽

As Gruber and White waited and the news leaked out, curious locals began to gather. Ebenezer Martin, justice of the peace for Sand Lake, arrived presently and started to direct them. Elias B. Boyce, a seventy-year-old country doctor who had been practicing medicine in these parts for nearly fifty years, was summoned in time to witness the removal of the body from the pond to the banks of the shore, so that the woman's face was finally exposed.

It was a gruesome sight—the skin wrinkled and blackened, her face frozen in a rictus. The woman's eyes bulged from their sockets, drooping onto her cheeks. Her swollen tongue protruded a good two inches from her mouth. The rotting corpse was severely bloated, water having seeped into the skin through the pores. Boyce figured it had been in the pond for several days at least.

He began cutting away at the shirtwaist, from the collar downward, noting a pink silk ribbon interlaced with the corset cover. The ribbon was about a quarter of an inch wide and wrapped tightly around her throat, just below the chin. The body was so swollen that the cord had embedded itself into the dead woman's neck.

In a tender act of mercy, Boyce cut the ribbon loose.

The doctor's mind raced. Was this string simply a decorative accessory the woman, whoever she was, had worn around her own neck? Or had the killer ripped it from her corset and used it to strangle her? A chill shot down the old man's spine.

Either way, Boyce was certain of one thing: foul play was involved. A criminal investigation was inevitable. He and Martin conferred: they would alert Rensselaer County coroner Morris H. Strope, who in turn would notify the office of the district attorney.

Boyce, who knew his way around a crime scene, began making mental notes. The hat, with the gloves inside, now lay on the bank about eight feet from the water, where Miller had placed it. No footprints were visible, and Boyce noted that the stones and flat rocks scattered around the shore showed no evidence of having been stepped on. Three feet from the shore a piece of linen, or cheesecloth, cut into a keystone shape, lay in a roll on the sandy bottom of the beach; at first he mistook it for a long white glove.

Among the onlookers at Teal's Pond that morning was a muscular seventeen-year-old Taborton farmhand by the name of Frank Smith. The boy gazed utterly transfixed at the human remains now on full display in front of him. Smith was an eccentric character even in these parts, so socially awkward that he was known by many of his neighbors on the mountain as a simpleton. The burly teenager, who had helped retrieve the body from the pond, knew the dead girl, and in fact had conversed with her in this very vicinity just five days earlier, when she was wearing the exact same clothing now sheathing her dead body.

And yet, he didn't say a word.

∿

The Larkin Brothers Funeral Home, a two-story white building off the Old State Road (now the Troy–Sand Lake Road) in Averill Park—the de facto town center of Sand Lake—doubled as the town morgue. Behind the house was a barn, where the coffins were assembled, and next to that a livery stable that proprietor Willis D. Larkin ran as a side business. On the afternoon of Saturday, July 11, Larkin was summoned to the pond, where he loaded the body onto his horse-drawn hearse, transporting it down the mountain and back to his funeral parlor, where the autopsy would take place.

In 1908, pathology was a relatively young science. The Baltimore Board of Health had broken ground in the investigation of suspicious deaths in 1890 by appointing two physicians as medical examiners and tasking them with performing all autopsies requested by the coroner. But even now, eighteen years later, autopsy results were unreliable. In 1912, after studying three thousand autopsy reports, a Harvard Medical School graduate named Richard Cabot found a "goodly number of classic time-honored mistakes in diagnosis." Sixteen years later, a National Research Council survey concluded that the coroner in most counties of the United States was an "untrained and unskilled individual" operating with "a small staff of mediocre ability, and with inadequate equipment."

The autopsy of the body discovered on Teal's Pond commenced at about 6:00 p.m. on July 11, in the dank, dimly lighted basement of the Larkin Brothers Funeral Home. Drs. Boyce and Elmer E. Reichard, also from Averill Park, performed the procedure, while Dr. Harry O. Fairweather of Troy witnessed and recorded notes. Coroner Strope, a country doctor from nearby Poestenkill, was also present. Although the basement's dingy must thankfully mitigated the day's blistering heat, the rotten stench emanating from the corpse was overwhelming, though not unexpected, since the body had been found floating in shallow water, left exposed to the flaming sun.

In the tension of the silent morgue, Boyce overcame any territorial feelings he had and worked collegially with the two younger doctors. Their first objective was to determine, to the best of their ability, the time of death. They would rely first on clues like the extent of rigor mortis, changes in body temperature, and the decomposition of the organs, although they were well aware that these clocks typically expired between forty-eight and seventy-two hours from time of death. The bloating, due to a buildup of gases produced by bacteria inside the corpse, would have begun within two to six days of her death.

Fairweather noted each item of clothing: a black overskirt; two underskirts; a white shirtwaist; white cotton underwear; a corset and corset cover; black stockings; suspender garters; and low-cut black patent leather shoes that bore the stamp *La Farge* and the case number 71,066. He also made a record of the jewelry, including the hatpin with the initial *H* on it and a brooch with the letters *H. I. D.* scratched on the back. All of these items would be bundled together into a parcel and handed over to the Rensselaer County District Attorney's Office in Troy.

There was no visible blood and no cuts, bruises, or scratches—nothing to suggest a scuffle. The victim's wrinkled skin had turned "as black as midnight," as Fairweather later described it, and her scalp and hair had loosened to the point of molting. A surface examination of the victim echoed Boyce's observations at the pond: the woman appeared to be between thirty and thirty-five years of age. She was of medium build, with blonde hair, and eyes still visibly blue beneath her clouded corneas. The doctors estimated that the body had been floating in the water for about a week. They found no wedding ring, but noted gold fillings between her upper middle teeth.

Boyce surveyed the surgical tools laid out on the table before him, steeling himself for the cruel final intrusion into the woman's body. The old country doctor proceeded to cut a Y-shaped incision from both of the shoulders, which connected over the sternum and continued down to the pubic bone. An examination of the stomach revealed only a few particles of undigested food, enough to fill a teaspoon if scraped together.

As they cleared away the skin and tissue, they removed the front of her rib cage to expose her organs, each of which was then removed from the corpse and examined for clues. Next they made an incision in the back of her head from ear to ear, peeling away the skin and removing the top of her skull with a vibrating saw.

The internal examination revealed all of the organs to be in normal condition except for the brain, which showed signs of a blood clot, likely triggered by a contusion about the size of a silver dollar that was discovered in the upper occipital lobe, or rear part of the cortex, hidden just above the hairline. The doctors believed the wound to have been caused by a powerful blow from a blunt instrument strong enough to bruise, yet too dull to pierce: perhaps a rock or club, many of which were found near the pond, although none was ever identified as the murder weapon. The skull had been bruised but not shattered. The blow, delivered at a point almost exactly between the crown and the base of the skull, would have knocked her instantly unconscious and in all probability resulted in instantaneous death—she "never moved a finger after it was dealt," as Fairweather articulated it—yet, remarkably, it had failed to dislodge the combs found on the back of the head, assuming the victim was in fact wearing them at the time she was struck.

The lungs were so full of air, the doctors noted, that they had kept the body afloat for a time after it was tossed into the pond. Both the lungs and stomach were free of water; thus, Fairweather concluded,

"The girl was dead when she was placed in the water, and of that there can be no mistake." This ruled out suicide or drowning as the cause of death and, combined with the severity of the head injury, led the doctors to also dismiss the possibility that she had struck her head after jumping or falling into the pond, ten feet deep at its nethermost.

"Positively not," Fairweather responded, when later asked about an accidental death. "It would have been an impossibility for a person to have received such injuries as we have found by a fall." Rather, he added, "such injuries might have been inflicted by someone taking her by the head and jamming it down on a stone or something of that kind. If she had injured herself she could never have reached the place where she was found alone."

Every doctor in the room agreed that the *primary* cause of death was the blow to the head.

Boyce, however, couldn't let go of his theory that the victim had also been strangled—though *after* being struck on the head. He was convinced her grotesquely distorted face, combined with the discovery of the cord that, in his opinion, had been ripped from her corset and wrapped several times around the throat, was persuasive evidence that the killer had endeavored to make "doubly sure" his victim was dead.

"The whole appearance of the body indicates strangulation," he said.

Fairweather and Reichard dissented, Fairweather vigorously so, arguing that the bulging eyes and protruding tongue could easily be explained by the body's extended exposure to the water and sun. As for the ribbon, they believed it was merely a feature of the woman's dress or else a decorative piece of apparel she had fastened around her own neck, and that it had become embedded in the throat as a result of bloating. In support of their position, they noted the absence of brass tips, which were customarily found on the end of corset strings.

"The girl was not strangled to death. She was beaten to death. Her face and body from her waist up were as black as midnight when we saw her."

A ghost hovered around the doctors in the autopsy room, and it couldn't have been far from the thoughts of each of the four men: Upstate New York had been rocked exactly two years earlier, on July 11, 1906, by the murder of twenty-year-old Grace Mae Brown on Big Moose Lake in the Adirondacks, about 130 miles northwest of Troy. Grace Mae—known as Billy, supposedly because of her love for the song "Bill Bailey, Won't You Please . . . Come Home?"—had been beaten over the head, allegedly with a tennis racket, by her boyfriend, Chester Gillette, after she had informed him that she was pregnant with their child, while out rowing on the lake. She then either fell or was shoved into the water and drowned by Gillette, who overturned the boat and swam safely to shore. (Billy's slaying would go on to inspire the 1925 Theodore Dreiser novel *An American Tragedy*, adapted into the 1951 film *A Place in the Sun*, starring Elizabeth Taylor and Montgomery Clift.)

In light of Billy's murder, everybody knew what angle reporters would be chasing: Was the victim pregnant at the time of death? Here at least the doctors were unanimous: the answer was no.

But was she *ever* pregnant? Was she a virgin? Had she been sexually assaulted on the night of her murder? The evidence here was murkier. And there is every possibility that the doctors were being deliberately evasive to protect the honor of the victim.

Reichard was a family doctor who had developed a reputation as an uncanny diagnostician. He had once been called on to treat what was believed to be smallpox, but he took one look at the patient and declared that it was in fact chicken pox and scarlet fever, and that the boy would be fine in a couple of days, which he was. Studying the body laid out before him, he noted a "slight rupture in the female organs" but said the body was so disfigured by bloating that he couldn't be sure if the tear was fresh. Fairweather and Strope also noted evidence of "an assault" but cryptically added that "the same injuries might also have been received in another way." The *Marion Star* of Ohio reported that the physicians determined she had been "outraged" before she was slain; the *Raleigh Times* of North Carolina said doctors reported that she hadn't been "mistreated" before death. What they did seem to agree on was that the condition of the body precluded any definite determination one way or the other. Fairweather, however, would insist to the very end that "there was no indication that the deceased was not a good girl"—an opaque statement that nobody ever pushed him to explain, or if they did the explanation was too sensitive to print.

In the days ahead, as the investigation kicked into high gear, the hours that these four doctors spent in the basement at Larkin Brothers Funeral Home on the night of July 11 would prove to be one of the most contentious aspects of the entire case. Physicians in Troy were said to be censorious of their "country" colleagues, which provoked newspaper reports demanding that the body be exhumed to determine if the victim, "like 'Billy' Brown, may have gone to her doom because her sweetheart, like Chester Gillette, found her a burden," as the *Evening World*, a New York City tabloid, phrased it. The crux of this argument was that the doctors who performed the autopsy had been cursory and overly delicate in their examination, focusing too much on the cause of death and not enough on a motive. But papers from New York City and elsewhere outside Troy also insinuated that the physicians were protective of the victim's reputation, and thus less than forthright about their findings.

Fairweather—the only one of the three doctors to hail from Troy—rushed to the defense of his colleagues, despite his differences with Boyce. "The process was thorough, every organ being examined," he said. "While the body's condition was not conducive to an infallible decision as to her physical condition, I believe a motive for her death such as accompanied 'Billy' Brown's murder is lacking.

"However," he added, "it is likely the girl was slain after an assault. Further than this I cannot say."

Ultimately, the decision about whether to exhume the body would be left up to the man in charge of the investigation: District Attorney Jarvis O'Brien. Would O'Brien, an elected official with deep ties to the Republican Party, be up for the challenge?

Chapter 2

THE RIGHT MAN FOR THE JOB?

Jarvis O'Brien, district attorney for Rensselaer County, whose juris-
diction encompassed both Troy and the surrounding countryside, to
include Sand Lake, made an immediate and lasting first impression:
he was tall, dark, and handsome, radiating stoic fortitude. At the age
of forty-four, he retained the outstanding physique of his youth—as
a young man he was crowned "best developed fireman in line" by his
fellow volunteer firefighters, earning a gag-prize silk hat in the process.
Peers and rivals alike sometimes referred to him as an "Adonis"—allies
admiringly, foes maybe less so. His only physical blemish was a missing
finger on his left hand, lost in a lawn-mowing accident while in his
early twenties.

O'Brien's jet-black hair was fashioned into a suave upsweep that
framed dark, piercing eyes capable of staring down a statue. His carefully groomed walrus-style mustache, suggesting a predilection for
theatrical flair, completed the public image of the righteous, heroic
crime-busting DA. Although he had built his reputation as being tough
on crime and somewhat of a moral crusader, battling public corruption
and shutting down houses of ill repute on the mean streets of early-twentieth-century Troy, he was actually born and raised in the small

town of Fort Edward, New York (population 5,300 in 1905), about fifty miles north of bustling Troy (population 76,910 in 1905). O'Brien's affinity for small-town life never left him—he would retain a cattle farm in Fort Edward and travel back and forth between the two locales, for both business and personal reasons, throughout his life.

Born to Irish immigrants Mary and James O'Brien, Jarvis was the youngest of five boys; their lone sister, Catherine, died at a young age. Their parents were modest, hardworking farmers, active in their town and church, but the O'Brien boys seemed destined for greater things. Even as young men they excelled in fields as diverse as engineering, business, law, statesmanship, and public service.

In some ways the O'Brien clan resembled an early-twentieth-century, regional version of the Kennedys, without the accompanying Hollywood glitz and titillation. John O'Brien, the second-eldest, was elected secretary of state of New York in a Republican sweep in 1902 and would later serve as president of the City National Bank in Plattsburg and, more informally, as a Republican boss in Clinton County, New York, while middle son Edward served as a brigadier general on Governor Eli Morton's staff before being nominated by President Theodore Roosevelt in 1905 as joint ambassador to Paraguay and Uruguay. As the youngest in the family, Jarvis had a lot to live up to.

Born in 1864, as the Civil War entered its final bloody year, he was educated at private schools: the Fort Edward Free School as a boy and later the Fort Edward Collegiate Institute, which offered college preparatory courses. Jarvis attended law school at Columbian University at Washington, DC—today known as George Washington University—a rare path in those times, when most lawyers learned their trade by apprenticing directly with a law firm. In 1892 he graduated with an LLB, or bachelor's degree in law, and followed his eldest brother, William, to Troy, where he secured employment with the prestigious law firm of Smith & Wellington.

George B. Wellington, one of the firm's partners, was prominent in local Republican politics and would go on to serve as chairman of the Rensselaer County party's General Committee, as well as city attorney (or, in the terminology of the area, "corporation counsel") and assistant US attorney. Years before O'Brien joined the firm, Wellington and Henry Smith had partnered with Frank Swett Black, who, for a brief period during the late 1800s and early 1900s, was as powerful as any Republican in New York State. Despite never having run for office before, Black was elected to the US House of Representatives in November 1894, largely on the strength of his role in spearheading the controversial prosecution of Bartholomew "Bat" Shea, who had been charged earlier that year in the shooting death of twenty-five-year-old Robert Ross, a Republican poll watcher, during an Election Day melee.

Shea, an Irish Catholic, was among those enlisted by the notoriously corrupt Democratic machine to do whatever it took to win Troy's Thirteenth Ward for the party, including engaging in ballot stuffing and repeat voting. Tapping into the community's near frenzy over Ross's murder, Black helped organize the Committee of Public Safety to pressure elected officials into exacting vengeance against Shea.

The only problem was that while Shea was indisputably one of those caught up in the brawl, which he had helped to instigate, in all likelihood he didn't fire the shot that killed Ross. Just days prior to Shea's scheduled execution, John McGough, Shea's associate, confessed to Dannemora Prison warden Walter Thayer that he had committed the crime. Despite being granted a temporary stay, Shea was electrocuted in front of twenty-seven witnesses at Clinton Prison on February 11, 1896, as a blinding snowstorm raged outside. Later that same year, Black was elected governor of New York State.

As demonstrated by his role in the Shea case, Black, along with some of his closest allies on the Committee of Public Safety, wasn't above forming alliances with less-than-savory parties, such as the infamous American Protective Association, which was the largest anti-Catholic movement in the country in the late-nineteenth century. Reputedly, the APA was linked to certain elements of the Protestant-led Republican Party, although the allegations were never substantiated. The influence of the APA, founded in 1887 by "Supreme President" Henry F. Bowers, a Clinton, Iowa, attorney, peaked at the tail end of the nineteenth century, with hundreds of thousands of members across the country, fueled partly by outrage over incendiary APA documents like a papal encyclical urging Catholics to "exterminate all heretics." The membership ritual included the following oath: "I do most solemnly promise and swear that I . . . will never allow any one, a member of the Roman Catholic church, to become a member of this order . . . that I will not employ a Roman Catholic in any capacity if I can procure the services of a Protestant . . . that in all grievances I will seek only Protestants and counsel with them to the exclusion of all Roman Catholics . . . and that I will not vote for, or counsel others to vote for, any Roman Catholic, but will vote only for a Protestant."

Given Frank Black's role in the Shea case, and his political battles with Democratic boss Edward Murphy Jr. and his Irish Catholic followers, it is somewhat ironic that he was one of the biggest boosters of an upcoming Irish Catholic politician in Troy by the name of Jarvis O'Brien.

⁓

As a young man in Fort Edward, Jarvis O'Brien, along with his brother James and other members of the local volunteer fire station, had helped to organize a Young Democrats Club. That O'Brien and his friends would initially be drawn to the Democratic Party is not a surprise. In the years following the Civil War, national politics were dominated by the largely Protestant-backed Republican Party. The Democrats enjoyed most of their success in urban centers, as various factions of disenfranchised people banded together into political coalitions, and Irish Roman Catholics were among the largest of these minority groups.

Once in Troy, however, O'Brien switched allegiances, no doubt influenced by his association with Wellington and Black, who would become two of his biggest supporters. Leveraging these connections, O'Brien quickly established himself as a prominent member of the Troy city establishment and a force in Rensselaer County Republican politics. On January 1, 1897, he was appointed assistant district attorney under DA Wesley O. Howard and was reappointed to the post three years later. In the fall of 1902, O'Brien was elected district attorney in a landslide victory, succeeding Howard, who had moved on to the state supreme court.

O'Brien made a splash soon after taking office when he uncovered an alleged scheme of jury fraud, giving birth to his reputation as a moral crusader on the tough streets of Troy. He would continue to make headlines in his first year as DA, waging war against owners of "disorderly houses," winning accolades from supporters and even rivals, such as the Democratic-backed *Troy Daily Press*, which in an editorial proclaimed, "We hope that he will continue as he has commenced until the city is purged of the pestilence breeding hell holes that contribute to everything that tends to blacken its once honored name."

O'Brien's reputation flourished throughout 1903, when Frank Black cajoled him into running for mayor of Troy, no doubt hoping that South Troy's dyed-in-the-wool Democratic Irish Catholic voters would be inclined to vote for a candidate named O'Brien. By ceding to his party's wishes, Democrats alleged, O'Brien had become a "perfect tool" of the Republican Party.

O'Brien originally had balked at running, insisting he was content as DA, but if you were a Republican in Troy and wanted a future in politics, you generally did what Frank Black and the party machine instructed you to do. Democrats scoffed at O'Brien's "modesty," pointing out that if he won the election he would have taken a pay cut of fifteen hundred dollars a year, which, they suggested, was the real reason for his reluctance to run for mayor.

Ultimately, Joseph F. Hogan—backed by the Democratic machine—squeaked out a razor-thin victory in a race that featured a little bit of everything, including election-day violence and allegations of tampering with the newly installed voting machines (in other words, a typical Troy election).

O'Brien was reelected district attorney in 1905 and continued to wield considerable influence, winning convictions in such high-profile cases as the 1905 trial of Samuel Cohn, accused of abducting women under the age of eighteen. In his closing statement, O'Brien once again demonstrated his eloquence and oratorial flair: "If these damnable sinks of vice are to be permitted in our midst, what chance is there for families to bring up boys and girls to become decent men and women? What protection is there for the family if such vile places are tolerated and such men as the accused allowed to go unpunished?"

Calling O'Brien "the best district attorney in the history of Rensselaer County," local Republican-controlled newspapers lauded his crusade against "scarlet evil," targeting tax-delinquent saloonkeepers and the proprietors of pool rooms, gambling houses, and "disorderly resorts"—code words for houses of ill repute. "He has driven the dive proprietors out of business and has cleaned a part of the city that for years was a stench in the nostrils of the decent element," the *Troy Sunday News* opined.

However, O'Brien was by no means universally revered, nor was he immune from criticism and controversy. More than once he ran into conflict-of-interest charges. Even after winning election, he served as the Troy counsel of the United Traction Company, an electric street railway operating in Albany and Rensselaer Counties. Then, in 1904, he was appointed counsel in charge of the Boston and Maine Railroad in New York State. A year later, he served as the transit company's defense attorney at a trial in the wake of a train accident that killed fifteen people and injured thirty more, while still serving as district attorney of Rensselaer County, which caused a huge uproar in the press.

Still, by the summer of 1908, the ambitious O'Brien had maneuvered his way into a position of even more prominence in the county's burgeoning Republican establishment. He regularly crisscrossed the state, rallying the GOP faithful in support of candidates, sometimes at the side of Frank Black.

O'Brien had built his career as a prosecutor, not as a detective. So when called on to investigate the death at Teal's Pond, he leaned heavily on his primary deputy and close friend, forty-two-year-old county detective Duncan C. Kaye, who had named one of his sons Jarvis, presumably in honor of the DA. Kaye was a clean-shaven man with diminishing dark hair and thin lips that seemed to curve into a smirk whatever the circumstances, and he was at the very least an APA sympathizer, if not an oath-taking member.

Although a law-enforcement officer, Kaye was an ardent soldier in the Rensselaer County Republican Party, and he, too, had played a crucial role in the arrest and execution of Bat Shea: On March 6, 1894, Kaye was among those accompanying Robert Ross as he confronted Shea and other Democrats over ballot stuffing and other illegal voting activity. Kaye claimed to have personally witnessed the shooting of Ross by Shea, his former schoolmate, and at Shea's trial he was accused by the defense of conspiring with Black to coerce witnesses. Soon after Shea was electrocuted, Kaye was named as a delegate to the Republican state convention, and his involvement with the Rensselaer County Republican Party continued to deepen as his law-enforcement career advanced.

Detectives William P. Powers and John H. Murnane, both of whom worked for O'Brien in the DA's office, would round out the Rensselaer County investigative unit looking into the murder at Teal's Pond. All three of the detectives who made up the close-knit, politically aligned team were active in Republican politics. Powers, in fact, would be elected Rensselaer County sheriff in 1914 with the backing of the Republican Party.

In Troy, politics influenced everything, including who was—or wasn't—arrested.

⸺

On the evening of Saturday, July 11, while the autopsy was being performed, O'Brien and Kaye rode out to Teal's Pond in the district attorney's automobile, drifting up through the rolling hills of Taborton, their windows rolled all the way down in the stagnant heat. O'Brien took stony Taborton Road, flexuous and narrow, bordered by ditches on each side, with care—the same way he planned to approach the spectators who were congregating at the scene of the crime. His strategy was to mingle among the locals—he was, after all, a small-town man himself, to whom folksiness came naturally—but he was anticipating a tough crowd; people in the countryside had no love of city folk, and they weren't shy about showing it.

The crowd had ballooned by now; even the pitiless heat couldn't keep them away. The investigators, sweating in their stiff dark suits, damp around the arms and collars, made the rounds, peppering each of the onlookers with questions. Frank Smith was still milling about, but claimed to have no notion of who the victim might be. Coon Teal, who had wandered down to the pond to see what all the fuss was about, chewed on a bit of dry hay as he informed authorities he had heard partiers in the vicinity from his piazza on July 4, but had noticed nothing alarming or strange since. The pond used to draw fishermen looking for bait, Teal said, but less so now that a new law had been passed requiring a state license. He could think of at least half a dozen men who used to come out, but not anymore.

Gilbert Miller recounted his summoning to the pond following the discovery of the body; another local, George Alberts, told of being at

Crape's Hotel that afternoon when people started chattering about the discovery of a woman's corpse in Teal's Pond, so he hurried up the road to check it out. He recalled wading into the pond and helping to flip the body so that Boyce, Martin, and others could endeavor to identify it. Like everyone else, he said he didn't recognize the victim and wasn't aware of any local woman who had gone missing.

O'Brien and Kaye appreciated the chatty Alberts, especially given the reticence of most of the locals to share their thoughts with two interlopers from the city, so they prodded him for more information, which is when Alberts mentioned the pink ribbon that had been discovered wrapped around the victim's neck.

"You're saying she was strangled?" Kaye asked.

"No, not saying that at all," Alberts replied. "If you ask me, it was just an ordinary silk cord that any woman might wear as decoration around her neck." Like Fairweather and Reichard, he noticed there were no brass tips on the ribbon, which would have been expected if it were a corset string.

After speaking with those lurking at the pond, O'Brien and Kaye fanned outward to the neighboring farms in search of relevant information. The interactions were tense, the answers often evasive. No one claimed to have heard or seen anything suspicious, or to have any clue as to the identity of the dead woman.

The detectives caught wind of the fact that two young women staying at the house of Edward Hohl on nearby Miller's Corner Road had disappeared on Saturday, July 4, so they paid Hohl a visit, but the tip turned out to be a dead end: the girls had returned two days later, saying they had spent the previous nights with friends.

Christopher Crape, proprietor of the stately twenty-two-room Crape's Hotel—famous for its home-cooked food and canned jellies and jams—mentioned that he was sitting on the long porch, by the circle of grass and imposing elms, in front of his hotel in the darkness of the wee hours one morning in early July (the exact date would remain a matter of confusion the entire length of the investigation) when a car flew by with its lights off. The vehicle sped up Taborton Road, a rocky, twisting country lane that was exceedingly jeopardous for automobiles even during daylight hours, and returned about fifteen to twenty minutes later. What got Crape's attention was there were four people—two men and two women—in the car on the way up, but only three on the way down, because one of the women was missing.

"What time was all this?" Kaye asked.

"Clock struck two as it passed," said Crape.

"Two in the morning?" O'Brien interjected. "You were still awake? And you could see all that?"

Crape turned to the DA. "Sure I could . . . was still up cleaning the place," he said.

O'Brien's interest was piqued, but the district attorney wasn't sure what to make of this: it was almost impossible for an automobile to climb the mountains in the vicinity of the pond, especially in the dark, unless perhaps the man behind the wheel was an expert driver who was intimately familiar with the road.

Kaye said thank you kindly, and the pair were on their way.

Exhausted, O'Brien and Kaye headed back to Larkin Brothers Funeral Home, knowing their day was far from over. They were greeted by the coroner and the three doctors, who shared their news: there was no doubt in any of their minds that the woman in the pond had been beaten to death.

~

Back in Troy, at the DA's office in the Rensselaer County Courthouse on Congress Street, Jarvis O'Brien and Duncan Kaye were in a sour mood. Their trip to Sand Lake had yielded many questions, but few answers: Who was the victim? What was she doing in the Taborton woods gussied up in fancy clothes and city shoes? Was she killed at the pond, or somewhere else and then disposed of there to hide the crime?

"Let's focus on what we do know," said O'Brien, in the soft white glow of the shaded lamp on his desk. Darkness had settled in for the night. O'Brien fingered his mustache, as he was wont to do in contemplative moments. Kaye was more a man of action.

The pond was secluded, surrounded by woods, a good four miles west of Averill Park; the killer surely had to either be from the area or be familiar with it some other way. Maybe a fisherman? Someone with a summer home nearby?

To reach the pond, it was necessary to cross a dam that some of the locals had cobbled together. There had been no evidence on the dam or along the path beyond indicating a struggle. The doctors had said the body itself hadn't been cut or scratched, and no blood was found on it or at the scene. Hence, it seemed probable that she had been killed somewhere else, and then her body was carried across the dam, a short way down to the pond, and tossed in. Her hat and gloves had been placed along the path—in all likelihood to create the impression that the victim had committed suicide, but the physicians had unanimously dismissed that possibility.

Was it robbery? Perhaps. No money was found on the victim. No purse or handbag. But then why leave the gold brooch attached to the shirtwaist collar?

Sexual violation? The female organ was slightly torn. The physicians were frustratingly indecisive about whether the girl had been criminally assaulted, due to the severe decomposition of the body.

"The condition of the clothes doesn't support it," said Kaye.

"Right," said O'Brien. "Not torn, not disarranged. Doesn't seem likely. Unless . . ."

"Unless what?"

"Unless she was undressed and then redressed?"

Kaye mulled it over.

"Maybe," he said, "but doesn't it seem too neat? Nothing out of place. Not even the hair combs."

"Which could mean just the opposite," said O'Brien.

"Maybe she was just in the wrong place at the wrong time," Kaye said. "Maybe it was just a random assault by one of those ruffians up there on the mountain."

O'Brien groaned. "They'll never give up one of their own."

They were convinced—at least for now—that they could rule out the so-called Billy Brown motive. The doctors, who hadn't agreed on much, seemed certain she wasn't pregnant at the time of death.

And there was cause for optimism. The killer was sloppy, not nearly as clever as he thought. Assuming that the placement of the hat and gloves was intended to suggest suicide, he had fooled no one—and even more significantly had left behind clues to his victim's identity, perhaps in his hurry to flee the scene.

O'Brien had stopped fingering his mustache and started rubbing his temples.

"Headache?" said Kaye.

"How about we call it a day?" said O'Brien.

Tomorrow would bring news, some good, some not.

⌒

The discovery of the body—and the likelihood of foul play—was reported in the July 12 morning edition of the *Northern Budget*, a Sunday-only paper (the major dailies in Troy did not publish Sunday editions). With the body rapidly decomposing, Willis Larkin—with all the sentimentality of someone who trafficked in death on a daily basis—was already planning a Jane Doe pauper's burial for the following day if no one came forward to claim the body; holding it any longer than that would be "objectionable."

That afternoon, a young couple visited the funeral home, asking to view the body. They were greeted by the wife of one of the proprietors, since both of the Larkin brothers were away at the time. The couple never identified themselves by name, but they told Mrs. Larkin they thought they might know the identity of the woman. After viewing the body, they said they believed it might be that of the young man's sister. They left almost immediately after and said they would be heading to the district attorney's office to view the victim's clothing.

At approximately eight o'clock that night, a man named John Drew of Troy arrived at Larkin Brothers to inquire about the body that had been retrieved from the pond. Drew, whose gaunt, craggy face made him appear considerably older than his fifty-three years, had heard chatter about the body discovered at Teal's Pond, and had an ominous feeling it might concern his daughter—Hazel Irene Drew. Both of the Larkin brothers were still away, as were the detectives who were canvassing the surrounding area, and Mrs. Larkin had taken to letting the morbidly curious help themselves to a view of the body. She listened patiently to the man's story, sensing something in his demeanor different from the others who had been through that evening, and then indicated he should follow her down the stairs so he could take a look for himself.

As John Drew descended into the basement of the funeral home, what was he thinking? That he had failed in his most basic obligation as a parent: to protect his child? That while his life had largely been an accumulation of failure and frustration, nothing would compare to what he was about to experience? Perhaps he was hoping that the body he was about to encounter wasn't Hazel at all, but rather some other unfortunate young woman.

As he was led inside the morgue, he was met by a blast of cool air. The abrupt change in temperature triggered a cold sweat. Drew's head was spinning; he grabbed hold of the first thing he could find—the slab on which the body lay—to steady himself. Larkin lifted the cover, revealing a bloated, discolored corpse.

Drew couldn't stand the sight of it. *Focus,* he told himself. He had never in his life wished so strongly for a gulp of whiskey.

Was it Hazel? He couldn't be sure. The body had deteriorated so drastically that it was, ultimately, beyond recognition.

Drew did, however, volunteer one vital piece of information: Hazel had gold fillings between her upper front teeth.

＜

Detective Kaye had heard about John Drew's sad visit to the Larkins' mortuary in Sand Lake, and the next morning he visited the Drews at their home in South Troy, bringing with him a collection of the jewelry and articles of clothing found on the dead girl's body. With a growing sense of dread, John Drew and one of Hazel's sisters inspected two of the pieces of jewelry—the hatpin with the initial *H* on it and the brooch with the letters *H. I. D.* on the back. As recognition showed in her father's tired eyes, her sister exclaimed, "That's Hazel's!"

To remove any lingering doubt, Eva Lapp Drew, wife of Hazel's older brother, Joseph H. Drew (and his second cousin—a fairly routine arrangement at the time, in which the couple would agree not to have children), and a local seamstress by the name of Mary Schumaker, who had custom-made garments for Hazel, were summoned to O'Brien's office.

Schumaker immediately recognized the shirtwaist worn by the victim as something she herself had made for Hazel—she had even retained a piece of the material and remnants of the trimming and lace, all of which matched. The dressmaker said Hazel had shown up unexpectedly at her house on the night of Friday, July 3, with fabric just purchased from the Boston Store in Troy, pleading with her to make her a shirtwaist immediately so that she could wear it during an out-of-town trip she was planning to Lake George for the Fourth of July weekend. She completed the garment at eleven o'clock that night and was stunned that Hazel would wait up so late for it. For some reason, Hazel was desperate to look her best that weekend.

Eva Drew, who was one of Hazel's closest confidants, then identified the black overskirt. She had one just like it; in fact she was wearing it at that very moment. Eva told the detectives that both her skirt and Hazel's were made from the same piece of cloth. Moving on from the garments, the detective brought out the small gold-and-enamel brooch the woman had been wearing at the throat of her shirtwaist.

The brooch was engraved on the front with the motto *Concordia Salus*—Latin for "salvation through harmony." It was surmounted with a crown and engraved with the emblems of the United Kingdom, Ireland, Scotland, and Canada—a rose, a shamrock, a thistle, and a beaver—each occupying a space marked by two white crossbars. The reverse side bore Hazel's initials.

Investigators would learn that the brooch had been gifted to Hazel by Adelaide Tupper, a former employer, who had purchased it while vacationing in Canada, her home country.

With the identity of the victim now confirmed, Hazel's parents were brought in to discuss their daughter and what might have led to her tragic demise. John Drew was no stranger to the Rensselaer County Courthouse, having brushed up against the law himself, like the time he galloped his horse around downtown after overindulging in alcohol.

During the meeting, O'Brien and Kaye were particularly struck by the manner of Hazel's mother, Julia A. Drew, who seemed remarkably unmoved, glancing at Hazel's clothing from a distance. In spite of the horrible tragedy unfolding before her, she never betrayed even a hint of emotion. Left disabled by a childhood battle with polio, Julia trudged to and from the room with crutches, her face frozen in what seemed a perpetual grimace.

Both John and Julia Drew told O'Brien that they did not know of their daughter keeping company with any man and could not imagine why she had been murdered.

Hazel hadn't spent much time at home in recent years, staying instead in the households where she worked as a domestic servant. The detectives got the impression that Hazel wasn't particularly close to her parents. (The detectives didn't realize it at the time, but the Drews misidentified Hazel's age as nineteen instead of twenty—she had celebrated the milestone birthday just over a month earlier, on June 3.)

The last time Julia had seen her daughter was on Thursday, July 2, when Hazel stopped by the house at 400 Fourth Street.

John Drew had last seen Hazel a few days later, at about 11:00 a.m. on July 4, with Minnie Taylor, Julia's younger sister, at Franklin Square in Troy. He, too, admitted knowing little about her friends and acquaintances or how she liked to spend her leisure time. The Drews did supply the names of Hazel's final employers, Edward Cary and his wife, Mary, as well as past families she had lived with and worked for.

At least the murder victim had finally been identified. But who was Hazel Drew? And how had she ended up like this, bludgeoned to death, her body unceremoniously dumped in Teal's Pond?

Her parents either did not know much about their daughter's life or were loath to reveal almost any information.

What was even stranger was that they had last seen Hazel nearly a week before her body was discovered, yet had never reported her missing or even inquired about her whereabouts.

Outside the courthouse, John and Julia Drew posed for newspaper photographers. On their way home, they stopped off at the offices of Metropolitan Life Insurance Company to cash a five-hundred-dollar industrial life-insurance policy they had taken out in Hazel's name.

Beating the reporters to the courthouse in the early morning hours, Duncan Kaye popped his head inside Jarvis O'Brien's office, where he found the district attorney staring off into space, apparently deep in thought, a wisp of steam rising from the piping-hot cup of coffee sitting on his desk.

"You see this?" Kaye said, tossing a copy of the *Columbia Republican*, a Hudson, New York, weekly, onto O'Brien's desk.

"Do I have to?" O'Brien said. Like any politician, he was fond of the press only insofar as he could control it.

"They're comparing it to the Lamp Black Swamp murder."

"Remind me," said O'Brien.

"Helena Whitmore, found dead in a remote swamp in New Jersey, out by Newark. They pinned it on the husband but couldn't get a verdict. Awaiting a second trial."

"Starting to come back to me now," said O'Brien. "Christmas Day. They quarreled; she disappeared."

"That's the one," Kaye said. "Pretty sordid. Both had lovers. He beat her all the time. Last words she said to her sister were 'I fear that he will kill me in the end.'"

"I seem to recall the name 'Gold Tooth' Billy."

"That's right. The prosecution called him as a witness. He testified that he and the husband had been partners in crime for years."

"Well," said O'Brien, "let's hope the *Columbia Republican* is wrong."

Chapter 3

HAZEL

Hazel Drew was courteous, respectful, virginal; she never missed a curfew or Sunday service and rarely if ever showed any interest in boys. She was a conscientious worker and exemplary role model for young children.

Hazel Drew was gregarious and flirtatious; she collected a menagerie of male admirers, dressed and dined extravagantly, and traveled extensively, way beyond her means. Acquaintances whispered that she had had a secret benefactor or lover; reporters even wondered if she had aborted a pregnancy.

The deeper the investigators dove into the life of Hazel Drew, the more they discovered a paradox of personalities, a Rorschach inkblot whose "true" identity depended on who was interpreting the image.

~

Hazel Irene Drew was born on June 3, 1888, in a farmhouse on Blue Factory Road in East Poestenkill, New York, about six and a half miles north of Sand Lake, where she would one day meet her death. Julia Drew was six months pregnant with Hazel when the Great Blizzard of 1888 dropped, without warning, fifty-plus inches of snow as winds gusted up to eighty miles an hour—an omen, perhaps, of arduous times ahead.

The Drews' comings and goings during those early years are difficult to trace, but if Hazel lived in Poestenkill during elementary school, she would have attended the District Number Four school on a farm in the hamlet of Ives Corner, one of eight one-room schoolhouses in Poestenkill at the time.

Her hometown was named after the mighty Poesten Kill creek (*kil* being Dutch for "riverbed"), which includes Mount Ida Falls. Local legend has it that a Mohawk warrior once fell in love with a young European woman who, to avoid being taken captive by her suitor, leaped to her death from the ledge of the falls. The creek itself was christened in honor of a legendarily shrewd seventeenth-century Dutch farmer and fur trader named Jan Barentsen Wemp, who had settled in the area and was sometimes referred to as Poest. The town of Poestenkill comprises four hamlets, one sharing the name of the town itself, plus Ives Corner; East Poestenkill, where Hazel was born; and Barberville, where she was buried, and where her grave still stands today.

Early on, Poestenkill and the surrounding areas were especially popular with German immigrants, tempted by the mountainous, densely wooded terrain that was so evocative of the Black Forest back home. Local legend—which may or may not be true—has it that Hessian defectors from the British Army during the Revolutionary War hid out in the mountains of Poestenkill and neighboring Taborton and liked it so much they never went home.

These were earthy, unpretentious, self-reliant people, mostly farmers and lumberjacks, due to the natural features of the land they inhabited. They lived insular, unhurried lives, without many of the luxuries of contemporaneous life that were common in neighboring cities like Troy. They knew their neighbors by name—in fact, many of them were related to their neighbors—and slept with their doors unlocked. City folk mocked them as slow-witted and naive, but they possessed a guileless, forthright sensibility ("If you breed a pa'tridge, you'll git a pa'tridge," was one folksy saying that got passed around), inflected by their distrust of anything—or anyone—affected or cunning. In their turn, they dismissed the urbanites from Troy and elsewhere as condescending windbags.

Hazel's maternal grandparents, Charles William and Mary Ann Thöle (their surname would eventually mutate into the Anglicized spelling Taylor), were hardy, industrious people. According to family lore, Charles Taylor, originally from Hanover, Germany, had nothing but an ax to his name when he married Mary Ann Lapp around 1850, but they were determined to build a life for themselves and their eleven children, of which Hazel's mother, Julia, was seventh. The Taylors lived and worked on a farm in Berlin, New York. It was a difficult life, made even more so when Charles was drafted to fight for the Union army in 1863. When their farm in Berlin burned down, they started over again, eventually making their way west to nearby Poestenkill, where they continued to farm. Charles served there as road commissioner until he cut his hand while building a bridge and wound up dying of blood poisoning at the age of fifty-one.

Less is known about the background of the vagabond John Drew, although by all accounts he was an irrepressible rascal who loved his liquor and couldn't hold a steady job. Hazel's father was a farmer and laborer who had never learned to read or write. He had migrated south from Vermont, eventually finding work at Barber Farm in Poestenkill, where he met Julia, whose family lived on nearby Blue Factory Road.

John and Julia married in 1885 and had seven children, though only five survived early childhood: Joseph, the oldest, was twenty-one years old in 1908; followed by Hazel; Carrie (fourteen); William, or Willie (eleven); and Emma (nine).

John Drew's inability to hold down a job would force the Drew family to uproot and relocate on a regular basis. By 1900 the Drews had moved from Poestenkill about five miles south, to the town of Sand Lake, but they didn't stay long; by the following year, they had moved to Troy, where John Drew found work as a laborer. The family returned to Sand Lake from 1905 to 1906 to live and work on the farm of William Taylor, Julia's older brother, in exchange for shares, but returned to Troy in 1906 after a heated dispute between Taylor and John.

Hazel did not return to Sand Lake: in 1902—at the tender age of fourteen—she had landed a job as a domestic servant in a wealthy enclave on Third Street in South Troy, working for a man by the name of Thomas W. Hislop, a prominent member of the Republican Party and, at the time of Hazel's hiring, the city treasurer of Troy.

How a poor country girl from the quiet little town of Poestenkill wound up working for one of the most powerful men in Troy is one of the enduring mysteries of Hazel's life.

~

At the turn of the twentieth century, Troy—located 150 miles north of New York City and eight miles north of Albany, on the eastern bank of the Hudson River—was, on the basis of per-capita income, one of the wealthiest and most culturally sophisticated cities in the nation. The US economy was thriving as the "Second Industrial Revolution" ran from about 1870 to 1914, and Troy was an economic juggernaut powered by metals and textiles.

Early in the nineteenth century, Troy was at the vanguard of progressive education. In 1821, Emma Willard, the wife of a physician, opened a boarding school, initially called the Troy Female Seminary but renamed after its founder seventy-four years later, as one of the first schools in the country to educate women only. Three years later, Stephen van Rensselaer, a descendant of the founding patroon of Rensselaer County, teamed with scientist Amos Eaton to establish Rensselaer Polytechnic Institute, the first university in the English-speaking world dedicated to engineering, in the former Farmer's Bank building at the northwest corner of Middleburgh and River Streets.

In 1827, Troy housewife Hannah Lord Montague—married to a local shoemaker named Orlando, a fastidious dresser who would come home several times a day to change into a freshly laundered shirt—grew weary of washing her husband's shirts over and over, when only the edges were getting soiled. She devised a novel solution: Why not just snip off the collars and cuffs so that they could be washed and starched separately, then reattach them with string, a ribbon, or buttons? Hence was born the detachable collar-and-cuff industry. By the early twentieth century, Troy, home to twenty-six collar-and-cuff makers—employing thousands of women (who could sometimes be heard while they worked warbling such tunes as "Wrapped in Red Flannels")—had earned its new sobriquet, "the Collar City." Cluett, Peabody & Company, the titan of the industry and manufacturer of the world-famous Arrow shirt, churned out more than four hundred assortments of detachable collars. In 1905, an artist by the name of Joseph C. Leyendecker, hired by Cluett, created the "Arrow Man," a universal symbol of urban sophistication, in a series of ads that appeared in playbills and on buses and trolley cars.

By the time Hazel Drew set out on her own, in 1902, Troy was a bustling, vibrant city, and in the midst of the largest population boom in its history: over seventy thousand people were squeezed into an area of about ten and a half square miles. Posh brownstone mansions lined Fifth Avenue—the "Tiffany of Streets," they called it; Washington Park, a rare privately owned urban green space, was surrounded by mansions erected during the Gilded Age.

Dozens and dozens of businesses crowded the downtown streets, which were covered in cobblestone, yellow and red brick, and large slabs of granite known as Belgian blocks. A plethora of department stores lined the sidewalks, displaying their wares through plate-glass windows. G. V. S. Quackenbush & Co. was among the oldest of them, having opened in 1824. Frear's Troy Cash Bazaar was the most famous, named after proprietor William H. Frear, whose motto, written on March 3, 1865, on a bronze plaque on the middle terrace of the store's ornate double stairway, with marble steps and cast-iron railings, was "One price and no deviation. Perfect satisfaction guaranteed or money cheerfully returned." Shoppers stepped foot inside Frear's through three arched marble entryways, leading to a two-story ground-floor arcade and a four-story atrium crowned by a huge sunlit dome.

On the weekends, so many people overcrowded the sidewalks of downtown Troy—both locals and out-of-towners—that pedestrians had to navigate their way through the streets, carefully avoiding trolley cars, horse-drawn carriages, and the automobiles that had just started appearing.

At times, the cacophony was astounding: Fiery socialists preached on street corners, shouting over the din of the steam-powered locomotives that ran right through the center of town twenty-four hours a day, seven days a week, ruffling the lines of laundry that families hung out to dry from the homes above their shops; suffragettes and union activists marched over to the factories up River Street, itself a beehive of activity as freight-bearing canal boats poured in and out of Troy. Occasionally you'd find an organ grinder cranking his barrel organ; other times a circus, newly arrived in town, might be parading from the train station up to Rensselaer Park at the northern end of the city, elephants in tow.

At night, the gaslighted streets were hardly empty—thanks to a vibrant theater scene—but were considerably less crowded, which, if you happened to find yourself wandering around downtown, meant exercising a degree of caution to avoid pickpockets or ruffians itching for a brawl after a night of drinking in one of the city's many taverns.

Unofficially, Troy was split into two sectors: the south, running below the Champlain Canal, and the north, above it. The north, along with downtown, was home to many of the collar-and-cuff businesses; the south, where Hazel Drew's family lived in 1908, was the industrial center of town, where immigrants, mostly hard-drinking, two-fisted Irishmen, worked "the heat"—hot metal foundries along the Wynants Kill. If you lived in South Troy, the saying went, you were one tough bastard; many years later, a Trojan GI, on the beaches of Normandy, would coin the phrase "South Troy against the world." South Troy was said to glow red at night from the multitudinous foundries churning out cast-iron stoves and bells, both local inventions.

Neighborhoods in South Troy, each several blocks long, sprang up around the different ethnicities—mostly Irish, Germans, Italians, Jews, Poles, and Ukrainians. Mom-and-pop grocery stores, where locals could "run a tab"—defer payment until payday—dotted every neighborhood, along with tailors, shoe-repair shops, and bakeries. Above these ground-floor storefronts the owners made their homes. Tensions between ethnicities were common, exacerbated by labor issues that repeatedly triggered strikes, especially in the steel and collar factories and among trolley brakemen and motormen. Every ethnic group had its gang, and if you belonged to one, you didn't want to find yourself in territory controlled by another—especially if you were outnumbered.

The epicenter of Troy's downtown district was Union Station, a bustling beaux-arts-style, block-long building featuring eight rows of train tracks, where over a hundred trains passed through every day, including thirty trains running between Troy and Albany, twenty-five minutes apart on the commuter "beltway." Troy was a popular destination not only in its own right, but also as a stopover, especially for businessmen heading south to New York City or military personnel called for deployment. Bounded by Union Street, Broadway, Fulton Street, and Sixth Avenue, the station featured high ceilings, huge windows, and a terrace overlooking a marble ground-floor waiting room with a built-in compass and a giant green ceramic clock perched above a staircase that led to a neoclassical subway tunnel that took northbound riders under the tracks and up to the trains on the Sixth Avenue side.

Bustling and noisy, Union Station was smack in the middle of where the action was, surrounded by hotels, restaurants, shops, commercial offices—and, not incidentally, brothels and gambling houses, where men congregated around huge card tables in clouds of cigarette smoke so thick you could barely see through them. Troy police weren't above looking the other way, in exchange for a cut of the pot.

The doyenne of this underworld was Mary Alice Fahey, better known as Mame Faye, who, in 1906, at the age of forty, had opened the first of what would become a string of rowhouse brothels along Sixth Avenue in the heart of Troy's red-light district—known as the Line—a run-down area full of noise and soot. In the following years, she would cater to clientele of every economic class, without discrimination—the marginalized and the powerful alike. Census reports from this time list up to six female boarders between the ages of nineteen and thirty-six living in Mary's original house, at 1725 Sixth Avenue, with occupations identified as "domestic" or "unemployed."

The house was perched just across the street from Union Station and three doors north of the police station, which made it convenient for the police to stand vigil over Mame's establishments in exchange for piping-hot cups of coffee (at least). The main stairway to Rensselaer Polytechnic Institute, a steep set of elaborate marbled steps and pillars known as the Approach, was situated at the corner of Sixth Avenue and Broadway, right behind the brothel.

Mame—the daughter of Irish immigrants and rumored to be a devout Catholic—recruited girls at local shops and restaurants, encouraging them to abandon their meager-paying jobs and come rake in mountains of cash working for her. She wasn't lying. Young, fetching prostitutes could earn up to fifty dollars a trick at a time when weekly incomes averaged between twenty and thirty dollars. Some women chose both: they kept their "day jobs" but turned tricks at night when the need arose.

It wasn't a glamorous life. Women might have sex with up to 150 men a week. Their careers were short-lived, often over and done with by the age of thirty, squeezed out by younger competition. Madams like Mame did better, though. They could earn up to $1 million a year in today's money—without paying a single penny in income tax.

Mame was said to stack her deposits into a carpet duffel bag and walk them over to the bank herself at the same day and time every week; once, on just such a sojourn, a lady on the other side of the street spotted her and called out, "Hey, Mame, how's business?" She replied: "It'd be a hell of a lot better if it weren't for amateurs like you!"

Mame was hardly the only game in town; the Line bustled with illicit activity. Mame, Jew Jenny, Big Flo, Little Flo—all of them openly advertised their services in the local papers: satisfaction guaranteed, "special attention given to high school boys and traveling salesmen." Prostitution was illegal in New York State—federally, it wasn't outlawed until 1910, with the passage of the Mann Act—but turning a blind eye wasn't. Few people of authority fussed over it, except for thundering Sunday preachers and rabble-rousing politicians who crusaded against it on the campaign trail, only to forget about their promises once the polls closed.

These were the two worlds of Hazel Drew—on one side the sleepy country towns of Poestenkill and Sand Lake, with their huckleberry farms, charcoal burners, and church picnics, and on the other, the teeming metropolis of Troy, sophisticated, intoxicating, and percolating with danger.

⌁

Hazel spent four years living and working at the Hislop home, from 1902 to 1906, as a domestic servant, a common occupation for young girls at the time, especially for those from poorer families, who would leave school at an early age to look for work. Families often forged close bonds with their servants, even considering them members of the family. But heaven help the servant who crossed the line; they'd be sent packing, often to a friend of the family. No explanation to the girl about what precipitated the breakup was necessary.

Thomas Hislop, Troy's first-ever city treasurer, was in his early forties and married with two children when Hazel started working for him in 1902. Born in Troy, Hislop studied business in college and took a job as a pharmacist at his father's neighborhood grocery shop after graduating. For a time he ran Foot & Thorne, a New York wholesale glass dealer, and co-owned the Troy and West Troy Ferry. Hislop served in the Spanish-American War and was a member of the National Guard, the Troy Citizens Corps, and Tibbits Cadets, an organization of war veterans who served with Troy military units as far back as 1876, named after Major General William Badger Tibbits, a prominent Civil War officer.

Hislop was known and respected around town; he belonged to all the right clubs, including the Masonic Veterans Association and the Troy Lodge of Elks. He was an officer at the Third Street Methodist Episcopal Church, and in 1902—the year Hazel was hired—the church's pastor, John M. Harris, was listed in the Troy city directory as living at 360 Third Street, the Hislop home, where Thomas Hislop resided with his wife, Nellie M. Hislop, and their two young children, Mabel and Thomas Jr. Hazel, too, worshipped at Third Street Methodist.

By the time Hazel drifted into his life, Hislop was done with private commerce—at least temporarily—and ready to take a shot at public service. It went well, at first. He won his first election, as city treasurer, on the Republican ticket, subsequently winning reelection. For years party standard bearers lauded him; Hislop, they crowed, was honest, efficient, and prudent, exactly the kind of man you wanted to entrust your money to. But in 1905, Hislop committed an unspeakable sin against the party, tossing his hat in the ring for mayor—as the candidate of the Citizens Party. In endorsing Hislop, attorney and former state senator Albert C. Comstock excoriated the same Republican establishment that up until that moment in history Hislop—and many other members of the Citizens Party—had belonged to, saying Republicans wanted a mayoral candidate who was "subservient, one who would obey commands. The organization wants obedience." Hislop came in third, behind Democrat Calvin E. Nichols and Republican Elias P. Mann, who was elected mayor.

The following year Hislop became embroiled in a particularly ugly scandal, resulting in the arrest, conviction, and imprisonment of his deputy city treasurer, Frank Carrington, for embezzling ten thousand dollars from the city. Hislop, who had erected his reputation as treasurer on the premise that he was an astute and cost-efficient guardian of public funds, was never charged with criminal wrongdoing, though he was sued by the Republican-run city over the missing funds in 1909 and never served in public office again.

It was during the same year that this scandal emerged that Hazel left the Hislop home after four years of service, for reasons that were never publicly revealed.

~

In 1907, Hazel took a job as a domestic servant at the home of John H. Tupper, a wealthy elderly Troy merchant dealing in coal—the "Black Diamond" of the times, used to power ironworks, the railroad industry, steamships, textile mills, and countless other essential industries. Like Hislop, Tupper was a prominent Republican and an officer in both the Troy Citizens Corps and the New York State National Guard.

A commanding, resolute businessman, Tupper served as a commissioner and secretary of the Retail Coal Dealers' Association of Troy, whose role was to crush the fiery labor movement that had resulted in a series of major work stoppages by miners seeking higher pay, shorter work days, and a seat for their union at the proverbial table. In 1897,

Tupper himself ran for mayor, nominated at the Troy City Republican Convention by Robert Cluett, a member of the influential collar-and-cuff family. In the run-up to the election, the *World*, a New York City paper, ran a less than flattering editorial saying that Tupper "knows more about coal than he does about politics." On a rain-drenched Election Day, Tupper was soundly defeated, losing by over two thousand votes to incumbent Francis J. Molloy, a protégé of Democratic Party boss Edward Murphy Jr., a former mayor of Troy and, at the time, a US senator from New York.

Hazel was reportedly close to Tupper's wife, Adelaide, who, in her early sixties, in many ways offered Hazel the maternal nurturing her own mother had struggled to provide. In the summer of 1907, the Tuppers vacationed in Canada, Adelaide's home country, returning with a gift for Hazel: the society pin bearing the Latin inscription *Concordia Salus*—"salvation through harmony"—with Hazel's initials engraved on the back. Hazel adored the brooch and was wearing it on the neck of her shirtwaist when her body was discovered in Teal's Pond, aiding her family in the identification of the body.

The Tupper home, at 711 Fulton Street, was in the shadows of Rensselaer Polytechnic Institute, which sat atop a hill overlooking the city. Past the slopes of RPI, the city landscape abruptly transitioned from stately residences, such as Hazel's new home, to the unhallowed red-light district, where Mame Faye and other madams ran their brothels. Less than two blocks from the Tuppers, on the corner of Sixth Avenue and Fulton, sat the notorious Comet Hotel, "frequented by girls of the street," as a private eye who had tailed a cheating husband there once described it.

On several occasions during her short tenure at the Tupper household, Hazel was stalked and assaulted on the street and once just outside the home by a stranger—she described him in a letter to her friend Mina Jones as either an Italian or Armenian—who apparently harbored an unhealthy obsession with the young beauty. Each time Hazel fended the miscreant off, once by smacking him vigorously over the head with her umbrella. According to Mina, the stranger told Hazel, "I will get you," as he fled from her beating. Hazel had written Mina that the strange man still bothered her at times.

It was into this cauldron of crime, sex, glamour, and corruption that eighteen-year-old Hazel Drew stepped when she moved to Fulton Street, the heart and pulse of the city. It was, perhaps, the beginning of a new life—and a new identity.

For better or worse, Hazel was determined to broaden her horizons.

On Christmas Day 1907, Hazel complained to her aunt Minnie that she was feeling sickly; Minnie volunteered to help her with her chores at the Tupper household that day. In early January, Hazel left the Tupper home, still complaining of feeling ill; she spent close to three weeks at her uncle William Taylor's secluded farmhouse in Taborton, where her brother Joseph and his wife, Eva, a confidant of Hazel's, lived at the time.

About two weeks into her stay at the Taylor farmhouse, Hazel received an envelope from John Tupper; inside was a sum of money and a letter informing her that he had replaced her with another girl—Hazel was now unemployed.

When Hazel finally recovered from her illness, she returned to Troy, securing work as a domestic for Edward Cary, a professor of geodesy at RPI and, like Hislop and Tupper, a prominent Republican, having twice been appointed Troy's city engineer in GOP-backed administrations. In 1908 Professor Cary lived with his wife, Mary, and their eleven-year-old daughter, Helen, on Whitman Court, on the city's East Side, a fashionable section of town that sat far away from the hustle and bustle—and grime—of downtown Troy. Many of the wealthy industrialists whose factories were tainting the air above the inner city had chosen to live there once the trolley lines opened up the hillsides.

Her stay with the Carys would last just over five months.

⁓

A few months before Hazel's murder, a fortune-teller had informed her that she would meet a sudden death sometime during the course of the year.

Hazel laughed it off. Confidence wasn't a problem; if anything, she possessed too much. She seemed to derive some perverse pleasure from tempting fate.

Even at the age of fourteen, she had been a striking, charismatic young woman with a flair for fashion, whose uncommon beauty garnered attention wherever she went. People spoke of her brilliant blue eyes and downy flaxen hair.

Somewhere along the way, Hazel realized that her beauty would open doors. And she intended to walk right through them.

Perhaps in reaction to the difficult lives she watched her parents endure, Hazel dreamed grand. Her roots were humble and her education slight—investigators would find frequent spelling and grammatical errors in the letters she left behind, which she'd draft first in pencil, before rewriting them in ink—and while only a lowly domestic servant, she had a degree of independence. For Hazel, the future was filled with unlimited possibilities.

And she was well on her way to reaching them. Despite her meager beginnings, she wound up working in the households of three of the most powerful men in Troy. She found a way, on a salary of $4.50 a week, to indulge her fancies. She dressed exquisitely, in custom-made dresses, extravagant hats, and Cuban heels. She loved to shop and dined at the finest restaurants. She traveled extensively—not just to New York City, Albany, Schenectady, and nearby resort areas like Lake George, but even out of state. In the last six months of her life, she had traveled outside of Troy three times—twice to New York City, staying two days each time, and once to Providence, for two days, before continuing on to Boston for three days.

Hazel wasn't just gregarious or convivial, she was socially driven. Her charm was prodigious, and she made friends easily wherever she went.

This, at least, was one facet of Hazel Drew's personality, though not everybody witnessed it. The longer the investigation continued, the more it would become evident that Hazel had lived a life filled with secrets, mysteries, and contradictions.

Chapter 4

Aunt Minnie

Staggered. That's how Jarvis O'Brien would have characterized his reaction to his interviews with Julia and John Drew, had anyone asked. How could the girl's parents have known so little about their own daughter's life? They hadn't even gotten her age right! At times they'd seemed not only clueless, but indifferent. Perhaps the shock of the tragedy had left them in a stupor?

Maybe, O'Brien thought, Mary and Edward Cary, Hazel's last employers before her death, would be able to provide some sorely needed insights into the life of Hazel Drew.

He turned out to be right about that, which is not to say he wasn't baffled by what information they did provide. Yes, Hazel had spent the previous five months working for the Carys, but on the morning of Monday, July 6—the day before she was last seen—she had tendered her resignation suddenly and walked out on the family. For some reason, she had chosen to keep the news from both her family and her friends.

Hazel had landed her job with the Carys in February 1908, likely through a shared connection with either the Hislops or Tuppers. All three families traveled in the same circles; like Hazel's previous employers, Edward Cary had ties to Republican politics and was active in fraternal affairs as a member of Apollo Lodge, Free and Accepted Masons.

A Troy native, Cary was a professorial-looking man with a prominent forehead, receding hairline, and bushy mustache. Born on December 19, 1865, he attended Rensselaer Polytechnic Institute from 1884 to 1888, graduating with a degree in civil engineering; as a student he worked part-time for Troy city engineer Charles Fuller. Upon graduating, he joined the faculty of RPI's department of surveying, simultaneously taking on a number of commercial projects. Cary married Mary Lyman, also of Troy, in 1892, and the couple had one daughter, Helen Elizabeth.

In 1902 he was appointed as an assistant professor, and two years later he was named professor of geodesy, railroad engineering, and highways, in which capacity he still served when he employed Hazel. Among faculty and students, he was considered blunt and straightforward. His colleagues included Dr. Arthur M. Greene Jr., head of the new department of mechanical engineering at RPI, who lived just one block away from the Carys, on Hawthorne Avenue, and employed a domestic servant named Carrie Weaver, one of Hazel's closest friends. (Upon learning of Hazel's death, Carrie, who was vacationing in Ohio at the time, sent her employer, Mary Greene, a copy of an account of the tragedy from a local paper along with a note saying, "Is this the Hazel that I know so well?")

Although a committed Republican, Cary wasn't nearly as politically ambitious as Hazel's previous employers. He was a delegate to the Rensselaer County Republican convention in 1900, but never ran for public office himself. He did, however, benefit from the prevailing spoils system, serving as city engineer under Republican-backed mayors from 1900 to 1902 and again from 1906 to 1908.

But his oversight of the engineering department, under Commissioner of Public Works Henry Schneider, a notorious political hack of dubious competence who was closely aligned with Rensselaer County Republican boss Cornelius V. Collins, surfaced as a campaign issue in 1907. According to the *Troy Daily Press*, "Many taxpayers have been heard to declare that the engineer's office represents one of the most glaring instances of bad government along the line of making public office a private map connected with the present administration." Elias Plum Mann, a Republican, was mayor at the time. The *Daily Press*—a Democratic newspaper—accused Cary, who was earning three thousand dollars a year from the city, in addition to his RPI salary, of overstaffing the department by handing out high-paying jobs to friends and colleagues at RPI, who were already overworked from their college obligations, resulting in both wasteful spending and a backlog in public improvements.

Further, the paper alleged that Cary and Schneider schemed to circumvent a city requirement that bids be solicited for any job over fifty dollars by artificially breaking them up into smaller projects, none totaling more than fifty dollars. "The plan is a simple one and might work well, but it is as bold a technical evasion of the intent, spirit and letter of the law as was ever concocted for enabling officials to pick favorites and turn jobs into the hands of men useful to the machine and who could be utilized at the expense of the city," the *Daily Press* argued.

One of those "favorites" was Robert T. Cary, Edward's cousin, who was awarded four jobs at a local school, for $42.85, $45.50, $49.86, and $49.84. Another was Frederick Schneider, Henry's brother.

Cary finished out his term but informed Mayor Mann he would not be interested in another reappointment if Mann was reelected in 1908, citing a new law that required the city engineer to confine all of his attention to official work, while boosting the annual salary from $3,000 to $3,500. However, he continued to serve as village engineer of Green Island, a small town across the Hudson River from Troy, in addition to his work at RPI.

～

At nine thirty on the morning of Monday, July 6, 1908, Hazel was in the backyard of the Cary home at 10 Whitman Court attending to chores when she was approached by Mary L. Cary. Hazel had returned from a holiday-weekend trip late the night before, sometime between ten and eleven o'clock.

"Hazel, that laundry is really piling up. I need you to take care of that today," Mrs. Cary told her. That meant dumping a ragbag full of dirty clothes into a sink; tossing in a pungent mixture of brown soap, starch, and ammonia; and scrubbing the clothes clean on a washboard in a cloud of steam. It was hard, unpleasant work, and apparently Hazel wanted no part of it.

She simply refused to do it.

Mary Cary was, by her own account, puzzled, but not nearly as much as by what happened next: Hazel announced that she was leaving her job, effective immediately. Within the hour she was gone, last seen by Mary fading into the distance, suitcase and large brown pocketbook (referred to by some witnesses as a handbag or shopping bag) in hand.

"There has been no trouble nor even slight unpleasantness," she claimed to investigators. "I did not question Hazel, and she departed without giving any explanation of her leave-taking."

Curious, thought O'Brien. The district attorney had already been made aware that Hazel had had her trunk—fully packed—shipped from the Cary house to her parents at 400 Fourth Street on Monday afternoon, suggesting, perhaps, that she had left less abruptly than he had been led to believe.

～

Although Mary Cary had nothing but kind things to say about Hazel—exemplary employee, indifferent to courting, regular churchgoer—she was baffled by Hazel's ability, on a weekly salary of $4.50, to afford to dress so extravagantly and travel so extensively, including those three trips in the previous six months, to places like New York City, Boston, and Providence, especially after having just endured weeks of unemployment while recuperating from an illness at the Taylor farm in Taborton.

"I could not understand where Hazel got the money to take these outings," Mary said. "She volunteered no information and was so enthusiastic in her descriptions of sights seen that my suspicion was disarmed if I ever harbored any. I recall now that Hazel never told me who, if anyone, accompanied her, whom she visited, where she stopped, or whether she defrayed her own expense."

And yet, Mary added, on another level she wasn't surprised at all that Hazel was gallivanting about the Eastern Seaboard whenever she got a chance: "As a matter of fact, the trips were such as might be expected from a girl of Hazel's temperament. She was constantly seeking to improve herself. She was a girl of more than ordinary intelligence for one in her station."

After leaving the Carys on the morning of July 6, Hazel took the short trolley car ride to the sprawling Pawling Avenue mansion of George B. Harrison for a quick visit with Minnie Taylor, her maternal aunt and, perhaps, her closest confidant. The two of them typically saw each other two or three nights a week.

It was an odd pairing: bonny young Hazel and her aloof, austere aunt, nineteen years her senior. Of medium height, Minnie had, like Hazel, light-blue eyes and blonde hair, which she wore piled atop her head. However, while Hazel was often praised for her beauty, the bespectacled Minnie, who dressed solemnly, in long, black taffeta skirts, was considered matronly. She was a haughty, formidable presence whom young nieces and nephews were warned never to beat in a game of dominos or Chinese checkers, and a notorious meddler who seemed to know everything about everyone in the family and was convinced that there were two ways of doing things: her way and the wrong way.

Born in 1869 in Berlin, New York, Wilhelmina Taylor was the tenth of Charles and Mary Taylor's eleven surviving children, seven years younger than Julia Drew. She moved around frequently as a young adult, staying with family members, though they unfailingly dreaded her visits. She was zealously loyal and protective of her family: when her sister Johanna was ill, Minnie went to Saratoga, New York, to look after her, until Johanna's death in 1895, at which time Minnie sought to prevent her sister's widower, Henry Ernst, from getting his hands on his deceased wife's share of the sale of Minnie and Johanna's parents' East Poestenkill farm.

In the late 1880s, Minnie worked as a housekeeper in Lansingburgh, a village in the north end of Troy, at the Phoenix Hotel, a popular gathering spot for prominent businessmen and politicians, especially Republicans. (Decades earlier, Kentucky's Henry Clay—"the Great Compromiser," who served in both the Senate and House and sought the presidency unsuccessfully five times—stayed there.) By 1897, she had moved to Greenfield, Massachusetts, to be near her older sister, Mary Ann Davis, whose husband owned a laundry business. Around 1905, she returned to Troy, landing a job with Harrison, a wealthy real-estate developer, attorney, and banker.

Harrison's father, himself an influential man, had owned the Troy Malleable Iron Company, which, like John Tupper, Hazel's second employer, clashed frequently with unions. Originally located on Congress Street between Fourteenth and Fifteenth in Troy, the company moved to Colonie around the turn of the twentieth century after union disputes, including one notorious showdown in 1883 (by which time Harrison had moved on) in which Pinkerton Detective Agency operatives wound up gunning down striking workers. Like every prominent Republican in Troy, he belonged to all the right clubs, including Pafraets Dael (a Dutch term interpreted by some historians to mean "lazy man's paradise"), the Laureate Boat Club, and the Island Golf Club, and (like both Tupper and Thomas Hislop) was an officer in the Troy Citizens Corps, having served on the front lines during the Spanish-American War.

Minnie, like Hazel, traveled on the fringes of elite circles. She was the last member of Hazel's family to see the girl alive. And, O'Brien would become convinced, if there was one person, other than the killer, who went to their grave knowing the truth about the circumstances leading to Hazel's demise, it had to be Aunt Minnie.

Late in the morning of Monday, July 13, County Detective Duncan Kaye returned with Minnie Taylor to Jarvis O'Brien's courthouse offices for questioning. They sat her down in a wooden chair and offered her a glass of water, which she accepted. She sipped from it daintily and rested the glass on a coaster on O'Brien's wooden desk. The district attorney studied the woman's face, which seemed frozen in something between a scowl and a grimace, and decided to proceed with caution.

"Now," he said, "we understand that you were with your niece on the Fourth of July in Troy, and that you then saw her again on the morning of Monday, July 6."

Minnie paused, collecting herself. "Yes," she said. "That is correct on both accounts."

"I see," said O'Brien. "Can you perhaps share with us some of the details of those occasions?"

At about 10:30 a.m. on July 6, Minnie said, Hazel showed up unexpectedly on the doorstep of the Harrison home. She was carrying her light-brown suitcase, monogrammed on the handle with her initials, H. I. D., and a soft brown pocketbook.

"Why was she there?" asked O'Brien.

"She still had some of my clothes from the weekend and wanted to drop them off. Nothing more to it than that."

"Over the Fourth?"

"That's right," Minnie said.

"I'm not following you, Miss Taylor," Kaye said. "Did you accompany Hazel on her trip to Lake George over the holiday weekend?"

"Not Lake George," Minnie said. "Schenectady."

O'Brien and Kaye exchanged a look. Hadn't Mary Schumaker, the dressmaker, said that Hazel had waited at her house for a new shirtwaist until 11:00 p.m. on July 3 because she was leaving for Lake George the following day?

Kaye intervened: "From what we were told, she was planning a trip to Lake George and was pretty excited about it."

That was true, Minnie said, without missing a beat. "She wanted me to go to Lake George with her on the Fourth, but I didn't want to go there on that day because the trains are so crowded on holidays. So Hazel abandoned that trip and we went to Schenectady instead."

"I see," said O'Brien. He paused for a moment before continuing. "Tell us about the weekend. We'd be most appreciative if you didn't leave anything out, no matter how insignificant it may seem."

"Take your time," Kaye said. "We're not going anywhere."

On the morning of Saturday, July 4, Minnie said, Hazel arrived at the Harrison house, believing that she and her aunt were about to embark on an overnight trip to Lake George. Hazel had been looking forward to it for some time. Minnie had packed lightly, so she suggested they consolidate their belongings into Hazel's single suitcase. As Minnie added her belongings to the bag, she slyly took inventory of its contents: a nightgown, a kimono, a golden heart-shaped locket, a black handbag, silken underwear, and several new shirtwaists, in addition to various toiletries.

After Minnie talked Hazel out of going to Lake George, they made alternative plans to attend the Independence Day parade in Troy, then catch a trolley to Schenectady, where they would spend the night with relatives, returning the following day.

On the way to the parade, they stopped at the home of Hazel's brother Joseph and his wife, Eva, to deposit the suitcase. They spoke briefly with Eva, but not Joseph, who, though home at the time, made no effort to greet his sister or aunt.

The parade of local and visiting militia and members of the Elks Club (grand-marshaled by Thomas Hislop, Hazel's first employer) began at ten o'clock that morning. Afterward Minnie and Hazel strolled over to Rensselaer Park in Lansingburgh, where they milled about, enjoying the fairgrounds. The park, stretching across forty-two acres, was packed—some forty thousand people wandered through the gates for the celebration decked out in colorful holiday attire. Automobiles of every make and color were displayed in battle-line formation on the grass. The park was almost intolerably noisy, with live music, the explosion of fireworks, the thunder of cannons, and the crackling of rifles from "sham" warfare.

"You're doing just great, Miss Taylor," O'Brien said. "Please continue."

"It was warm," she said, "and crowded, so we languished for a time in the grove of trees in the midway section of the park. It was cloudy and they talked of rain, but it never came, thank goodness."

"How late did you stay?" O'Brien asked.

"We stayed for a good long while," Minnie said. "We left at five o'clock, give or take."

"Did you meet anyone there? Speak to anyone?"

"Whatever do you mean?" Minnie said sharply. "We nodded hello at people, of course, but no real conversations."

"Nobody at all?" Kaye said.

"I just told you no, didn't I?" replied Minnie.

Kaye couldn't help himself from smirking.

"Miss Taylor, your brother-in-law says he ran into you and Hazel on the street on July 4," O'Brien said. "Is that correct?"

"That's right, at Franklin Square."

"Did you and Hazel have a conversation with him?"

"Not much to talk about with him."

About an hour later, shortly before the beginning of the sunset parade, Minnie and Hazel returned to Joseph and Eva's house to retrieve the suitcase. Next, as planned, they boarded a trolley car to Schenectady. They spent that night and most of the following day at 4 Pearl Street, in the four-room house of Hazel's maternal cousin (and Minnie's niece), twenty-seven-year-old Annie Becker Weinmann, who lived there with her husband, John; their three children; and Annie's eighteen-year-old sister, Etta Becker. Annie and Etta were particularly close to Hazel; their mother, Eliza Taylor Becker, who had passed away in 1895, was the older sister of Minnie Taylor and Julia Drew.

Enjoying their stay, Minnie and Hazel didn't leave Schenectady until about 9:00 p.m. on Sunday, arriving back in Troy about ninety minutes later. From there, they boarded the Berman Park trolley (an account subsequently confirmed by conductor Roy Beauchamp, who was working that night). Hazel alighted first, at Whitman Court, between ten and eleven; Minnie stayed on until she reached the Harrison home.

"Did anything out of the ordinary happen in Schenectady?" O'Brien asked. "Did you meet up with anyone, other than family?"

"No, no one," replied Minnie flatly.

"What kind of mood was Hazel in?"

"Cheerful, as always."

"Wasn't she disappointed about Lake George?" said Kaye. "Why was she so eager to go there in the first place?"

Minnie insisted she hadn't a clue.

"OK," O'Brien said. "Tell us about the morning of Monday the sixth. She shows up unexpected at your door and then what?"

"That was it," Minnie contested. "She stayed just a few minutes, then left."

"Did she say anything else? Like where she was going?" prompted Kaye.

"She said she was going to Watervliet to spend the day. She left and took a car down the street. I saw her go off in that direction."

"What's in Watervliet? Why there?" O'Brien pressed.

"There are a couple of girls out that way Hazel knows."

Kaye scribbled down the names of two women.

"Did she mention anything to you about having quit her job?" O'Brien asked.

Minnie locked eyes with her interlocutor. "Hazel didn't say anything about that to me. What gave you that idea?"

"So you didn't know she left the Carys?" Kaye said.

"I told you no," Minnie answered. "But when I went to see Julia a couple of days later—that Thursday, I think it was—I heard then that Hazel had had her trunk sent home. I knew something must have happened at her job," said Minnie, trailing off.

"I see," O'Brien said. "Let me come right out and ask you, Miss Taylor. Can you think of any reason at all why Hazel might have been in some kind of trouble? Why anyone would want to hurt her or see her dead?"

"Goodness, no," Minnie said. "The girl was a peach; not an enemy in the world. It's a terrible tragedy, what happened to her."

"Indeed it is," the DA said.

"We understand that your niece lived and worked in Troy. Do you have any idea why she might be out in the woods of Sand Lake?" interjected Kaye, who was far less interested in exhibiting any sort of decorum with the fractious aunt.

"She might have been out that way to visit my brother Will. He lives out there, by the pond. Though I can't imagine why anyone would want to visit him."

O'Brien and Kaye were momentarily flummoxed. Her brother? How could John and Julia Drew have neglected to mention family living near the scene of the crime?

As the questions continued, Minnie's patience wore thin. The more O'Brien and Kaye pressed for details about Hazel's personal life, the more reluctant Minnie seemed to become. She refused even to share the names of any of Hazel's friends, other than the two women in Watervliet, insisting that they couldn't have had anything to do with the crime.

"You say you saw your niece often—three times a week, on average?"

"That's what I said," Minnie responded.

"And the last time you saw her was on the morning of July 6, six full days before her body was identified?"

"Do you have a question I have not already answered?"

Yes, I do, O'Brien told himself. *Why on God's earth wouldn't you have reported her missing?*

He motioned for Kaye to escort her from the courthouse, and as he watched them depart, he was as certain as he could be that Minnie Taylor would be back here in this very same room—maybe more than once. As unpleasant as the prospect seemed, he wasn't through with her yet.

On her way out of the courthouse, Minnie was pounced on by a gaggle of reporters, who sprayed her with questions.

"She was a good girl," snapped Minnie. "I won't tell you who her friends are, because it could get a lot of girls into trouble. It's none of your business, anyhow."

O'Brien, who overheard the exchange, found the comment puzzling. Why would releasing the names of Hazel's friends get them into trouble?

He packed the question away for another day.

Did Hazel ever make it to Watervliet on Monday, July 6, as Minnie had implied?

According to *most* press accounts, the answer was no. Investigators tracked down Sarah Moran and Ida Rowe, two of her friends who lived in Watervliet (formerly West Troy), a gritty and bleak factory city across the Hudson River.

Both women, who had met Hazel the previous summer at the Bly boarding house on Plank Road in Poestenkill, said they weren't expecting Hazel on July 6 and hadn't seen her in over a month.

However, the July 14 edition of the *Binghamton Press and Leader* claimed that Hazel had spent the afternoon of July 6 at the home of Amelia Huntley, at 383 Third Avenue, then left without announcing her destination.

Two days later, the Albany *Times Union* reported that a Watervliet man had told John Drew that he had seen Hazel in town on the night of Monday, July 6. According to John Drew, this man—whose identity was never publicly revealed—had written his name on a card, which Drew passed along to Duncan Kaye. Kaye claimed to have scoured Watervliet in search of him, but he either never found him, dismissed the lead altogether, or decided for reasons unknown not to share whatever it was he had discovered, because nothing was ever made of it again—though John Drew never stopped believing it to be true. "Best look in Watervliet," he told an *Evening World* reporter. "She went there Monday night for some reason."

In an interview with reporter William M. Clemens in the July 22 *Thrice-a-Week World*, Amelia Huntley said Hazel had visited her "only a few weeks ago and was happy and contented, and I am sure she did not have a care in the world." Unfortunately, Clemens never provided his readers with an exact date.

In the end, investigators were convinced that Hazel hadn't been to Watervliet on July 6. Which meant she had either abruptly changed her plans or lied to her aunt. Or that the fiercely protective Minnie Taylor was lying to O'Brien and Kaye.

~

The interrogation of Minnie Taylor was excruciating, but not fruitless. She had more to say than either of the parents and left investigators with a handful of tantalizing leads to pursue. Hazel's cousins in Schenectady, with whom she had apparently spent the night of the Fourth and most of the following day, would be questioned to see if they could add anything to what Minnie had already told them. Even more promising was the fact that Julia's older brother William owned a farmhouse in Taborton less than a mile from the pond where Hazel's body had been found. Perhaps, as Minnie said, Hazel had been on her way to see him?

O'Brien and Kaye would have to head back out to Sand Lake to speak with William Taylor; based on their previous interactions with the locals at the pond, they weren't savoring the prospect. As Trojans, they were pariahs in the area, and it wouldn't help if the people on Taborton Mountain started thinking they were trying to pin the murder on one of their neighbors.

Just as O'Brien was preparing to leave his office to head out to the country, he received an urgent phone call from Harry Fairweather, one of the doctors who had been present during the autopsy, calling from Sand Lake. Not realizing the DA was about to embark on a trip out there himself, Fairweather pleaded with him to get to Sand Lake immediately.

"Harry, what's all this about?" O'Brien said. "I am heading out there right now to follow up with the uncle near the pond."

"Jarvis, there's a boy here! I just had a chat with him. He says he saw Hazel up near that pond about a week ago. Strolling about without a care in the world!"

Chapter 5

Mountain or Molehill?

Early in the evening on Tuesday, July 7, as he rolled down Taborton Mountain, on the outskirts of Sand Lake, Rudolph Gundrum noticed a shadowy figure hailing him from farther down the road. Gundrum, dressed in his customary collarless white shirt, jeans, and suspenders, took another sip of hard cider and then stashed the jug under the seat in his carriage. Gundrum was on his way into town to pick up some friends from Troy at the Averill Park trolley terminus for a planned fishing trip, more than likely stopping off at Harris's Hotel for a round or two (or three) of drinks. As he drew nearer, the shape gradually took form, and he recognized the grinning face of Frank Smith—one of his neighbors up on the mountain. Smith, who was just seventeen—a good eighteen years younger than Rudy—wasn't very bright and could be a bit annoying, but he was a good enough kid, and it meant Rudy had someone other than his horse to talk to for a bit.

"Whoa there, Frank, what are you up to . . . no good?"

"Hahaha, no, no, no . . . very funny, Rudy. You heading into town?"

"Hop in, buddy," said Gundrum, warmly offering the boy a swig from his jug.

The pair chatted about their day as the carriage rumbled down Taborton Mountain, with the sun overhead gradually fading into the muggy evening sky. They passed a few of their neighbors as they continued beyond Conrad Teal's farm and the turnoff road to Will Taylor's place. Less than a mile from the foot of the mountain, near a twist in the road known among the locals as the Hollow, they saw a figure heading up toward them.

Squinting in the approaching twilight, Gundrum could see that this wasn't another local farmer. Rather, a beautiful young woman, extravagantly dressed—as if on her way to a ball at the governor's mansion—was walking up the hilly slope.

"Hey, Frank," said Gundrum, slowly turning to his companion. But the boy seemed not to hear him. Instead he was staring ahead, transfixed by the girl.

"That's old man Drew's oldest daughter," Smith muttered.

Rudy remembered the Drews, who had lived in Taborton a few years back, but not this girl. She strode forward casually and confidently, swinging an ornate black hat in her hands. She smiled briefly at Rudy before making direct eye contact with the boy.

"Hiya, Frank."

"Howdy-do, Hazel."

After this brief encounter, Smith and Gundrum continued on their way down the mountain. Rudy glanced to his right, noting that Smith still seemed a little dazed; then again, that was nothing new with the boy. He cast a last glance back over his shoulder at the pretty young girl, who looked to be heading up the path toward Will Taylor's, and then turned once again to Smith.

"You OK there, Frank? Nobody working up at the Browns' looks like that, huh?" teased Gundrum. "Tell you what, pal. You look like you could use a drink. First round at Harris's is on me."

It was a harmless enough beginning to the night of July 7, 1908, but in the end neither of them would ever forget it.

For Jarvis O'Brien and his team of investigators, events transpired at a vertiginous pace from July 13 to July 15, and by the time the dust had settled, three cardinal suspects had emerged:

William Taylor, Hazel's morose fifty-four-year-old uncle, spoken of around town as a crotchety old man who had once attempted suicide; Frank Smith, the seventeen-year-old Taborton farmhand who was derided by his neighbors as a "half-witted" dullard and was apparently obsessed with Hazel; and Rudolph Gundrum, a thirty-five-year-old charcoal burner renowned on the mountain mostly for his drunken escapades.

Rensselaer County had posted a thousand-dollar reward for the arrest and conviction of Hazel's killer, and newspapers were demanding arrests.

The *Evening Journal* of Wilmington, Delaware, headlined a front-page United Press story: Talk of Lynching Girl's Murderer.

"The greatest indignation is felt here, and should the expected arrests be made to-day [*sic*] every precaution will be taken to avoid lynching, which was openly talked about by the scores of people who visited the little home at No. 100 [*sic*] Fourth Street, where the father and mother of the girl are almost distracted with grief," the story read.

Both Troy and the town of Sand Lake were percolating with a strange brew of frenzy and fervor. Hundreds of tourists visited the crime scene daily, plucking cattails as souvenirs from "the marshy, watery waste where the young woman's body was found," as the *Evening Telegram* of New York phrased it.

In the midst of this circus atmosphere, on the afternoon of Tuesday, July 14—exactly one week after her last-known sighting—Hazel Drew was buried in a quiet churchyard ceremony at Poestenkill, where her life had begun just twenty years earlier. The Reverend J. H. E. Rickard of the Third Street Methodist Church, where Hazel had attended services in Troy, presided in what was described in the press as a "heavy electrical storm," drenching the ten or so mourners at the sparsely attended ceremony. The rapidly deteriorating state of the body had forced her family to hastily prepare for the funeral. Roses adorned the casket as it was lowered into the earth. The family had originally planned to bury Hazel at Mount Ida Cemetery in Troy, but reconsidered at the last moment, opting for Brookside Cemetery in Barberville instead. (One of the many incongruities in the life and death of Hazel Drew is that her death certificate misidentifies her resting place.)

Minnie Taylor was bereft. "If I could only cry!" she was overhead to say. "Tears will not come to relieve my grief." At one point she collapsed by the bier and had to be revived with stimulants.

William Taylor attended the funeral service earlier in the day at the Larkin Brothers mortuary, but skipped the internment (he claimed he wasn't even aware of the location change until reporters told him). On his way out, a newspaper reporter hollered at him: "What do you think happened to Hazel?"

"Well," Taylor replied flatly, "I think she was waylaid and done away with."

A day earlier, on the evening of July 13, District Attorney Jarvis O'Brien and Detective Duncan Kaye were back in Sand Lake, driving up the winding lane that twisted through the slopes of Taborton Mountain. Kaye indicated to O'Brien to take the turn a little before the pond where the body was found, and they were soon marching in the country heat up to the stoop of William Taylor's farmhouse. Three hard knocks later, the door swung open, and the detectives were greeted by a man with beady eyes set within a compact face, topped by tousled hair that partially obscured his receding hairline.

"What the hell do you want?" he asked.

Hazel's uncle William Taylor lived in a farmhouse on what the locals imaginatively referred to as Taylor's Turn, about a quarter of a mile from Teal's Pond. He was a sullen, cantankerous man who seemed to make a habit of alienating everyone he came in contact with. With family, he fought; neighbors preferred to avoid him altogether. Libbie Sowalskie, a sixty-year-old widow, had rebuffed his marriage proposal a year earlier; he called on her at her home unexpectedly, popped the question in a hurry, and—upon being rejected—apologized and left. His own mother found living with him so unpleasant that she eventually left and moved in with one of her daughters.

William was the second of Charles and Mary Ann Taylor's eleven children. He was said to be a "huge" man, though, like most farmers, he had picked up a stoop from years of hard labor on his Taborton farm, where he had lived for the past eighteen years. Taylor fought severe bouts of depression, and after the death of his first wife, Emelia Pollack, in 1903 at the age of fifty-nine, he had attempted suicide by slitting the arteries at his wrists.

Misery seemed to follow William Taylor everywhere.

~

After first demanding proof of identification, Taylor had allowed the detectives to enter, and now they shifted uncomfortably in their seats, taking in the home and this strange, aloof man.

"Mr. Taylor, I expect you know what we came out here to talk to you about," O'Brien started. "We need to ask you about your niece. Specifically, when was the last time you saw her?"

"Been some time . . . last winter, it was," Taylor said.

"You didn't see her last week, then?" interjected Kaye.

"Last winter, I said."

"Did you have any knowledge of Hazel being out this way on the seventh of July?" Kaye asked.

"Sure I did."

Kaye and O'Brien waited, expecting Taylor to elaborate. Awkward silence ensued.

"Well?" Kaye finally prompted.

"Young Frank Smith's been talking all over the neighborhood about seeing her out near the pond that evening."

Frank Smith—that was the boy Dr. Fairweather had called so urgently about. O'Brien had assured him he would track Smith down right after they finished their chat.

"I'm told he even asked the Richmonds about her."

"Who's this?" asked Kaye.

"Couple staying here with me on the farm, working shares."

"You never asked around about Hazel, after hearing that Frank Smith had seen her? Not even after the body was pulled from the pond?" O'Brien said.

"You can't put much stock in what somebody heard Frank Smith say. That boy has his issues."

"What *did* you do when you heard about the body, Mr. Taylor?" asked Kaye.

"Well, I went into town," he said. "To Crape's Hotel."

"Crape's?" Kaye said. "Why there?"

"I needed a shave," Taylor answered.

"So you heard rumors of your niece being up here and a dead body being found and you went into town for a shave?" asked O'Brien, trying not to betray any trace of astonishment.

"That's right."

"Well, weren't people buzzing about the body at the pond?" Kaye asked.

"Sure they were."

Even now, Taylor wasn't betraying a hint of emotion; O'Brien couldn't fathom what was going on inside this man's mind.

"You know there's a telephone down there, at Crape's?" Kaye said.

"Sure I do."

"Did you ever think to call your sister? Maybe tell her about what you were hearing?"

"Why, no, I never did. I don't care to get involved in things that don't concern me."

"OK, Mr. Taylor, so just to set the record straight, you weren't expecting Hazel here on July 7, and you never did see her on that day. Is that correct, sir?" the district attorney asked.

"That's what I said, ain't it? Hadn't seen her since the winter."

Taylor was a taciturn, unpleasant man—he might have sweated icicles for all they knew—but there was something about the way he responded to their questions that led O'Brien and Kaye to suspect that his strangeness was more a function of insularity and self-absorption than deception. Though Taylor certainly didn't seem in any way upset or grief-stricken by his niece's death, nor did he seem remorseful that he hadn't paid more heed to the ramblings of Frank Smith, or even been curious about who could have been responsible for Hazel's death.

"Perhaps we can speak with the Richmonds?" O'Brien said.

"If you want to, go ahead," said Taylor. "That's nothing to do with me."

Frank and Frederika Richmond told the investigators that they had run into Smith at the Averill Park trolley terminus at about nine o'clock on the night of July 7. Smith told the couple that he had seen Hazel on Taborton Road earlier that night and believed she was heading up to the Taylor farm.

When the Richmonds asked Taylor about it the following morning, he told them Hazel hadn't been expected and had never appeared.

O'Brien and Kaye knew what they had to do next: find Frank Smith.

Frank Smith and Rudy Gundrum most certainly did encounter Hazel on July 7; in fact, other than the killer, they were likely the last people to see her alive. Smith knew the girl and, according to villagers, harbored an unhealthy fascination with her. According to Taylor, the boy would pop by his farm unannounced, asking if she was there. He talked about her frequently and was overheard to say she was the prettiest girl in that section of the country. Smith had met Hazel years earlier on the Taylor farm, having been introduced by John Drew. He met her a second time while passing through the farm on his way to hunt. Their final encounter—prior to July 7—was the previous winter, during a two-hour visit to the Taylor home. William Taylor and Joseph and Eva Drew were all there, along with Hazel, who was perched on a chair, reading. (In typical Smith fashion, he later told another version of the story, in which he and Hazel played cards.)

Rudy Gundrum, on the other hand, had never met Hazel Drew; more than anything else he was simply the victim of the devil's own luck, winding up in the wrong place at the wrong time. And for the next few weeks of his life, nobody let him forget it.

Born in Albany to German immigrants, Rudy was a pipe-smoking, suspender-wearing charcoal burner who lived with his wife, Carolina "Carrie" Wilhelmina Karl, in a farmhouse on Stagecoach Road, about three and a half miles from Teal's Pond as you climbed up Taborton Road. The Gundrums had five children crammed into two bedrooms in their mountain cabin, which had a stove pipe but no running water or indoor plumbing. Rudy's children knew enough to steer clear of the old man whenever he overindulged in liquor; he once put a couple of holes in the floor with his shotgun because he didn't like the way his daughter was cleaning it. But if he was in a good mood, he'd let the kids climb up onto his lap and squeeze the shotgun trigger.

The one thing Rudy loved more than that gun was his hard cider; many of his wild nights ended with a saloonkeeper having to drag him to his wagon unconscious, urging the horse to go, hoping that the pair would find their way home. He had plenty of time to imbibe while charcoal burning. Making charcoal was tedious, arduous work that involved chopping wood and hauling it to a pit—maybe twenty feet wide, its walls lined with mud and dirt—stacking it, and finally sitting vigil for hours on end to ensure the fire was kept under control. ("There goes a pit!" people in town would point out whenever they spotted a fire out on the mountain.)

Fires could smolder for two to three weeks if the pit was big enough, and the wait was more bearable with a jug of hard cider and a plate of "Rudy's potatoes"—grated and fried up with salt, pepper, and bacon fat in a cast-iron pan—close at hand.

On the evening of July 7, Rudy Gundrum headed into Averill Park to pick up a couple of friends and, in so doing, unwittingly carved himself a role in one of Sand Lake's most enduring mysteries.

Although Smith and Gundrum may have been the last people known to see Hazel Drew alive on that fateful evening of July 7, they weren't the only ones.

On Saturday, July 18—a full week after the discovery of the body—Henry Rollman and his wife, Charlotte, of Bears Head Road, at the tip of Glass Lake, came forward to reveal that they, too, might have spotted Hazel on Taborton Road on July 7, as they drove their horse and buggy down the mountain and into town.

As the investigation continued, other eyewitnesses who were out on Taborton Road on July 7 would gradually come forward to tell their stories. Finally O'Brien and his detectives were able to piece together a fairly reliable outline of the events as they unfolded on the mountain that night—the final hours of Hazel Drew's life—and in the days that followed:

6:00 p.m.: Rudy Gundrum glances at his watch—plenty of time to make it to the Averill Park trolley station to pick up his buddies from

Troy, who are visiting Sand Lake on a fishing expedition. He hitches up his buggy and starts down the mountain. The night is warm. Rudy glances up at the sky; it rained and thundered during the afternoon and is still overcast, but with any luck the rain will hold off.

6:50 p.m.: Frank Smith, hot and thirsty after a hard day's work on the farm, stops by the Brown house to chat with Brown's two daughters but misses them, as they are out walking.

7:00 p.m.: The Rollmans turn onto Taborton Road just a few feet below Teal's Pond, where they spot a pretty young woman matching Hazel's description plucking raspberries from a bush by the side of the road, at a spot known as the Two Chestnut Trees. They're about a quarter mile west of the recessed stretch of road known as the Hollow or, more colloquially, Piss Hollow, because Taborton mountain men—a rugged, uncouth bunch—often stop there to relieve themselves after a night of drinking in Averill Park (as do their horses).

Charlotte Rollman admires the girl's wardrobe, especially her hat: large and black, adorned with black plumes. She'd love one just like it.

"What a pretty girl!" she says to her husband.

"Yes, and a fool to walk along this road alone at this time of night," Henry replies. "She is taking a long chance with all the campers and charcoal burners that pass along this road."

After passing the Two Chestnut Trees, Charlotte looks back and sees that the girl is still standing in the very spot she was when they had passed her.

"My, but that girl is having a good time with those berries," she says.

7:05 p.m.: Just minutes after spotting the girl, the Rollmans, continuing down the mountain, encounter Julia and Henry Rymiller, who are heading up the road, about a quarter mile above Crape's Hotel at the foot of the mountain.

"We were driving away from the village Tuesday night," Henry Rymiller told investigators later, "and we passed Mr. and Mrs. [Rollman] coming into town only a little way from the hotel. We went right on up the road, but we did not . . . see anything of the girl."

Trailing directly behind the Rymillers is Marie Yeabauer, also heading up the mountain. She meets Smith and Gundrum just above the pond but doesn't see the girl.

7:10 p.m.: The Rymillers are passing the chestnut trees. In the course of ten minutes or so, Hazel Drew has disappeared from sight.

7:11 p.m.: Frank Smith, dreaming of an ice-cold beer, heads out on foot down the rocky slopes of Taborton Road on his way into town.

7:15 p.m.: The Rymillers pass the Hollow.

7:20 p.m.: Frank Smith flags down Rudy Gundrum for a ride.

7:22 p.m.: Rudy and Frank pass the Rymillers on the corner of Routes 43 and 66 and Taborton Road.

7:30 p.m.: Frank and Rudy reach the Hollow, about a third of a mile past Teal's Pond. They spot a young woman strolling idly toward them, on the left side of the road. She's alone, carrying nothing but a black-trimmed straw hat with three large plumes in her gloved hand, which she swings by her side. (This suggests that the suitcase and brown pocketbook she carried at her last-known sighting—leaving Minnie Taylor's place of employment—are no longer in her immediate possession.)

This is the first sighting of Hazel in thirty minutes, since the Rollmans spotted her at the chestnut trees.

8:00 p.m.: Smith and Gundrum arrive at Harris's Hotel for a couple of beers; Gundrum leaves Smith to pick up his friends.

8:13 p.m.: William Taylor sits on his porch, passing the time in his favorite rocking chair, smoking his pipe.

8:15 p.m.: Frank and Frederika Richmond leave the Taylor farm to drop Frank's brother Harry, of Lansingburgh, New York, off at the Averill Park trolley station. Again, no sign of Hazel.

8:30 p.m.: The Richmonds pass the Hollow.

9:00 p.m.: William Taylor retires for the evening—or so he says. The Richmonds arrive at the Averill Park station. While waiting with his wife and brother for the trolley back to Troy, Frank Richmond notices someone peering at them through a slit in the station window. He rises abruptly and marches outside to demand an explanation. As Richmond steps back into the summer night, Frank Smith is already fast approaching from the spot where he had been crouching down near the window. Richmond isn't sure if he should be relieved or worried to discover that it was Smith who was spying on them. Before he can even confront his teenage neighbor about his odd behavior, Smith assaults him with a barrage of questions.

"You got some company up at the house tonight, huh?" he burbles excitedly.

"Whaddya mean?" Richmond shoots back.

"I just met John Drew's daughter on the road, and she asked if Will was home," Smith says. "He is, ain't he? I told her he probably was."

"Will wasn't expecting any visitors that I knew about. I never met his niece, but we didn't pass anyone along the road on our way here."

Smith seems puzzled. Then again, Smith always seems puzzled.

9:15 p.m.: The Richmonds say goodbye to Harry and set off for Taborton. They pass no one on the way home except a few charcoal peddlers also making their way up the mountain.

When asked later if one of these burners might have committed the murder, Frank Richmond replied, "The charcoal burners are not in condition to do anything on their way home but sleep."

10–11:00 p.m.: The Richmonds arrive back at the Taylor farmhouse. They look for Taylor, to fill him in on their conversation with Frank Smith. Asked later by O'Brien if he conversed with Taylor upon returning that night, Richmond replied, "I did not see him until the next morning."

"Where was he that night?" O'Brien asked.

"I suppose he was sleeping. I don't know."

The following morning over breakfast, Frank Richmond tells Taylor of their encounter with Smith.

"I hear that Hazel Drew is up here," he says.

Taylor looks confused. "If she is up here, I have not seen her," he replies.

Smith, meanwhile, spends the next couple of days asking around the neighborhood if anyone has seen Hazel Drew. Nobody says they have.

Less than a week later, on July 11, when Hazel's body is discovered in Teal's Pond, Frank Smith is there to help retrieve the body. The corpse is dressed in the exact same clothes Hazel was wearing when he and Gundrum last saw her; that was less than a quarter of a mile from the pond. Yet, he says nothing to the detectives he speaks with about any suspicion that the victim is Hazel.

On the morning of Sunday, July 12, Smith tells his parents he believes the victim is Hazel Drew—even before her identity has been confirmed by the Drew family or reported in the papers. Frank's father, John, visits the Taylor farm to break the news to William, yet Taylor never bothers to tell his sister that her oldest daughter might be dead.

⌒

After leaving the Taylor farm, O'Brien, and Kaye, joined by Detective William Powers, tracked down Frank Smith in Taborton; it was now close to 10:00 p.m. Still, they spent the next two hours roasting him—it would be the first of many such interrogations involving Smith over the course of the investigation, each one leaving them more exasperated than the last.

"Now Frank, we understand that you may have seen the dead girl that wound up in the pond down the road sometime last week," O'Brien said.

"Yes, sir, I reckon I may have."

O'Brien and Kaye were livid: the young farmhand hadn't said a word to them about suspecting that the victim was Hazel Drew when they queried him on July 11 by Teal's Pond.

"When did this occur?" O'Brien said.

"I'm trying to think back. Maybe a week ago Monday morning."

"So that would have been Monday, July 6. In the morning?"

"Yes, sir."

"Are you sure about that, Frank?"

"Wait," Smith said. "No, I think it was Tuesday. July 7. Definitely Tuesday."

"In the morning?"

"Yes, sir."

"Now Frank, didn't you meet the Richmonds, who work the farm for Hazel's uncle, that night and say you had seen Hazel and asked her whether she was stopping at their house?" pressed O'Brien.

"Hmm . . . well, yes, I guess I did. I met them on the flats up near Sand Lake about half past ten."

"At night?"

"Yeah, that's right. Tuesday night."

"Hold on a second," interjected Kaye. "The Richmonds said they met you at the station in Averill Park, not out on the road."

"That's right, that's right! Now we got it straight," Smith said.

The awkward youth coughed and wrangled his hands nervously, while O'Brien and Kaye exchanged weary glances.

"OK, Frank, what about Hazel's hat? Did you see her wearing a hat that . . . Tuesday night, was it?"

"Yeah, ya know, come to think of it, I think she did have a hat with her."

"What kind of hat?"

"Fancy black one . . . with feathers."

"Like that hat we all saw Saturday night up by the pond when the body was pulled out?"

"S'pose so."

The boy, who couldn't help but squirm in response to the investigators' disbelieving stares, excused himself momentarily to fetch a glass of water.

"Frank, didn't you hit Hazel on the head and throw her body into the pond?" O'Brien demanded upon his return. "Tell the truth now."

"No, sir, I didn't! Why, I wouldn't do anything like that to a dog. I had nothing to do with such a thing," spluttered Smith.

"Why were you so curious about Hazel, asking if she was at her uncle's house, and all around at your neighbors'?"

"Shucks . . . I only wanted to know if she was at Taylor's so that I could stop by and say hi. Honest, that's all," he stammered.

Smith seemed lost in his own world. O'Brien thought he caught a whiff of liquor on his breath. The damn boy seemed congenitally incapable of being forthright. He thought the body might have belonged to Hazel, but he didn't really think about it. He alighted from Rudy's wagon to walk with her, or he didn't. Sometimes he remembered her saying she was going to her uncle's; sometimes she didn't. Maybe she had taken the trolley from Troy, maybe she hadn't. They barely chatted, beyond saying hello; she stopped and chatted with him for a bit.

After a debriefing by O'Brien, a reporter for the *Binghamton Press and Leader* described Smith's testimony as "an intricate mass of corrections and misstatements, so that William P. Powers of the District Attorney's office could scarcely make coherent stenographic notes."

Smith was an odd duck, O'Brien said. His statements were "unsatisfactory." Though not "overbright," he was "a deep one in some respects and guards his answers with what may be called cunning." It was impossible not to view him with suspicion.

"So far," the DA added, "Smith comes in closest touch of anyone we have spoken to with Hazel just before her death. I do not say he has knowledge of the way she met death, but I do say his conduct has been, to say the least, very peculiar. From what we learn, the girl was evidently on his mind . . . Why? I don't undertake to answer that inquiry, but it is full of suggestion."

Sand Lake postmaster George Shriner didn't do Smith's reputation with the investigators any favors when he came forward on Tuesday, July 14, to tell of his own bizarre encounter with the young man on the night of July 7: Shriner and Alfred Carmen were sitting on the post office porch on the northeast corner going up Taborton Road, shortly before 11:00 p.m., when Smith madly raced past them, stopped at Dr. Isaac Wright's Averill Park drugstore, and began rapping on the door.

"He was hatless and excited and gasping for breath. He rushed to the drugstore across the street and pounded vigorously. Getting no reply after two minutes' kicking and knocking, he ran across the street to us and exclaimed, 'Where's the drugstore man? Quick, I must get in the store at once. Hurry, tell me! Oh, tell me, help me get in there!'

"It was Frank Smith. Both of us knew him. We told him shortly that the place was locked. His eyes rolled in his head; he turned and looked again at the drugstore and then at us, and the next second was gone back up the road like a flash. We watched him racing madly by the Chris Crape Hotel and then lost him up the road toward Teal's Pond. I have often seen him the butt of the village loungers, but never saw him so strangely affected before. His advent and departure were so sudden that we were really astonished, even at Smith, of whom we were accustomed to expect almost anything stupid or erratic."

Shriner concluded by saying neither he nor his friend Carmen "can be mistaken in point of day, time, identity, and incident."

Had Frank Smith inadvertently harmed Hazel and rushed to Wright's in search of medical supplies to treat her?

Confronted by investigators in a follow-up interview, Smith—who originally said he had gone straight home after Harris's—conceded that Shriner's story was true, but there was an innocent explanation. After departing the trolley station, he had moved on to Crape's Hotel, where he met two campers from New York who bet him he couldn't run to the pharmacy and back within fifteen minutes. For proof, they demanded that Smith procure a postcard from the drugstore. As more memories flooded back to the boy, he recalled that he took another bet even later that night, requiring him to run around a tree in the village seventy-five times.

Leaving Smith after that particular follow-up interview, Kaye confided to Powers, "I really can't wait to get back to Troy."

~

The investigators left their initial marathon interview with Smith on the night of July 13 exhausted and completely unsure about the boy's story. Until they were able to speak with Rudy Gundrum and corroborate Smith's version of events, who could tell fact from fiction? The main problem now facing detectives was tracking down Gundrum: everyone wanted to talk with him, yet no one could find him. One newspaper, the *Evening Journal* of Wilmington, Delaware, reported that there was a "hot search" underway and that he "has disappeared," but his wife reported that he had merely gone into Troy to peddle his wares that morning. He had been expected back hours earlier; she couldn't imagine what was keeping him—maybe he was out drinking again? Carrie Gundrum didn't sound very happy about the prospect.

By midnight, there was still no sign of the wayward Gundrum, so investigators decided to wait until morning to resume the search. O'Brien left for Troy—he had a funeral in Fort Edward to attend the next day. Detectives Kaye and Powers remained in Sand Lake, booking a room at Crape's Hotel. Eager to get hold of Gundrum, the detectives set off back up the mountain before sunrise and finally caught up with Rudy on the road leading to his home in the early morning.

Initially, the detectives did not reveal to Gundrum that they had already spoken to Smith. Yet he essentially confirmed the details of their encounter with Hazel as related by his teenage companion.

Where did that leave the investigation? Gundrum seemed to be off the hook; Smith appeared to have an alibi.

That left one person of extreme interest unaccounted for: William Taylor. Smith had said—in one of his many versions of events—that Hazel told him she was heading up the road to Taylor's place. Taylor said he never laid eyes on her that night, wasn't expecting to, and would have been surprised if she was headed there. Smith spoke gibberish, but Gundrum backed up the gist of his account.

Kaye and Powers headed back to the farmhouse of Hazel's uncle.

~

As the door of the Taylor farmhouse opened, Kaye and Powers strode through purposefully, brushing aside a bemused William Taylor. This and subsequent discussions with William Taylor would be far less cordial than their initial encounter.

"Morning, Mr. Taylor," began Kaye.

"You boys forget something?"

"Yes, sir, we did. We have a few more questions for you. That Smith boy says when he talked to Hazel she was on her way to see you for a visit."

"Well, she never came here. I told you that."

"Do you think there's any possibility that she was on her way out here to see you on July 7?" Kaye asked.

"Now how am I supposed to answer a damn-fool question like that?"

"Give it a try," Powers urged dryly.

It turned out John Drew and William Taylor were not on the best of terms. Furthermore, the detectives learned that the Drews—except for Hazel, who had already moved out on her own to Troy by that time—had lived on the Taylor farm, working for shares for two seasons, from 1905 into 1906, until the arrangement had ended in some sort of dispute, forcing the Drews to vacate the premises. Hazel's older brother, Joseph, and his wife, Eva, would return to the farmhouse sometime later in 1907.

Taylor claimed his niece had been to the farm just four times since: once in the summer of 1906, twice in 1907 (once in January, once over the summer), and once in early 1908, when recuperating from her illness under Eva Drew's care.

"Hazel was out here last winter for three weeks while she was not working," Taylor said. "She seemed to enjoy herself in her own quiet way, but had no company. She seemed contented and left promising us another visit. That was the last time I saw her."

Taylor insisted he had never asked Hazel what was ailing her; he was helpless around sick people, he said, and assumed he would have been informed if it were anything serious. Eva and Joseph moved out of the farmhouse shortly after Hazel's visit, following a quarrel with their uncle, the subject of which William couldn't seem to recall.

"Now, Mr. Taylor, I want to ask you again, and I want you to think carefully before you answer me: When was the last time you saw your niece?" Kaye asked.

Taylor didn't hesitate a second: "Last winter, like I told you."

"That's your story, and you're sticking to it?"

"Sure, why wouldn't I?" Taylor said. "It's the truth, I tell you."

⌒

The detectives left the Taylor house that day not sure what to think. Taylor was a peculiar, thoroughly unpleasant character, but was he capable of murdering his own niece?

His whereabouts on the night of July 7, beginning at 8:15, when the Richmonds left for Averill Park, were unsubstantiated. He claimed to have retired for the night at nine, but nobody could confirm it. The

Richmonds returned around eleven, but didn't see Taylor again until the following morning.

Did Taylor have a motive for killing his niece? He was a bellicose, unstable man, with a history of violence, self-inflicted at least. He and the Drews had feuded. A year before Hazel's death, he had treated a young farmhand so brutally that authorities had to intervene. Taylor was a lonely widower looking for companionship; he had recently proposed to the widow Sowalskie, who rebuffed him. His actions—on both July 7 and July 11—were supremely baffling. On the day everyone in Sand Lake was talking about the discovery of a body that might very well have belonged to his niece, Taylor went for a shave.

Pushed by reporters to explain why he didn't attempt to identify the body, he responded, "What for? You say the features can't be recognized. I could only tell by the clothes. I have not seen Hazel for so long that I have not any idea of what she wears, so what's the use?"

Most bizarre of all, he ignored a neighbor's suggestion to let his sister know that her daughter was dead.

On Friday, July 17, County Detective William Powers and Troy police detective Louis Unser were instructed to keep a watch over Taylor. According to press reports, the uncle was perilously close to being arrested.

Chapter 6

Final Days

As unanswered questions accumulated, Jarvis O'Brien became obsessed with one mystery in particular: How had Hazel passed the night of Monday, July 6? After being closeted half the night with County Detectives Duncan Kaye and John Murnane, he told reporters, "Until I know the secret of Monday night, an arrest is out of the question." But in fact, investigators at this point had absolutely no idea how Hazel had spent the bulk of her last two days on earth.

When Hazel Drew had left the Cary house on Whitman Court that morning, she was carrying a light-brown suitcase with her initials engraved on the handle and a brown shopping bag, or oversize pocketbook. According to Minnie Taylor, Hazel arrived at the home of her employer, George B. Harrison, on Pawling Avenue, about a half hour later, still carrying both of the bags.

Yet when Hazel was spotted thirty-three hours later on Taborton Road, at about seven thirty on the night of Tuesday, July 7, by Frank Smith and Rudy Gundrum, she apparently had neither the suitcase nor the shopping bag in her possession. O'Brien and his stable of detectives wanted to know why. Had she left the bags behind, wherever she had come from? Or had she brought the bags with her to Sand Lake and hidden them among the bushes? Where were they now? In the possession of the murderer?

If Hazel had come to Taborton without her bags, she almost certainly hadn't intended to spend the night there. Julia Drew, for one, was convinced of this: Hazel was so fussy about her sleepwear that she refused to retire for bed in anything but her own nightgown. "Wherever she went, she always took her nightgown with her unless she was sure she would be back home to sleep," Julia said. "She would even take it when she went to her sister's overnight. Hazel would never have left the nightgown behind unless she expected to call for the bag again before bedtime." (By "sister," Julia likely meant Eva Lapp Drew, her sister-in-law.) John Drew, who appeared to know almost nothing about his eldest daughter, including her birthday, agreed with his wife about this.

There was another possibility: What if Hazel had brought the bags with her to Sand Lake and the murderer had tossed them into Teal's Pond, to prevent anyone from finding them? Was some crucial piece of evidence hiding inside one of these bags?

It was a long shot, but worth a try, O'Brien reckoned: he would instruct his detectives to drain the pond.

Thunder rolled around the mountains of Taborton on the morning of Tuesday, July 14. The crime scene had emerged as a popular attraction for tourists and locals alike—some merely gawkers, some amateur sleuths who believed they could solve the crime themselves—and today was no different, despite the clouds looming in the pewter sky.

So many had shown up, the *Troy Record* reported, that "the mountain road is blocked with every kind of a conveyance known—automobiles of all grades line the highway, which is narrow, and farm wagons, and high priced city vehicles, runabouts and surreys made up the picture. Women and men from the city visiting in the vicinity and residents throng the north shore of the pond, which is only a step from the road." The audacious tourists even ventured into the pond itself, crowding the small body of water with a macabre flotilla. Newspapers dubbed it an "invasion." In this chaotic environment, Hazel's untimely demise was nearly mirrored when a young woman lost her balance in one of these boats and almost drowned. One never-identified bystander was even suspected of planting a "Dear Hazel" letter, signed either Larry or Harry, on the bank of the pond, inviting her to a rendezvous in Averill Park. Because the note was neither soaked nor soiled and the writing, which was in lead pencil, was still legible days after the body was found, authorities never paid it much attention.

The investigation into the murder of Hazel Drew had become the social event of the season.

District attorney's officer William Powers and Troy police detective Louis Unser were heading up the case in the countryside and had already spoken to Conrad Teal about temporarily dislodging the dam he had erected to create the small pond. Powers looked up at the menacing sky and pondered their options: Postpone or move ahead? If the clouds burst, the pond might fill up faster than they could drain it. But a full week had passed since the likely night of Hazel Drew's murder, and any possible trail of clues was getting colder by the minute. An unnecessary delay could be disastrous.

"Well," Unser said, "what's the verdict, Bill?"

"Let's do it."

They had managed to sluice off about two feet of water before the rains came, and they were torrential. Disappointed onlookers scurried for cover. Before long, it was clear that today was not going to be the day to find the missing luggage. Powers turned to his partner and said, "Lou, I'm starting to wonder if anything's going to go right for us on this one."

The following day, with clearer skies overhead, the detectives set out once again to drain the pond. Undeterred by the previous day's downpour, the spectators returned, in numbers equal to the earlier crowds. As the pond was slowly bled, Powers started for the surrounding woods, taking only Unser with him.

"Hey!" a reporter called out. "Where're you going?"

Powers was evasive. "Stay here," he replied. "Lou, come on with me."

The two men conducted a laborious search of the area surrounding the pond. All they found was a man's handkerchief with the letter P embroidered on it.

"Mean anything to you, detective?" Powers asked.

"Not unless you killed Hazel Drew and dropped your pocket handkerchief in the process," Unser shot back.

By noon, the pond had been drained and dragged from one end to the other. The detectives, wading thigh deep in their rubber boots, spent hours raking through two feet of muck. By 2:00 p.m., they had just about given up when Powers noted two officers engaged in deep conversation, one of whom had just arrived from Troy.

"Why all the hubbub?" Powers asked them.

"They just found the suitcase," the newly arrived officer said. "The darn thing was in the city all along!"

Go figure, Powers thought.

He turned to commiserate with his partner, only to find him struggling to pull his boot from the quicksand-like quagmire they had inadvertently created. Shaking his head, he left Unser to his own devices and sullenly began the climb to surer ground.

⌒

While Powers and Unser had been contending with the elements and locals in the countryside, County Detective Duncan Kaye was on a mission to check every single parcel room and hotel in the city of Troy to locate the two bags.

At about 4:00 p.m., he got lucky, thanks to a man with the unlikely name of Adelbert Atwood, the parcel clerk at Union Station, who recalled a young woman checking in a piece of luggage on the afternoon of Tuesday, July 7.

"Nothing strange about it at the time, but here it's been ever since." Kaye's heart skipped a beat. "Let's have a look," he said.

Atwood led him into the back room, where he rummaged around in search of the missing bag.

"I reckon it's still here," he said. "Just got to find it . . . Ah-ha!"

He pulled a light-brown suitcase from beneath a jumble of luggage.

It *looked* like Hazel's bag. Flipping the luggage over, Kaye found exactly what he was hoping for: engraved on the handle were the letters *H. I. D.* Written in ink on the ticket stub was the time and date of the transaction: 1:49 p.m., Tuesday, July 7—about six hours before Hazel Drew was last seen some fourteen miles away in Sand Lake.

"What do you remember about the person who checked this?" Kaye said. "Was it a girl? What did she look like?"

"Young girl. Blonde. That's about all I can remember. It gets kind of busy around here, especially in the summer."

"I understand. Take a look at this," Kaye said, flashing Atwood a photograph of Hazel.

"Maybe. Can't say for sure. I think so."

"Was she alone? With somebody?"

Atwood rubbed his chin, deep in thought. His silence seemed to last an eternity.

"I wish I could say, mister, but I honestly can't remember. She was just another customer checking a bag."

Kaye thanked Atwood, grabbed the suitcase, and bolted so fast the bemused clerk didn't even have a chance to shake the curious detective's hand.

Returning with speed to the Rensselaer County Courthouse, an excited Kaye tracked down O'Brien in his office.

"Look what I found," he said, holding up his prize discovery.

O'Brien's deep, dark eyes gleamed. He jumped up from his chair. "By golly, I could use some good news."

Kaye laid the suitcase down on top of O'Brien's desk and popped it open. Together, the two men dug eagerly through its contents. On a yellow legal pad, Kaye jotted down everything they found: black leather purse, heart-shaped gold locket with a diagonal brace of imitation diamonds, comb, toothbrush, Japanese printed kimono, nightgown trimmed with pink ribbon, washcloth, undergarments, handkerchief.

"This has got to be it," said Kaye.

"Right," O'Brien said.

"So, what next, chief?"

O'Brien gave it a moment's thought. He sighed.

"Let's get the aunt in here again in the morning, just to confirm it."

⟜

Minnie Taylor verified what O'Brien and Kaye both already knew: the suitcase, and the contents therein, belonged to Hazel.

When questioned later, Julia Drew was initially surprised that the luggage included only one handbag; she was certain that Hazel had owned two, one of which—a brown imitation-leather bag about six inches long by four inches wide and shirred with brown ribbon—she never went anywhere without and was where she kept her coin purse and handkerchief. This wound up creating quite a stir at first, until Hazel's friend Carrie Weaver eventually explained it: Hazel had lost the brown purse during a Memorial Day weekend trip to New York City. But there was no disputing this: both the oversize pocketbook (the brown shopping bag she had in her possession when Minnie last saw her) and Hazel's half of the baggage ticket were still missing.

For O'Brien and Kaye, the presence of the suitcase at Union Station eliminated any doubt about whether Hazel had planned to spend the night of July 7 in Taborton. She must have been planning to return to Troy that very night. But how? The only money she had on her was a five-cent coin in the finger of her glove, leaving her fifteen cents short of the fare for the trolley ride back to Troy (fifteen cents to Albia, another five back home). True, the shopping bag was missing, and it was conceivable that the killer had absconded with whatever funds she had had on her, but Hazel was said to keep her money in her purse, which she had deposited back at Union Station in Troy inside the suitcase. Kaye at least was convinced the nickel was all the money she was carrying at the time of her death. How, then, would she even have been able to pay to retrieve the suitcase? And, having quit her job with the Carys, where was she planning to go once she had retrieved it?

⌐

Days had passed, and investigators still had made little progress in tracing Hazel's movements from the time she left Minnie Taylor on Pawling Avenue in Troy on the morning of July 6 until she was seen strolling along Taborton Road at about seven thirty the following evening. O'Brien and his investigators would soon go from being starved for clues to being deluged with them.

Eventually, sifting through everything that was thrown at them, they were able to piece together a more complete picture of her final days in Troy.

Henrietta Robertson—whose daughter Lillian was friends with Hazel—came forward to reveal that she had encountered Hazel between 11:20 and 11:30 a.m. on Monday, July 6, at Union Station. She was certain it was Hazel, who seemed cheerful and relaxed. They exchanged greetings.

"Where are you headed?" Henrietta asked.

"I'm going down the river a ways," Hazel said.

Hmm, Henrietta thought to herself. *Why so evasive?*

"How far down?" she asked Hazel.

"I am going to New York."

Their chat was interrupted by an announcement: a train was about to depart. Henrietta couldn't recall the destination, but said Hazel bade her farewell and hurried to the ticket window. Henrietta then watched as Hazel descended underground, presumably to board her train on the other side of the station.

Lawrence Eagan, an employee at the W. E. Kerin's grocery store, claimed to have seen Hazel walking west on Congress Street, toward Fifth Avenue, sometime between 11:00 a.m. and noon on Monday. Eagan said he turned to Anna O'Donnell, a cashier, and said, "Ain't she a daisy?" Anna confirmed the conversation, but since she didn't know Hazel, she couldn't verify her identity.

The timing of this supposed sighting is conceivable, given Hazel's encounter either shortly before or shortly after with Henrietta Robertson and the proximity of the location to Union Station. But Edward J. Knauff, a Troy resident who claimed to have known Hazel, told detectives Eagan had both the time and the identity of the woman wrong. Knauff, who was shopping in the grocery store when Eagan pointed out the woman to O'Donnell, was certain she wasn't Hazel.

"I was in the store a few minutes before six o'clock, making some purchases, when I heard one of the employees say, 'Isn't she a daisy?' referring to a girl who was passing. I glanced at the girl, who was a blonde, wore glasses, and had on a white dress. A few minutes later the same girl boarded an Albia car on which I was going home, and I am positive she was not Hazel Drew."

Pressed, Eagan recanted, saying he couldn't be sure of either the time of day or the identity of the woman.

At about 1:15 p.m. that Monday, a woman matching the description of Hazel—though her identity was never definitively confirmed—walked into the office of Westcott Express Service at Union Station, placing an order for her trunk to be picked up from the Cary house and delivered to her parents on Fourth Street.

This had to mean one of two things: either Hazel had never boarded the train Henrietta Robertson saw her heading toward, or she had returned to Troy immediately after arriving at her destination.

Between 1:00 and 2:00 p.m. Monday afternoon, Jeanette Marcellus, a Troy resident who was waiting for a friend to arrive on the 1:45 train from Schaghticoke, New York, saw Hazel in the waiting room at Union Station and exchanged greetings with her. Soon afterward, Marcellus ducked into the ladies' room, where she ran into Hazel again, gazing into a mirror, adjusting her hat and fixing her hair.

There were also vague reports floating around that a prominent Troy real-estate man had knowledge that Hazel and Minnie had an engagement with two young men in Averill Park on Monday, which was likely the day before Hazel's murder. O'Brien dispatched Duncan Kaye to a saloon at Congress Street and Sixth Avenue to interview a man identified only as Lindermann, who supposedly knew the two men, but strangely, the results of this interrogation were never publicly revealed.

Sometime on Monday night, according to a purser aboard the *Saratoga*, a New Hudson Line steamship cruiser—a three-hundred-foot-long, sixty-eight-foot-wide "floating palace"—en route from Albany to New York, a young woman identifying herself as Miss Drew approached him and asked for a stateroom. The purser replied that all the rooms were booked, though he eventually found her one that went unclaimed. The purser's logbook confirmed this; the name *Miss Drew* had been entered on July 6. Another crew member aboard the ship also reported noticing a young blonde woman—"but not of the bleached variety."

The detectives reached out to New York City police and checked with all the Drew families they could find in and around Albany to see if they could eliminate this somewhat tenuous lead, but no one they talked to had anything constructive to say. Assuming, as investigators did, that the passenger on board the ship was not Hazel, her whereabouts on the night of Monday, July 6, remained unknown. (The fact that the purser would not be called as a witness at the inquest days later seems to indicate that O'Brien didn't believe Hazel had boarded the ship.)

Between 11:00 a.m. and noon on the following day, Tuesday, July 7, Hazel was spotted on the south side of Congress Street, walking alone toward Fifth Avenue, three to four blocks from Union Station, by Thomas Carey. Carey, a fireman who knew Hazel and lived a block away from her parents on Fourth Street, was certain of the identification.

At 1:49 p.m. on Tuesday, Hazel—or someone looking like her—checked her suitcase with Adelbert Atwood at the Union Station parcel room.

At about 3:00 p.m. on Tuesday, Peter Cipperly, an elderly farmer from the North Greenbush hamlet of Snyder's Lake, boarded a trolley in Albia—a four-wheel "Dinky" with open cars—heading for Averill Park. Although there was no direct trolley from Troy to Averill Park, Hazel could have taken the line from downtown Troy to Albia, then walked a block or so to the Averill Park trolley, which ran every thirty minutes in the summer (and hourly in the winter). As he got on, Cipperly noted with some irritation that, as usual, the younger folks had monopolized the seats up front, where the view was better and the breeze, such as it was, stronger. Cipperly knew that as the car trudged into the depot, the youngsters would hop off and run alongside it, just for fun, though he never understood the point of it.

These open cars had benches that could seat up to six passengers each, with standing room up front and in the back. Cipperly's attention was drawn to a young woman seated directly in front of him, about nineteen or twenty years old. He had never met Hazel Drew, but, as he would recall later, she seemed to resemble the dead girl that had appeared in the photos in the papers since her murder. The woman he saw had a hat but wasn't wearing it at the time. Her light hair was done up in a pompadour. A young man, about the same age, accompanied her. He was tall and slim—about five feet ten inches tall and 150 pounds—with a dark complexion, brown hair, a long, thin face, receding hairline, sharp eyes, and a prominent nose. He wore black clothes, a black hat, and tan shoes.

What a peculiar-looking fellow, thought Cipperly.

The man, sitting sideways and facing the woman, appeared absorbed by whatever she was saying. Peering a little closer, he saw that the girl held a large sheet of paper with notes of some kind jotted on it—they were reading or looking at the page together, much to their amusement. The man seemed extremely interested in something she was pointing out.

"She and the young man sat well in front," Cipperly told O'Brien on Saturday, July 18, after stepping forward voluntarily—a full week after the discovery of the body. "It was a fearfully hot day, and she held her hat in her left hand. The man's right hand was about her shoulders. It was not until I alighted and looked up at her that I got a good view of her face, but I had plenty of time to study his and will know it in a minute if I ever see it again. He leaned close to her and frequently toyed with the lace on her shirtwaist sleeves. I left the car at Snyders Corner, and they continued on toward Averill Park. Four other persons sat in the car behind them and should recall the couple."

Shown a photo of Hazel by O'Brien, Cipperly noticed a resemblance, but couldn't say for certain it was the woman he saw on the trolley. The girl in the photo seemed younger, he said. O'Brien was actually relieved; the picture, though the newest in his possession, had been taken four years earlier, when Hazel was just sixteen, before she wore her hair in a pompadour.

This particular trolley car would have reached Averill Park—the closest stop to Teal's Pond—at 4:30 p.m.

Aurilla E. Horton, who owned a general store across from Crape's Hotel at the bottom of Taborton Mountain, claimed to have seen a young woman matching Hazel's description walking along the left side of the road between 6:15 and 6:30 on Monday night. Aurilla, sitting out on the porch at the time, did not know Hazel Drew but took notice of the woman's appearance, particularly her blonde hair and the black hat she carried in her left hand, with a large plume of feathers.

"I am fond of feathers and I noticed the drooping black plumes on the hat and her bright hair," she said. Although her description of the girl's hat was promising, investigators seemed to dismiss Mrs. Horton's story as a credible sighting. There was also talk in Sand Lake about a local woman who looked so similar to Hazel that the press referred to her as a "double," and the detectives might have concluded that this was in fact the woman whom Horton had seen.

Hazel Drew wasn't seen again until around 7:00 p.m. on Tuesday evening when the Rollmans saw a girl picking raspberries on Taborton Road.

～

O'Brien and Kaye had a lot of unpacking to do, separating the wheat from the chaff. Maybe these witnesses meant well; maybe they didn't. Ever since the county had posted that thousand-dollar reward for information leading to an arrest, which several newspapers had since enhanced with bounties of their own, they were hearing all kinds of stories, some believable, some not.

Henrietta Robertson and Jeanette Marcellus, who claimed to have seen Hazel around 11:30 a.m. and 2:00 p.m. on Monday, respectively, seemed reliable witnesses. Both knew Hazel and claimed to have spoken with her. Assuming that it was Hazel who placed the order at Westcott to have her trunk picked up from the Cary house, which seemed likely, she was also at Union Station at 1:15 p.m. on Monday. Thomas Carey, who saw Hazel walking in downtown Troy on Tuesday between 11:00 a.m. and noon, also knew Hazel and claimed to have seen her not far from Union Station shortly before she—or another young woman looking like her—checked her suitcase. Also believable.

"So what do we know?" O'Brien said. He and Kaye had once again closeted themselves in the district attorney's office. "She leaves Minnie Taylor around ten thirty on Monday morning, saying she is going to Watervliet, but then shows up at Union Station an hour later. Did she change her mind? Did she lie to Minnie? Did Minnie lie to us?"

"All possible," said Kaye, tired. "I don't know about Minnie."

"So Hazel presumably boards a train to . . . somewhere but is back in Troy in less than two hours, placing the order for her trunk. Where'd she go?"

"I looked into that," Kaye said. "The only train leaving Union Station at that time was the Belt Line, which arrives in Albany at 11:55."

"Then what?"

"Well, if she's telling Henrietta Robertson the truth, she went on to New York, but that doesn't make sense if she was at Westcott at 1:15."

"Could she have caught the Belt right back to Troy?" O'Brien asked.

"That's a yes," Kaye said, checking his notes. "Leaving Albany at 12:30, arriving in Troy at 12:55, which fits the timeline."

"So the question is, what could have happened in Albany that made her turn around and head right back to Troy?"

"Probably not something good," Kaye deduced.

~

O'Brien now assumed that Hazel had intended to go from Albany to New York on the afternoon of July 6 but was dissuaded by something—or someone. The fact that Hazel didn't have her trunk delivered to her parents' home until *after* she returned to Troy seemed to affirm this theory. Perhaps the original plan had been to have the trunk sent somewhere else.

Was Hazel expecting to meet a man in Albany? Did he not arrive? Did he meet her in Albany but call off whatever arrangements they had made? Perhaps they had agreed to rendezvous again the following day in Troy—or the following night by Teal's Pond?

The Taborton woods seemed an odd choice for a meeting point, though perhaps not for Hazel. Gilbert Miller, who lived right by the pond and knew the Taylor and Drew families, told Detective William Powers that he had seen Hazel in the woods by the pond "three or four Sundays" during the summer. "She was always alone. I never spoke to her on those occasions . . . Sometimes she would remain in the woods three and four hours, wandering around or sitting down."

The *Evening World* reported that Hazel's friend Lillian Robertson "has told District Attorney O'Brien that Hazel has said that she frequently visited the farms in the locality up to a year ago, and that Hazel suggested many times that they go to Teal's Pond.

"The place apparently had a fascination for her," the paper concluded.

There were still huge holes in the timeline: Hazel's confirmed whereabouts between 2:00 p.m. Monday and 11:00 a.m. Tuesday and then again from 2:00 p.m. Tuesday until she was seen on Taborton Road at about 7:00 that night by the Rollmans remained shrouded in mystery. According to Mary Greene, the employer of Hazel's good friend Carrie Weaver, Hazel had promised to see Carrie off on her three-week vacation to Ohio at Union Station on Monday evening, but she never showed up, which seemed disturbingly out of character. Carrie would never see her friend again.

O'Brien and Kaye weren't at all sure what to make of Peter Cipperly's story. Detectives had checked him out; he was an unassuming man with a solid reputation in Snyder's Lake. Dr. Elias Boyce, who was the first doctor at the scene after the discovery of Hazel's body and had conducted the autopsy, claimed to have seen a similar-looking couple in Sand Lake on the afternoon of July 7. But neither was in any way certain the woman was Hazel. Cipperly was never called as a witness at the inquest (nor was Aurilla Horton), which would seem to suggest that O'Brien discounted his report.

Frank Smith claimed—in one of his many versions of the events of July 7—that Hazel told him she caught the trolley out to Averill Park on July 7, but O'Brien could put no stock in anything the youth said. Investigators had queried every conductor and motorman on the line, many of whom knew Hazel by sight; none recalled seeing anyone resembling her on July 7. Later in the investigation, liveryman John Abel claimed to have seen an attractive young woman deboard the trolley and walk briskly in the direction of Taborton, but that was a bit before 7:00 p.m., hours after the Cipperly sighting, and Abel—who knew Hazel—couldn't make a positive identification.

There was a report by William Clemens, the arrogant and injudicious *Evening World* columnist, that all four of the regular conductors for that run had taken the day off—one camping and the other three attending a baseball game in Albia—and their substitutes had no reason to recognize Hazel. But as investigators would learn, anything that man wrote had to be considered suspect.

The Averill Park station, the last of the twenty-odd stops on the nine-mile trek from Albia, was about a mile from Crystal Lake, which was packed during the summer months. Homes and hotels surrounded it. Could a woman dressed as Hazel was walk all the way to Taborton Road from the terminus without being noticed by multiple people?

Perhaps Hazel had caught a ride out to Averill Park by carriage or automobile? Yet no one had come forth to say they had given her a ride, and nobody had reported a strange car or runabout on the road that night.

The unfortunate reality was that, based on the evidence collected so far, it was impossible for O'Brien and his detectives to say with any confidence how Hazel had gotten to Teal's Pond on July 7. Or, for that matter, why she had gone there.

Early speculation that she had been visiting her uncle William Taylor now seemed unlikely: Hazel appeared to have no emotional attachment to the morose old man, and her brother and sister-in-law, Joseph and Eva Drew, had left the farm months earlier for Troy.

What other explanation was there?

A secret rendezvous? Perhaps.

Respite from all the stress that had accumulated in the preceding days—the aborted trip to Lake George, leaving the Carys, the disappointment of whatever had happened in Albany? It couldn't be ruled out.

Whatever Hazel's plans had been on the final two days of her life, nobody—not her family, not her employer, not her closest friends—seemed to know anything about them.

Unless someone was holding something back.

The district attorney had a habit of making audacious comments. Some believed it to be grandstanding. Yet, being the successful politician that he was, he was equally deft at withholding information whenever the need suited him.

Over the next three days, the public was about to witness both sides of Jarvis O'Brien.

On Friday, July 17, with O'Brien away in Albany on business, County Detective William Powers, demonstrating an independent streak that at times seemed to have him working on his own authority,

MURDER VICTIM IS IDENTIFIED

Body of Young Woman Found Near Lake.

DISCOVERED Bth/_y FARMER.

He Noticed What He Thought Was Bundle of Rags Lying In Shallow Water at Edge of Pond and Investigated Through Curiosity—Innkeeper Tells Story of Automobile Party Which Rushed Through Village and Returned Without Woman Member. Death Caused by Fractured Skull.

Troy, N. Y., July 13.—The body of the murdered young woman found in Teal's pond, about ten miles from this city, was identified as that of Hazel I. Drew of this city. Death was caused by a blow on the head, and the body was later thrown into the water. Miss Drew was nineteen years old and had been missing from home since last Monday. The police have no clew as yet to follow. The parents can offer no reason for the murder. The identification was made by means of a brooch worn by the girl.

Newspapers across the country jumped on the Hazel Drew murder from the start, but not always accurately (the article on the left misidentifies the discoverer of the body as a farmer). (Left: "Murder Victim Is Identified," *Pittston Gazette*, Pittston, PA, July 13, 1908, p. 1. Digital reproduction courtesy Newspapers.com; Below: "Murder Mystery That Baffles New York—Who Murdered Hazel Drew?" *Fort Wayne Journal-Gazette*, Fort Wayne, IN, July 25, 1908, p. 5. Digital reproduction courtesy Newspapers.com)

Sand Lake, about 160 miles north of New York City, was once a popular summer get-away for urbanites seeking refuge from the oppressive heat. (Photo © 2021 Bob Moore)

A picturesque view of tree-lined South Street in West Sand Lake, since renamed Route 150. (Courtesy Sand Lake Historical Society)

A view of Sliter's Corners (also known as Sand Lake Corners or Four Corners) showing Taborton Road, where Hazel was seen walking the night of her murder. (Courtesy Sand Lake Historical Society)

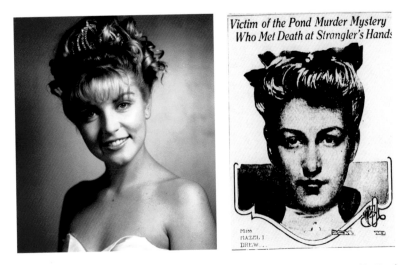

Above, left: Twin Peaks*'s haunted Laura Palmer (portrayed by Sheryl Lee), partially inspired by Hazel Drew.* (© Spelling Entertainment / Courtesy Everett Collection); *Above, right: "My Lady of the Blond Hair," one admirer called Hazel, shown here with her trademark pompadour.* ("Victim of the Pond Murder," *Evening World*, New York, NY, July 14, 1908. Digital reproduction courtesy Newspapers.com)

The groundbreaking TV series Twin Peaks *was cocreated by Mark Frost, who first learned of Hazel Drew as a child from his grandmother.* (© CBS Photo Archive/Getty Images)

Woodsy Taborton, where Hazel was last seen alive, has inspired its share of ghost stories and folktales. (Photo © 2017 Daniel William McKnight)

Teal's Pond, where Hazel's body was discovered, as it looks today. (Photo © 2017 Daniel William McKnight)

POND IN WHICH THE BODY OF HAZEL DREW WAS FOUND

Teal's Pond, Near Troy, N. Y., in Which the Body of Miss Hazel I. Drew Was Found. Her Hat and Gloves
Were on Shore at Point Indicated by Cross.

Troy, N. Y., July 27.—The suicide theory in regard to Miss Hazel I. Drew's death was exploded at the coroner's autopsy. It is now clear that Miss Drew was killed before she was thrown in the water by her assailant. Who the assailant was is still a hiden mystery which may never be solved.

The south bank of the pond. The cross marks the spot where Hazel's hat and gloves were found. ("Pond in Which the Body of Hazel Drew Was Found," *Lima Times-Democrat*, Lima, OH, July 27, 1908, p. 2. Digital reproduction courtesy Newspapers.com)

Pictured, from left: Gilbert Miller, a local who alerted authorities to the body; Conrad Teal, owner of the pond; and William Taylor, Hazel's cantankerous uncle. ("Hazel Drew's Tragic Death Baffles Troy Police; Inquiry Seeks to Reveal Identity of Sweetheart," *Buffalo Courier*, Buffalo, NY, July 19, 1908, p. 6. Digital reproduction courtesy Newspapers.com)

HAZEL DREW'S TRAGIC DEATH BAFFLES TROY POLICE;
INQUIRY SEEKS TO REVEAL IDENTITY OF SWEETHEART.

TRAIN HITS
AUTO; SIX
KILLED

Prominent Indiana Politician, Wife, Two Daughters, Guest and Chauffeur Dashed to Instant Death—Mangled Bodies of Pleasure Party Are

ANOTHER GILLETTE ATROCITY

Body of Girl Found Floating in Lake---Marks of Outrage and Murder on Decomposed Remains

A pregnant Grace Mae "Billy" Brown was murdered by her boyfriend in Upstate New York two years to the day before Hazel's body was discovered. (Left: "Another Gillette Atrocity," *Medford Daily Tribune*, Medford, OR, July 12, 1908, p. 1. Digital reproduction courtesy Newspapers.com; Above: FLHC10 / Alamy Stock Photo)

DA Jarvis P. O'Brien: hailed by local papers, hounded by New York City tabloids demanding an arrest. ("Hazel was Hypnotized Then Foully Murdered," *Lima Times-Democrat*, Lima, OH, July 28, 1908, p. 1. Digital reproduction courtesy Newspapers.com)

Jarvis O'Brien, district attorney of Rensselar County, N. Y., who is actively engaged in ferretting out the mysterious murder of Hazel Drew.

County Detective Duncan Kaye, who is actively engaged in the search for Hazel Drew's murderer.

County Detective Duncan C. Kaye, fiercely loyal to O'Brien and to the Republican Party. ("Hazel was Hypnotized Then Foully Murdered," *Lima Times-Democrat*, Lima, OH, July 28, 1908, p. 1. Digital reproduction courtesy Newspapers.com)

William Powers, District Attorney prominent in the search for Hazel Drew's murderer.

DA's officer William P. Powers, O'Brien's man in the countryside. Did he have a personal agenda? ("Hazel was Hypnotized Then Foully Murdered," *Lima Times-Democrat*, Lima, OH, July 28, 1908, p. 1. Digital reproduction courtesy Newspapers.com)

1528—Rensselaer County Court House, corner 2nd and Congress Sts., Troy, N. Y.

DA Jarvis P. O'Brien spearheaded the investigation from the august Rensselaer County Courthouse. (Courtesy private collection)

Dr. Harry O. Fairweather, the Troy doctor who assisted in the autopsy of Hazel Drew, shown in 1906. ("The Troy Elks," *Troy Daily Times*, June 30, 1906, p. 1. Digital reproduction courtesy Troy Public Library)

D. H. O. FAIRWEATHER
Esteemed Lecturing Knight,
Troy Lodge of Elks.

$4,200 FOR ARREST OF GIRL'S SLAYER.

Troy Police and Citizens Trying to Solve Mystery of Mamie Killion's Death.

Newspapers dredged up the notorious investigation into the 1901 murder of Troy "factory girl" Mamie Killion, whose killer was never discovered. ("$4,200 for Arrest of Girl's Slayer," Evening World, New York, NY, September 17, 1901, p. 10. Digital reproduction courtesy Newspapers.com)

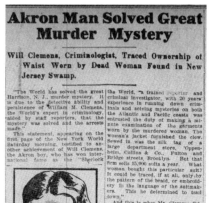

Akron Man Solved Great Murder Mystery

Will Clemens, Criminologist, Traced Ownership of Waist Worn by Dead Woman Found in New Jersey Swamp.

"The World has solved the great Harrison, N. J., murder mystery. It is due to the detective ability and persistence of William M. Clemens, the World's expert in criminology, aided by staff reporters, that the mystery was solved and the arrests made."

This statement, appearing on the first page of the New York World Saturday morning, testified to another achievement of Will Clemens, the Akron boy, who has won international fame as the "Sherlock

the World, "a trained reporter and criminal investigator, with 20 years' experience in running down criminals and solving mysteries on both the Atlantic and Pacific coasts was entrusted the duty of making a minute examination of the garments worn by the murdered woman. The woman's jacket furnished the clew. Sewed in was the silk tag of a large department store, 'Oppenheim, Collins & Co.,' Fulton and Bridge streets, Brooklyn. But that firm sells 15,000 suits a year. What woman bought this particular suit? It could be traced, if at all, only by the pattern of the braid, or embroidery in the language of the suitmakers. This he determined to trail down."

And this is what Mr. Clemens did. Through the house of Oppenheim, Collins & Co., the suit was then traced to the customer by Clemens. After long hours of labor, the sale slips of every one of the 23 suits in lot No. 573 of this design were found and every purchaser located. The sale slip of the red suit showed that it was bought by Mrs. H. Whitmore, 290 Adams street, Brooklyn. Clemens' work was then done. The World reporters found the house and learned that Mrs. Whitmore had had a quarrel with her husband Christmas day, and had not been seen since. Neighbors identified the photographs of the body, Theodore Whitmore admitted that the body was his wife's and one of the greatest mysteries of identity in New

WILL M. CLEMENS.

Holmes of America." The police

The infamous William M. Clemens, newspaperman and "criminologist," who stirred things up with his sensationalist reporting. ("Akron Man Solved Great Murder Mystery," Akron Beacon Journal, Akron, OH, January 8, 1908, p. 8. Digital reproduction courtesy Newspapers.com)

The Troy Times, headquartered at Broadway and Fourth Street, was one of O'Brien's heartiest cheerleaders. (Courtesy Don Rittner)

Hazel's parents, John and Julia Drew, seemed surprisingly uninformed about their daughter's life; Aunt Minnie Taylor almost certainly knew more than she was telling. ("Parents of Hazel Drew, Pond Mystery Victim, and Aunt Who Figures in Case," *Evening World*, New York, NY, July 16, 1908, p. 4. Digital reproduction courtesy Newspapers.com)

Hazel and Minnie were among the thousands who thronged to Rensselaer Park to celebrate July 4, just days before her death. (Reading Room 2020 / Alamy Stock Photo)

Investigators "sweated" tight-lipped Minnie Taylor after she refused to spill the beans about Hazel's male acquaintances. ("Aunt of Slain Girl to Get 'Third Degree' in the Pond Mystery," *Evening World*, New York, NY, July 15, 1908, p. 2. Digital reproduction courtesy Newspapers.com)

AUNT OF SLAIN GIRL TO GET "THIRD DEGREE" IN THE POND MYSTERY

Troy Police Determined to Make Miss Minnie Taylor Tell Who Were Men Companions of Hazel Drew Before She Was Murdered.

Minnie Taylor, Hazel's quirky aunt and close confidante. ("Here are some of the figures in the Hazel Drew murder . . . ," *Muskogee Times-Democrat*, Muskogee, OK, July 24, 1908, p. 1. Digital reproduction courtesy Newspapers.com)

Hazel, Uncle William Taylor, and the Richmonds, the farmhands who made the fateful decision to go into town on the night of the murder. ("Girl Who Was Slain, Uncle and Employes on Farm Near Which She Was Last Seen," *St. Louis Post-Dispatch*, St. Louis, MO, July 20, 1908, p. 3. Digital reproduction courtesy Newspapers.com)

Snowy Sand Lake illustrates the kind of terrain Hazel would have braved to reach her uncle's farm in December of 1907 during her mysterious illness. (Courtesy private collection)

"Half-witted" farmhand Frank Smith, allegedly obsessed with Hazel, emerged as an early suspect. ("Hazel Drew's Aunt, Minnie Taylor, Frank Smith and the Taylor Farm," *Passaic Daily Herald*, Passaic, NJ, July 17, 1908, p. 1. Digital reproduction courtesy Newspapers.com)

Frank Smith and charcoal burner Rudy Gundrum had what appeared to be a chance encounter with Hazel just minutes before her death. ("Youth Is Watched in Murder Mystery," *Washington Times*, Washington, DC, July 14, 1908, p. 1. Digital reproduction courtesy Newspapers.com)

Frank Smith's odd behavior on the night of the murder included a mad dash to and from Wright's pharmacy. (Courtesy Bob Moore, Sand Lake Town Historian)

The Gundrum farmhouse, where Rudy burned charcoal and took potshots at marauding beavers. (Courtesy Bob Moore, Sand Lake Town Historian)

Rudy Gundrum and son Lawrence, posing for a newspaper article on the art of charcoal burning. ("Taborton Mountain Known as Charcoal Burning Center," *Knickerbocker Press*, Albany, NY, July 12, 1931, p. 2. Digital reproduction courtesy Sand Lake Historical Society)

Right: In 1908, Troy was a vibrant, prosperous city, with much of the action centered here on bustling River Street. (Courtesy Don Rittner); *Below: A locomotive chugs along Sixth Avenue through the "Line," Troy's infamous red-light district, where legendary madam Mame Faye ran her string of brothels. Hazel lived only a few blocks away when she worked for the Tuppers.* (Collection of the Hart Cluett Museum at Historic Rensselaer County, Troy, NY)

The baronial steps of one of Troy's crown jewels, the prestigious Rensselaer Polytechnic Institute. (Pictures Now / Alamy Stock Photo)

announced that he was on the verge of arresting three unidentified people: two men living near the scene of the crime and a woman from Troy—not on suspicion of committing the crime, but for withholding information that could lead to the apprehension of the murderer.

"I am satisfied that the time has come to make three arrests," he told reporters. "I will act just as soon as I can communicate with my superior. Of course, the arrests will be made solely to prevent the suspects from getting away and to force them to tell all they know. A more serious charge will depend on the evidence developed at the inquest."

Powers never identified his targets, but speculation centered on Frank Smith, William Taylor, and Minnie Taylor.

Later that day, upon his return, O'Brien found five letters waiting for him in his office, two of which were said to contain valuable insights into the whereabouts of Hazel on the night of Monday, July 6, a puzzle that had vexed detectives from the start. Some of the missives were anonymous, some weren't, but O'Brien refused initially to comment on any of the information contained therein.

However, when reporters persisted, the district attorney grudgingly compromised, releasing some details but not others. Four of the letters listed names and addresses of people who had been seen with Hazel and Minnie. All five questioned the veracity of statements Hazel's relatives had made to investigators. One new lead was especially tantalizing: one of the letters claimed that Hazel was seen in the company of a man— never publicly identified—just a few hours before her death on July 7. Prodded by reporters, O'Brien acknowledged that the letter contained the following lines: "Hazel Drew met a man at the depot. They drove to Averill Park. He returned in a delivery wagon after midnight."

This, O'Brien knew, was not the first time someone was suggesting that Hazel had an engagement with a man in Averill Park, though earlier it had been maintained that it was two men instead of one, and that it had transpired not on July 7, but on July 6, the day before her murder.

The *Washington Herald* reported on July 18 that O'Brien "does not consider that the letters will bear on the identity of the slayer, but hopes they will show that Hazel Drew was occupied in harmless pastimes from the time she left the home of Minnie Taylor, early on Monday, until she was recognized on the Taborton road, on Tuesday night."

If true, it was a curious conclusion by O'Brien, who had been harping all along about how important it was to know Hazel's whereabouts on July 6 and July 7, and who was unusually tightlipped about information he was publicly dismissing as incidental to the investigation.

However, he considered the letters important enough to summon his detectives back from the mountains of Taborton, where a hefty complement of ten officers, under the supervision of William Powers, had been chasing down leads, including one that two drunken mountaineers—who had since disappeared—had returned home on the night of the murder and spoken of encountering a pretty young woman on Taborton Road. (Yet another dead end; the two men were found and were able to satisfy the officers that their only knowledge of the crime was through the gossip of the villagers.) On Saturday, July 18, after spending half the night closeted with Duncan Kaye and DA's officer John Murnane, O'Brien emerged with another of his brash announcements: "My mind is made up concerning the murder of Hazel Drew," he said. "I know who killed her."

Who was it?

O'Brien—surprise!—wouldn't say. But he did volunteer this: "I am certain that the murderer lives in the neighborhood where the crime was committed."

How certain was he? Certain enough to postpone the inquest, which had been tentatively planned for later that day, because to convene it "at this time might be fatal to the ultimate bringing to justice of the person responsible for the terrible tragedy." Yet even O'Brien admitted the evidence was merely circumstantial, and postponing the inquest would, he hoped, enable him and his team of sleuths to "complete every link in the chain of evidence."

After days of lamenting the stagnation of the investigation, O'Brien now was suddenly peddling hope.

Given the newfound focus of the investigation, it made sense that detectives stepped up their activity in the area of Teal's Pond. This included pursuing a tip Powers had received that a party of young men was camping out at the pond on the night of the murder.

Meanwhile, reports emerged that investigators were also seeking a young man in Schenectady—also unidentified—who reportedly had been seen with Hazel a few hours before her death. According to a report by the Hearst News Service, detectives were theorizing that Hazel had met this Schenectady man by appointment at Union Station on the afternoon of July 7, ready to elope. He then prevailed upon her to check her suitcase at Union Station and accompany him on a drive to Averill Park. This man then clubbed Hazel over the head, tossed her body into the pond, and returned to Troy alone. Hearst said this entire theory had surfaced from the letters in O'Brien's possession.

So who *was* O'Brien fingering? Had he jumped the gun by announcing he knew the identity of the killer? And was the Schenectady lead believable or simply another flight of fancy by the press?

Complications were mounting. The labyrinth seemed to sprout a new branch every day. And then this: enter the man on the train, who, despite evidence that seemed to suggest otherwise, insisted he had never met or spoken to Hazel Drew or any other woman at Union Station, and was then caught lying about it by the press.

Chapter 7

Cherchez L'homme

Three days into the investigation, District Attorney Jarvis O'Brien and his sleuths uncovered another side of Hazel Drew: as an object of male obsession. And not just one male. Inside the trunk she had had shipped from the Cary home on Whitman Court to her parents on Fourth Street on the afternoon of July 6 was a treasure trove of letters and postcards. Although most of the authors had identified themselves only by their initials, many of them were clearly from men. The missives were simultaneously flattering and alarming.

Six of the postcards, bundled together, were signed *C. E. S.* This person seemed particularly smitten with Hazel, declaring his love for the girl and telling her, "Your merry smile and twinkling eyes torture me. Your face haunts me. Why can't I be contented again? You have stolen my liberty. Please don't forget a promise to write. When I reach Albany again I will meet you at the tavern. I must see you soon or I'll die of starvation." But in another postcard, he hinted at being irritated with her, chiding her for "broken promises."

Beyond those snippets, however, O'Brien was tightlipped.

The missives from C. E. S. were postmarked Boston and New York, which didn't mean anything to investigators—at first.

On July 14, the day of Hazel's funeral, a postcard intended for her, from her friend Carrie Weaver, arrived at the Cary residence. The Carys returned the note to the post office, which forwarded it to Hazel's parents, who subsequently shared it with investigators. Detectives learned that Carrie was out of town on vacation, not due back until early August. However, her employers, Professor Arthur Greene and his wife, Mary, were able to provide valuable insights into the girls' friendship, including details about a trip the pair had made to New York City over Memorial Day weekend in anticipation of Hazel's twentieth birthday. Speaking to family and friends, the investigators soon learned that Hazel had also traveled recently to Boston and Providence, where her friend Mina Jones was living at the time (before moving to Waterville, Maine).

During that trip, Hazel had left Troy on Friday, April 24, and spent the day and night in New York with unidentified friends. On Sunday, April 26, she arrived in Providence, where she stayed with Mina and her husband, Frank, until Tuesday night, April 28. According to Mina, Hazel arrived alone, left alone, and didn't meet up with anyone while in town. During her stay, Hazel asked Mina to mail several postcards for her, including one to a man who worked for the B. F. Sturtevant Company in the Hyde Park neighborhood of Boston, which manufactured fans and ventilation systems. Mina claimed she was unable to recall the man's name.

From Providence, Hazel went on to Boston, where she spent the day of April 28 sightseeing in a tour group led by local expert F. A. Waterman, returning to Troy that night. Soon after, she dashed off a "chatty, gossiping letter"—the *Boston Globe*'s words—telling Mina all about her trip. On May 1, Mina wrote back, encouraging Hazel to come again soon and to "bring your friend."

Who was C. E. S.? And was it possible he had arranged a tryst with Hazel on at least the first two legs of her trip? According to O'Brien, one of the postcards clearly established that Hazel and C. E. S. had met in

New York prior to June 13. This meant their meeting happened either during the April trip or during Hazel's May visit to New York with Carrie Weaver (who insisted that she and Hazel did not meet with any men during their travels).

If O'Brien ever resolved either of these questions, the findings were never publicly shared. The identity of C. E. S. remains a mystery to this day. However, there is one intriguing possibility that was never explored: on the day after Hazel's funeral, another mystery man surfaced—with the initials C. S. (middle name unknown). According to the July 15 Albany *Times Union*, a man identifying himself as Con Sullivan reported that he had seen Hazel and her aunt Minnie Taylor riding in a carriage with two young men in Averill Park on the evening of Sunday, June 21—just over two weeks before Hazel's death—and had overheard them planning for another trip after the Fourth of July.

Mulling over this lead in O'Brien's office, the DA and County Detective Duncan Kaye figured they had nothing to lose in pursuing it.

"Bring the aunt back in?" Kaye asked.

"It has to be done," said O'Brien, ruefully anticipating another grueling session. "And this time, let's third-degree her."

O'Brien had reached the limit of his patience with Hazel's bullheaded aunt, and he let the press know it. On July 15, he told gathered newshawks: "She has not told everything. To my mind she is shielding someone. She's of a determined, cold puritanical disposition and a peculiar woman. She has refused to tell who Hazel's male friends are, saying they had nothing to do with the crime."

O'Brien was preaching to the converted. The press had had its own share of run-ins with Aunt Minnie. Once, when a reporter for the *Evening World* approached her outside her place of work, at the George B. Harrison residence on Pawling Avenue in Troy, and asked, "Were you Hazel's chum?" Minnie replied, "Yes, she fancied me more than others. She wanted my company."

"You and she took auto and carriage rides?"

"None of your business," Minnie snapped. "I refuse to tell you or anyone else our private affairs. None of our friends had anything to do with the murder. I won't drag innocent persons into this. I don't know how she died and can't explain why she went to Teal's Pond."

The reporter scurried off with his prize quotes, but O'Brien, Kaye, and Detective John Murnane weren't so easily scared off. Their grueling interrogation of the aunt lasted for hours—Minnie was taken home in a "state of collapse," escorted by two detectives. An *Evening World* reporter phrased it like so, poison dripping from his pen: "Her breakdown was pitiful. She wept and prayed that Hazel's slayer would be taken. Several times stimulants were needed to keep her calm."

Bottom line: the harsh tactics worked. Minnie cracked. She revealed the names of the two men she and Hazel had gone riding with. On the way out, she pleaded with reporters: "Don't bring innocent persons into this terrible affair!"

The press dutifully jotted down her words, then dashed off to demand that O'Brien cough up the names.

"One problem, boys," the DA said. "The only way I could get 'em was to promise her I wasn't going to share them with you all."

The reporters raised a rumpus, but O'Brien wasn't budging.

"Calm down, everyone," he pleaded. "The way some of you have been dragging innocent people through the ringer, it's scaring folks off—people who may know something that could help put an end to all of this.

"Here's the deal," the DA added. "My men will track these fellas down and get everything there is to get out of them. If anything comes of it, you'll be the first to know."

Nothing ever did—at least nothing that was shared publicly.

And what of the mysterious Con Sullivan? Could he have been one and the same as C. E. S.? Detectives and reporters fanned out searching for him, but apparently no trace of the man was ever found, since he was never reported on again.

Con Sullivan, it seemed, had vanished into thin air.

⌐

While rummaging through Hazel's suitcase, investigators also came upon another item of interest.

"What's that?" Murnane asked.

"What's what?" said Kaye.

"That," said Murnane, pointing to the edge of a newspaper clipping peeking out from underneath one of the flaps.

Kaye tugged at it gently. "A newspaper clipping."

"I can see that. What does it say?"

"'Edward Lavoie has departed for Chattanooga, Tenn., where he will remain for the winter.'"

The clipping was dated October 27, 1907.

"Edward Lavoie. Mean anything to you?"

Kaye poked his tongue around the interior of his mouth, a habit of his when he got to thinking.

"Sounds French. But there's a date on it, written in pencil," he said, showing Murnane the clipping.

"October 7, 1907." (This handwritten date preceded the article's publication by twenty days.)

"Looks an awful lot to me like Hazel's hand," said Kaye. "Let's go show it to the boss."

This time, O'Brien did share the information with the press, and an enterprising reporter for the *Evening World* tracked down the twenty-six-year-old Lavoie, a US Army soldier stationed in Chattanooga. Lavoie said he was flabbergasted by news of Hazel's death.

"I had been told that she disappeared on July 6, but did not believe that the poor girl had been murdered," he said. "I do not think that she had an enemy on earth, and there is no cause I can think of for the murder."

Lavoie hadn't seen Hazel for about a year, since a "pleasure trip" to Troy, and although he had received letters from her since, their correspondence had become irregular of late. Asked if Hazel might have committed suicide because of not hearing from him, Lavoie dismissed the suggestion outright, saying their relationship was never that serious.

The *World* also interviewed Edward Rice, Lavoie's uncle and foster parent, who resided in Troy. "Yes, Eddie and Hazel were sweethearts," he said. Lavoie was born in Watervliet but raised in Troy. He enlisted in the army in 1900 and reenlisted on October 25, 1907—eighteen days after the date scribbled on the newspaper clipping. "He met Hazel when but a child, and I guess the young folks fancied one another. Last fall he went South. Hazel would ask me where he was. When she got a letter she would read it to me and cry. But Eddie is an adventurous lad and not sentimental. He wouldn't love any girl long."

Rice's revelations to the press about his nephew's relationship with Hazel didn't really matter from the perspective of investigators. Lavoie had been in Tennessee on July 7, and thus couldn't have had anything to do with Hazel's murder. But, they noted, it was yet another indication that Hazel was more active romantically than they had been led to believe by her employers, family, and friends. Even Carrie Weaver—said to be one of Hazel's closest friends—was insistent. "As far as I know," she said, "Hazel did not associate with any men, and I think if she had I would have known it."

How had Hazel managed to keep so many secrets from so many of her closest associates?

Something else about the Lavoie connection bothered O'Brien: Why clip the newspaper article, stash it away, and handwrite the date on it? Surely there had to be some significance to October 7, 1907. But what?

October 1907 would have been about three months before Hazel came down with the illness that led her to William Taylor's remote farmhouse in the woods of Taborton in the dead of the previous winter. Nobody seemed to know what was ailing her.

Was she pregnant, as the tabloids from New York City were implying? Was Edward Lavoie the father? And could October 7, 1907, possibly have been the date of conception?

～

On July 22, William M. Clemens of the *Evening World* would publish in full a letter she had received from another admirer, calling himself "KNIGHT OF THE NAPP KINN AND YOUR ARTIST FRIEND, HARRY," and writing that Hazel "seemed to belong to a higher sphere, and [was] considerably more sensible, modern, and [had] more pleasing ways" than her girlfriends with whom he had encountered her over the course of a week during the summer of 1908. Harry apologizes for being forward with her and possibly bruising her wrists, and signs off with "'If Knighthood Were in Flower' I should live only for and have fond clinging memories of 'my lady of the blond hair' and be faithful unto death." (Harry, like so many potential suspects in the case, went forever unidentified, at least publicly.)

Mina Jones's husband, Frank, emerged briefly as a person of interest, once detectives discovered he had been boarding in Troy during the early summer—even with Mina living in Maine—before disappearing from town around the Fourth of July weekend.

Mina Jones had initially come to the attention of investigators after sending a dispatch to the *Troy Record* requesting additional news on the case, upon reading about the murder. Soon, papers were peppering the Joneses with questions, and their family drama was intermingled with the rest of the headlines.

Frank had left Mina behind in Waterville in search of work; he landed a job at Fuller & Warren Company in Troy over a month before Hazel's murder and was boarding at the home of Martha Fuller, daughter of the company's deceased former owner. Understandably, Mina wasn't thrilled with these arrangements. She wrote to Hazel on June 16: "Please do find Frank and tell him he has a wife down here in Waterville and he shouldn't forget it either."

Jones, back in Waterville by the time investigators caught up with him, insisted he had left Troy on July 3 to visit friends in Boston and hadn't returned since. Yes, he could account for his whereabouts on July 7. Despite having spent six weeks in Troy, he never once called on Hazel.

Why not?

"Mina's a jealous woman," Frank said. "She might've gotten the wrong impression."

However, Frank Jones did hand investigators a tantalizing new lead: Hazel, he said, had once confided to Mina that she had rebuffed a marriage proposal from a man who lived in Troy. Mina confirmed it: Hazel had met her suitor at a church Christmas party in 1906. She knew few details but remembered he worked in a dentist's office.

"She told me she could marry him anytime she wanted," Mina said. "I asked her, 'Who is your fellow now?'" Hazel, however, refused to identify him, other than to say he was "young and good-looking."

While O'Brien himself downplayed the relevance and credibility of the story, which continued to develop primarily through dispatches back and forth between Mina and the press, the newspapers were off and running. Reporters rushed out to Hazel's parents', but neither John nor Julia could remember their daughter sharing the name of her dentist. However, Mary Cary recalled an evening several weeks before the murder when Hazel had requested permission to leave the Carys' to see a dentist.

"It was after supper," Mary said, "and I thought it a rather unusual hour to visit a dentist's office, as I would gladly have permitted her to make such a visit during an afternoon. For that reason I refused to let her go, and she did not leave the house that night."

Hazel had identified the dentist, Mary said, but she couldn't remember his name. She did, however, recall that his office was on Third Street, in downtown Troy.

~

Reporters fanned out all over Troy in search of the mysterious dentist who had wanted to marry Hazel Drew. Nobody they spoke to could recall having worked on Hazel's teeth, let alone proposing to her. Those who kept written accounts willingly produced them as proof; others, who ran a cash business, simply denied ever having met Hazel.

Finally, they located Edward J. Knauff, a forty-nine-year-old dentist who lived and worked at 49 Third Street—not far from the home of Thomas Hislop, Hazel's first employer, at 360 Third Street. Coincidentally, this was the same Edward Knauff who had been inside Kerin's grocery store on Monday, July 6, when Lawrence Eagan believed he spotted her walking along Congress Street. Knauff was adamant that Eagan was mistaken about the girl's identity, and Eagan subsequently recanted.

"Hazel Drew had some work done here several months ago," Knauff said. "I do not remember the exact date. About two months ago she called again one Thursday afternoon with another girl who I did not know and asked if I would make an appointment to do some work in the evening. I told her that I did not do any work evenings, and she said she would see when she could get away during the day and would return later and make an appointment. She never came back. Possibly she did not have the money to have the work done, or she may have gone to some other dentist."

Had he ever proposed to Hazel? Or even been romantically involved with her?

Knauff smiled.

"I'm a married man," he told the reporters. "With children." (One of those children was William, a year younger than Hazel and a student at RPI, where Hazel's final employer, Edward Cary, taught.)

"So is that a 'no'?" he was asked.

"Yes. It's a 'no.'"

⌇

Toward the end of the first week of the investigation, a curious scene took place at the Cary home on Whitman Court: Mary Cary, who was in the process of being queried by two detectives, heard the doorbell ring and went to answer it. Opening the door, she was stunned to find John Drew standing on her doorstep. The poor man—who felt a bit out of his element in this part of town—appeared weary and gaunt. The wrinkles etched into the corners of his eyes were pronounced, and his cheeks seemed sunken almost to the point of concavity.

"Why, Mr. Drew, what a surprise," she said, taken aback. "Please do come in."

"I apologize for the intrusion, Mrs. Cary," John said.

"Of course not," Mary reassured him. "I must tell you, though," she added quickly, "that the police are here, in the drawing room. They have some additional questions about Hazel."

"I don't mean to stay long," John said, stepping inside. He removed his creased hat and gripped it tightly with both hands. "It's just, I understand you had already paid Hazel her wages for her next week's work and, well, I wanted to make that right."

He started to reach into his pocket. Hearing murmurs from the drawing room, Mary took a quick look behind her, then turned back to face Hazel's father.

"Don't be silly, Mr. Drew," she said. "I wouldn't dream of taking any money from you. I can only imagine what a terrible hardship this must be to bear for you and your family. Hazel was a marvelous, marvelous young woman."

She stood there in awkward silence, trying to think of something else to say, but nothing came to her. John Drew stared at the floor, shuffling his weight from one foot to the other, saying nothing—the detectives were waiting.

"Is there anything else I can do for you?" Mary asked.

"Actually, Mrs. Cary, if it's not too much of a burden, it's been days since I had a proper accounting of the investigation. Would you mind if I listened in while you speak to the detectives?"

Mary let out a brief sigh. What a sad, lonely-looking man. She paused and, deciding to be charitable, took his hat and ushered him back to the drawing room.

As John Drew sat quietly in a corner, Mary conversed with the detectives, trying to remember everything she could. Most nights, she said, Hazel stayed home, curled up with a book. She loved to read. She had friends, but never had a gentleman caller and, as far as Mary knew, had not kept company with a man since she began working for the Carys in February of that year.

"Well, you know, she was engaged once," said John Drew.

Every head in the room turned to him. Engaged? Hazel?

"She did have a man, once."

Drew couldn't recall the man's name, or whether Hazel had even shared it.

That was all investigators got out of John Drew, but Julia later confirmed his recollection. Her husband was right that Hazel had been engaged, she said, but the man stopped calling on her just over a year ago—in the spring of 1907—when she came down sick with the grippe, and he had gone on to marry another woman. A friend of Hazel's, no less. Julia couldn't summon up the man's name, either.

She and Hazel had spoken not long before her death about her love life, Julia said: "Hazel to my knowledge has not had a beau for more than a year. I asked her recently, 'Haven't you got a fellow yet, Hazel?' And she replied, 'No, I don't care for one. If I got one, some other girl would cut me out.'"

Julia also remembered Hazel once sharing that a young law student—the name Wolf came to mind—wanted to marry her, but not for another three years, when he was financially secure. She said Hazel had no interest in the man and no intentions of marrying him.

As it turns out, there did live in Troy a man by the name of Lawrence Wolf—who, as of 1905, was working as a clerk in a dentist's office. In 1902, when Lawrence was twelve and Hazel fourteen, the Wolfs and the Drews lived next to each other on Second Street in South Troy. By 1905, he had moved to 187 Third Street, four blocks north of the Hislops, for whom Hazel was working at the time. Wolf was baptized at St. Jean Baptiste Church. While Hazel's church—the Third Street Methodist—was being constructed, congregants were allowed to worship in the St. Jean Baptiste chapel.

As Mina Jones had recalled, Hazel had met the man who wanted to marry her at a Christmas party at her church in 1906. Was Wolf that man?

The answer to that question remains unknown, because the name Lawrence Wolf never surfaced during the investigation.

~

On Monday, July 20, William C. Hogardt, seventeen years old, of Dedham, Massachusetts, told the *Troy Times* in a dispatch from Boston that he was grieving over the death of Hazel Drew, "one of his most intimate friends." "Hazel was a quiet and refined girl whom anyone would greatly admire," he said. Hogardt, employed by B. F. Sturtevant and stationed in Hyde Park, turned out to be one of the mystery men whose writings, signed only with initials, were found in Hazel's trunk.

"Refreshing to actually *solve* a mystery," O'Brien said.

"Not sure that's the solution everyone is looking for," answered Kaye. "Remember, you're up for reelection in the fall."

For the past six summers, Hogardt had vacationed with a relative named Feathers in East Poestenkill. He met Hazel in the summer of 1907, when she boarded out in the woods on Plank Road with the Blys, about a mile away. Hazel spent about a week there, before moving to another boarding house run by John Link at Snyder's Lake (where she met her devoted artist friend, Harry).

Hogardt and Hazel got to know each other at dances and parties, and corresponded regularly once Hogardt returned to Massachusetts. Approximately a month before her death, the letters stopped coming. Hogardt had received twelve in all, beginning in September 1907, when Hazel was employed by the Tuppers; writing from Schenectady, she said, simply, "Having a fine time here." A second postcard, dated a few days later, was postmarked Troy and depicted the Rensselaer Polytechnic Institute. "Just a step from where I live," Hazel wrote.

On January 8, 1908, Hazel wrote Hogardt from the Taylor farmhouse, where she was recuperating: "Owing to illness, was unable to get you a New Year's card. But I wish you a very happy New Year. Thanking you for your kind remembrance, I remain H. I. D." A few weeks later, on February 3, she sent him another letter, saying, "I received your card. Am taking a few months' vacation. I never hear from Gordon [a reference to their mutual friend, nineteen-year-old Gordon Hull of East Poestenkill; by her own words, Hazel seemed more preoccupied with Gordon than Hogardt]. I hope to see the girls soon, but I have not seen any of them lately. We are having very cold weather. I will be up to Poestenkill with Bell this summer. My address is at the present time 400 Fourth Street, Troy, NY. H. I. D."

There's no indication of who this Bell is—yet.

On March 7, 1908, shortly after taking the job with the Carys, Hazel wrote Hogardt again: "Received your postal. I like my new home very much indeed. It will be very lonely here in the summer. We are having quite cold weather here for this time of year. I never hear from Gordon. H. D., Whitman, West Troy, N.Y." (Hazel curiously refers to Whitman Court as being in West Troy, when in fact it was in the eastern part of the city; the area previously known as West Troy had been renamed Watervliet.)

Hogardt received two postcards from Hazel in April, one from Troy and one from Providence, which would have been the one Mina Jones mailed for her. The Troy postcard had only the initials *H. I. D.* According to Hogardt, this was his last contact with her.

The back-and-forth between Hazel and Hogardt seemed harmless, and investigators quickly dismissed him as a serious suspect. And yet their image of Hazel continued to evolve, a judgment that was reinforced when Walter Spreat, an employee in the Troy Post Office who claimed to be Hazel's friend, furnished O'Brien with the names of several young men who, he said, had accompanied her to dances and picnics.

Clearly the quiet churchgoer the detectives had originally been told about was simultaneously a confident, outgoing woman, with a wide social network that just about *everybody* had trouble keeping up with.

⚊

In her haste to depart the Cary residence on Monday, July 6, Hazel had left behind a pile of letters and postcards that had been ripped into pieces and tossed into a rubbish pile. Detectives had to tape some of them back together just to decipher their contents. One that caught their eye was a torn piece of paper with the name John E. Magner written on it, along with an address: 449 Lexington Avenue, New York City.

Magner, detectives soon pieced together, was a Pullman car conductor on the New York Central Railroad's so-called Fast Mail trains running between New York City and Montreal, with stops in both Troy and Albany—two places with connections to Hazel's whereabouts on July 6. The New York Central train left New York City at 8:45 a.m. and reached Albany at noon, giving Magner twenty-five minutes to kill before the train was hitched up to a Delaware and Hudson–line engine that would drive it the rest of the way north, up through Troy and Saratoga and into Montreal.

There were reports that Magner had an alternate run, heading west from New York and through Syracuse on the way to Chicago, which would have also taken him through Albany but bypassed Troy. Like the northern run, that train hit Albany at noon. If in fact Hazel had been looking for Magner on July 6 and thought he was on the New York–Chicago run, she would have headed to Albany to meet him, rather than waiting for him in Troy.

On Monday, July 20, an *Evening World* reporter tracked down Magner at the Union Station lunch counter.

"John Magner?" the reporter asked, noticing the name on his uniform.

"Who's asking?" Magner said.

"I'm a reporter, with the *Evening World*."

"Really. What of it?"

"Can you respond to the reports that you have been coming into Troy to see Hazel Drew?"

"Reports?" Magner said. "What reports?"

"They found your name on a piece of paper with her things. Your address had been scrawled on it, too."

Magner scowled. "Look," he said, "I never met any Hazel Drew. I never even heard the name before all this stuff in the papers."

Magner said he'd been working the New York–Montreal Line for about a month, including on July 6 and 7.

"Did you run through Troy on July 6?" the reporter followed up.

"Yeah, so?"

"What time?"

"Got here at 1:25."

"Meet anybody?"

"No, sir, I didn't."

"So you're sure you didn't know Hazel Drew?" the reporter asked. "And you have no idea what your name was doing on that paper we found with the rest of her stuff?"

"I said I never knew her, or any other girl in Troy," Magner said, emphatically ending the impromptu interview.

He was lying.

~

Minnie Taylor provided the investigation with their first clue that something was amiss with Magner's story. Hazel's aunt, stubbornly defiant up to this point, except under extreme duress, suddenly found her voice.

On the morning of Tuesday, July 21, Minnie was hauled back to the courthouse by Detectives John Murnane and John W. Lawrenson for another round of questioning. In order to avoid the press, she was brought in through the back entrance and into the grand-jury room, which O'Brien could covertly access via a private entrance from his office; the meeting was brief but intense, lasting about thirty-five minutes.

"You ever hear the name John Magner?" the DA asked, getting right to business.

Minnie took a moment to consider the question. O'Brien noticed that the woman had the same look she did whenever she was being investigated, as if her mind were far off in another place or time. The gingerbread clock ticked, like water dripping from a faucet.

"I don't believe so, no. Should I have?"

"Maybe," O'Brien said. "That's what we're trying to find out."

"I could use a glass of water," Minnie said.

O'Brien disappeared for a moment, then returned, glass of water in hand.

"Magner is a Pullman car conductor," O'Brien said, standing but resting his right leg up on the chair across from her. "We found his name and his address on a sheet of paper Hazel left behind at the Carys'."

"Yes," Minnie said, after a beat. "Now that you mention it, I do have a dim recollection of Hazel mentioning that she had called on a conductor in New York on one of her trips. I believe he apologized for not being able to show her the sights because he had to be at work early the next morning."

"Did she tell you his name?"

"Hmm. For the life of me, I just can't remember his name."

"When was this?" O'Brien said.

"Sometime or other. I can't recall."

Hazel had taken those two recent trips to New York, O'Brien remembered: the one in late April, when she supposedly spent the day with still-unidentified friends, and the other over Memorial Day weekend, with Carrie Weaver. Carrie would later insist, still from Ohio, that she and Hazel never met up with any men while there: "I don't see why the reporters, without exception, have asked me if any men accompanied us. We went entirely alone and were unattended, while there and on our return. Yes, we made a trip together to New York City, and I saw so many things there that I can scarcely tell what we did see. We rode over the city in an automobile, but we paid our own fare every time. Really, I do not believe I should have gone to New York with Hazel if I had known what kind of men were there. I would have been scared to death if I had been alone. Most of them looked as if they would as soon strike a woman as not. New York is certainly a wonderful place, but I am sure I would not like to go there to see the sights again. I saw them enough that time to last me."

Minnie swore what she told them was all she knew about any conductor, and for once O'Brien sensed that maybe that was all there was to it. In this case, at least, he couldn't think of a good reason for Minnie to be withholding, since she didn't appear to have any connection to Magner herself.

"Thank you for your help, Miss Taylor."

Minnie was free to go. Murnane escorted her out the back way, through the cellar, and into the alley.

"Come along, ma'am," he said. "We'll see you safely to your trolley."

Photographers, however, had learned of her presence and literally chased after her.

"Come on, Minnie!" one reporter shouted at her. "Who were those men with you and Hazel? Who are you protecting?"

Photographers jostled for the best angle to capture the scene, but Minnie's oversize hat and Murnane's protective shielding thwarted their efforts.

She halted momentarily and snapped back, "I've told you all a hundred times. Hazel was a good girl. Why can't you let her poor soul rest in peace?"

"Let 'em be, Miss Taylor," Murnane said. "This way, ma'am," he added, pointing across the thoroughfare toward Fifth Avenue, where she could catch a trolley car on the Albia Line.

The brief confrontation had caused a delay that allowed some of the photographers to slip ahead, and as Murnane led Minnie across Fourth Street, a wagon resting on the corner forced her from her intended path, right into the view of the cameras, as the photographers snapped away.

"Safe travels, Miss Taylor," said Murnane.

She boarded the car to take her home, exhausted, slowly shaking her head.

The battle between Minnie and the press raged on.

From there, the Magner story got messier. Minnie Taylor had a rare epiphany, suddenly remembering John Magner's name after all.

"Hazel Drew knew and loved John E. Magner, the Pullman car conductor," she announced. "I have heard Hazel talk about Magner. When the girl came home from one of the trips to New York, she told me she had met him and was greatly disappointed because Magner had to leave her early to make his train run."

O'Brien didn't trust Minnie to begin with, and his apprehension had been reinforced by the recent discovery that the aunt had sent Mina Jones a letter on July 16—the day after investigators sweated her at the courthouse—requesting that she destroy all her correspondence from Hazel, without any explanation as to why. (Contemporaneous reports were conflicted over whether Mina in fact destroyed most of Hazel's correspondence.) The district attorney was suspicious of the timing of Minnie's revelation about Magner and disinclined to believe it.

However, two men who worked at Union Station—George Peterson, a manager at the Westcott Express Company, and William Humphrey, a baggage clerk—came forward to say Magner was in the habit of meeting a young woman who answered Hazel's description during his frequent stops at Union Station.

Also on July 21, a young General Electric employee named Peter Ross, who lived and worked in Schenectady, stepped forward with news that he had left New York City on a return trip home at 9:20 a.m. on July 6, aboard the train. Ross found a seat in the rear of one of the day coaches; when the train reached a station a few miles south of Albany, he noticed a young woman who, in retrospect, strongly resembled Hazel Drew. A young man in uniform, who answered the description of Magner, approached Ross and asked him if he and the young woman could have his seat, since they needed to have an important conversation. Ross complied, vacating the rear seat and moving to an unoccupied one in the front part of the car.

The man in uniform then took the girl's suitcase and sat down next to her; the pair proceeded to converse earnestly. He believed both the man and the girl left the train at Albany.

Later that day, Murnane and Lawrenson questioned Magner during a layover on his return from Montreal to New York. Pressed by investigators in the wake of the reports from Peterson and Humphrey, Magner relented, admitting he had been meeting with a young woman at Union Station in Troy, whom he identified as Anna LaBelle, a salesclerk at the lace counter at Frear's department store, about four blocks from the north side of the train station. But Magner remained steadfast that he had no idea who Hazel was before reading about her in the papers, and no clue why his name and address were discovered on the piece of paper found among her possessions.

"I've never met Hazel Drew and I've never talked to Hazel Drew, and I'd thank you to stop pestering me about it," he said.

As it turned out, Anna and Hazel were acquainted, from Hazel's frequent shopping trips to Frear's. When an Albany *Times Union* reporter showed up at the store to grill Anna on July 22, she "became embarrassed and asked to have the interview occur at her home," at 190 Third Street, in the same South Troy neighborhood where Hazel had lived. Surrounded by her family, she "coolly denied" knowing Hazel, except as a customer. Yet she indignantly defended Hazel against allegations that her behavior was anything less than virtuous.

How would she know that if the two were barely acquainted?

LaBelle's credibility issues didn't end there: she told the *Times Union* she had no idea how Hazel had known about Magner's name and address, but she subsequently claimed she was the one who had shared the contact information with her. After learning that Hazel was planning to visit New York, LaBelle had suggested she drop in on Magner and ask him to show her around town.

Trying to make sense of everything that had happened, O'Brien huddled up with Detectives Kaye, Murnane, and Lawrenson, who were his eyes and ears in the city.

"Anna LaBelle," said O'Brien. "Wasn't she arrested a couple of times for disorderly conduct in the Line?"

"Hope it's not that Anna LaBelle," said Murnane. "That woman is crazy."

"The devil's water," said Lawrenson.

"You know," said Murnane, "I can't help wondering if Anna LaBelle and Hazel were better acquainted than Anna is letting on. What if the two of them spent some time together with Magner in New York last April?"

"Here's another thought," said Kaye. "What if Anna LaBelle is the 'Bell' Hazel refers to in her postcard to Hogardt? 'I will be up to Poestenkill with Bell this summer.'"

"Maybe," said O'Brien. "I can't think of another Bell having anything to do with this case, can you?"

The room was completely silent. O'Brien had his answer.

⁓

While the Magner lead stalled out, detectives hunted down another Pullman conductor, Samuel LeRoy, whom they suspected might have authored one of the anonymous letters found in Hazel's trunk—a missive indicating that the writer had once been a waiter in Averill Park. The thirty-eight-year-old LeRoy had in fact waited tables at the Averill Park Hotel when he was younger. Ten years earlier, he had landed a job as an usher at Union Station and hadn't returned to Averill Park, or waiting tables, since. Eventually he was promoted to Pullman car conductor, like Magner; his current route ran between Albany and New York. He currently lived with his wife, Rose, at 1621 Seventh Avenue in

Troy—just steps away from Hazel's brother Joseph and his wife, Eva—with two teenage sons, Martin and Harold.

LeRoy was located at his house and escorted by Kaye to the county courthouse, where he and his wife were interviewed on the morning of Saturday, July 25. The two were separated and interviewed apart by O'Brien, as stenographer Louis Lowenstein recorded their comments.

LeRoy acknowledged knowing Magner, though only as a fellow conductor; he had never boarded with him or even stayed at the same house. He denied ever meeting Hazel Drew or hearing of her before reading all the coverage of her murder.

"Tell us about July 6 and July 7," O'Brien said. "That would have been a Monday and a Tuesday. Be particular."

"It's my custom when I leave in the morning to prepare for my run from Albany to New York to take either the 10:40 a.m. regular or the 11:00 a.m. local from Troy, and I'm certain that I took one of those trains on the morning of Monday, July 6."

"Go on."

"I left Albany at five minutes after twelve o'clock Monday afternoon . . . I reached New York at fifteen minutes of three and spent the afternoon hanging around the Pullman office. I went out to get some supper and returned to the company's office, where I hung around until it was time for the train to leave at half past twelve. I reached Albany at half past five and took the first local, reaching Troy at seven o'clock."

Samuel and Rose LeRoy told essentially identical stories about what happened the rest of the day. Samuel had spent July 7 lounging on the couch at home, sleeping a good portion of the day. In the early evening, they sent their older son, sixteen-year-old Martin, to the home of their neighbor, Alice Coleman, to ask if she wanted to play cards that night; Mrs. Coleman responded that she was unavailable, since she was planning to help a friend prepare for her wedding, scheduled for the following day. Since their younger son, Harold, was ill, the LeRoys wound up staying in that night; Samuel went to bed sometime between ten thirty and eleven o'clock.

After his interrogation, LeRoy was stopped outside O'Brien's office to field questions from the omnipresent press.

"There are reports going around that your wife says you have a habit of running around with other women," one reporter asked. "What about it?"

"Ridiculous and untrue," LeRoy said. He was angry about the whole affair.

"So you're sure you never met either Hazel Drew or Anna LaBelle?" asked another reporter.

"I never knew either one of them from a side of sole leather," LeRoy said. "I never even met or talked with either of those girls."

Numerous people confirmed the LeRoys' account, including Alice Coleman and her mother, Esther Prangley, who lived with the Colemans. In the end, O'Brien absolved him of any wrongdoing.

The *Washington Times*, however, didn't. The paper clearly intimated that LeRoy was the killer, without ever actually identifying him by name. The *Times* spun an incredibly intricate yarn, claiming that Hazel had fallen "victim to the wiles of a married man," not knowing that he was married, and hoped desperately to elope with him—"to her a fond dream, but to the man merely a trap and a snare." As the paper argued it, the two met in Albany on Monday, July 6; the man planned a tryst for the following night at Teal's Pond, where the elopement would begin, but which in fact became the scene of her murder at his hands, as he was desperate to get rid of the girl.

In presenting this argument, the *Times* made a big deal out of the fact that LeRoy had used a distinct type of pencil at work, of unusual color and size, and Hazel Drew had used the same size and style of pencil, based on scraps of paper found among her belongings.

LeRoy, eventually queried about this by reporters, simply stated that like other Pullman car conductors (including John Magner), he used an indelible pencil, which he sharpened flat.

Meanwhile, on Saturday, July 25, the *Syracuse Journal* ran a story headlined Railroad Man Is Suspected, conflating LeRoy with Magner, or else suggesting that LeRoy was using John Magner as an alias in his dealings with Hazel.

This and other, similar reports infuriated LeRoy, who wound up hiring George B. Wellington—partner of O'Brien's old law firm—to slap the *Evening World* with a twenty-five-thousand-dollar libel suit.

The whole Magner saga was enough to drive O'Brien mad—except that he had other things to worry about. Like the latest lead that had emerged out of the blue: wild sex parties were being staged in the Taborton woods, about five miles south of Teal's Pond.

Chapter 8

SEX, LIES, AND REAL ESTATE

It was known, unironically, as Alps: a hilly area that included a cluster of summer homes—camps, the locals called them—located in the southeasternmost corner of Sand Lake, about five miles south of Teal's Pond and beyond Crooked and Glass Lakes, popular resorts for the wealthy from Albany, Troy, and New York.

Gossip on the mountain was that riotous sex parties were "common occurrences" at a sixteen-and-a-half-acre secluded camp, named Tsatsawassa, after a local creek, in a sector of Alps known as Dunham Hollow. Detective William Powers had been hearing such rumors since early in the investigation but had largely discounted them, as there was nothing concrete connecting Hazel to the area.

But the stories persisted.

An unidentified man told reporters that young women were being picked up and taken to the camp under the pretense of being offered leisurely automobile rides. Within certain circles, the camp had developed notoriety as "a spot where purity and virtue are held but lightly"; anyone who cared anything about their reputation steered clear of the place.

The camp was said to be owned by a pair of brothers, wealthy businessmen, one of whom had been the subject of a complaint filed with authorities by a young woman; according to a private detective involved in the case, this resulted in a large settlement paid out by said fat cat. Newspapers, including the *New York Evening Telegram*, surmised that the situation "strongly resembl[ed] the story of Evelyn Thaw"—the young actress whose husband, Harry, had famously shot and killed the prominent architect Stanford White in front of a crowd of people at Madison Square Garden's roof garden theater in 1906, after learning that White had sexually assaulted his wife.

On Thursday, July 23, Powers and Detective Louis Unser, still operating out in the countryside, paid a visit to Minnie Clifford, who had at one time worked at the Tsatsawassa camp as a caretaker, along with her husband, William, and still lived nearby. Minnie was a magpie, with a chilling story to tell.

On the night of either July 6 or July 7—she couldn't remember which—while lying in bed with her husband, Minnie was jolted awake from a deep sleep. A woman's shrill scream echoed in her ears as she bolted upright, suddenly awake and alert.

That was no dream, she told herself.

"Billy . . . Billy," she whispered, poking her sleeping husband in the ribs.

"Grrmphh," responded William, rolling over.

"William! You had better get up. They are liable to be killing that young girl out there!"

Minnie rolled her husband over so that he faced her, rousing him in the process.

"OK, OK," he said. "What's the rumpus?"

"Shhh," Minnie whispered. "Listen."

The Cliffords sat in silence for a full minute, listening for unusual sounds but hearing only the sporadic buzzing of insects.

"Probably another racoon messing about," William said. "Like that time last month."

It didn't take William long to drift back to sleep; Minnie wasn't so lucky. She tossed and turned but couldn't get that scream out of her head. About an hour later, she was roused again, this time by the sound of a passing automobile, fading off into the night as it headed down the mountain.

That wasn't the end of her story.

Back in early May, Minnie recalled, two young women had come out to the country for a stay.

"One, who had light hair and a slight build but a well-developed figure, came over shortly afterward to buy butter [off] of me," she told Powers. "This girl said her aunt, who was with her at the camp, was ill. Afterward she came again and begged me to let her take our team [of horses], as she said she had an engagement to spend Decoration Day with friends and afterward go to Lake George."

"That so?" said Powers.

He was tantalized, but a voice in the back of his head cautioned him to simmer down: something about her story sounded too neat. Hazel's aunt Minnie Taylor was her frequent traveling companion. Hazel had spent Memorial Day weekend in New York City with her friend Carrie Weaver. And she had been chattering for weeks about a trip to Lake George on July 4—though she wound up visiting Schenectady instead. All of which was now common knowledge, thanks to the newspapers. Plus, the county had posted that thousand-dollar reward for information, not to mention the additional bounties offered by newspapers; suddenly people seemed to be jumping out of the woodwork to report sightings of Hazel.

"Anything else?" he asked.

"She also said her life had been threatened by one of the men, who was intoxicated," Minnie continued.

Powers and Unser exchanged a look. This was getting wilder by the moment.

"What happened there?" prodded Unser.

"Because she did not blow out a light when ordered, he threw her against the wall with great violence!"

"So what happened to the young woman?" Powers prompted. "When she paid you that visit?"

"She borrowed our rig, wanting to go to Brown's Hotel, to telephone for someone to take her home."

She returned the rig later, Minnie said, and that was the last she saw of her.

⁓

From there, the detectives headed over to Brown's Crooked Lake House, well known in those parts as a frequent vacation spot for Theodore Roosevelt, who enjoyed hunting in the nearby woods.

Mabel Brown, the proprietor's daughter, was another chatterbox. She confirmed Minnie Clifford's story about the two young women, who had shown up unexpectedly at the hotel one day in May, one of them only partially dressed, wearing a men's rubber overcoat. They asked to use the telephone; Mabel obliged. One of the women, the one with light hair and large, expressive eyes, placed a call to Albany, to a name Mabel recognized as belonging to one of the owners of the Tsatsawassa camp. The girl wanted a doctor to come out to the camp to look after her aunt.

Not long after, Mabel recounted, one of the young women showed up again, this time accompanied by a different woman. The woman Mabel recognized from the previous visit wore a pair of men's trousers. The other wore a heavy blanket around her shoulders. It was a hot day. This woman appeared to be wearing only underclothes beneath the blanket.

Again they asked to use the phone; they said they had ended up at the camp after accepting a ride from a man. Now they were broke and desperate to go home, but nobody would take them because everyone was afraid of being implicated in *whatever* was happening at the camp, if word got around.

Both Minnie Clifford and Mabel Brown were shown photographs of Hazel Drew. The girl they'd seen resembled Hazel, but they couldn't make a positive identification.

Mabel had never liked that camp being so nearby. Neighborhood residents had complained to the sheriff about it. Some nights she'd hear shrieks coming from out that way. It was unholy.

Unholy, that's what it was, Powers agreed. And he wasn't one to abide sinners. He was excited about reporting back to O'Brien and Kaye.

—

O'Brien didn't like the sound of these outrageous accounts relayed by Powers. Orgies on the mountain, indeed! But outside of vague, innuendo-laden stories, perhaps inspired by the rewards being offered, there wasn't much to go on.

True, it had been established that Hazel liked to go riding, and her means of transport out to Taborton on the day of her murder was still unknown. And yet, as the district attorney told reporters, "It was not reasonable to suppose that a person would drive a touring car over the Taborton mountains, although it could be done." He described the route one would need to take as "almost impassable," with the "roadbed in places being rough and dangerous."

Furthermore, following up on the lead, investigators had discovered that the Cliffords had left the Tsatsawassa camp after a dispute with its owners, perhaps prejudicing Minnie's version of events.

But even if Hazel had never been to the camp—or was unaware of its existence—could one of its inhabitants have wandered out to Teal's Pond and committed the murder? From the sound of things, these campers were exhibiting signs of predatory behavior and were used to getting what they wanted. What if there was an unexpected encounter? A scuffle? What if Hazel had resisted?

At the very minimum, there was enough smoke to check for fire.

O'Brien had built his reputation as a DA by crusading against houses of ill repute in Troy, shuttering establishments alleged to be holding girls, including minors, against their will, and he still considered that his mandate. If camps were being run like disorderly houses and the law could stop the practice, he said, it would be done at once.

He would conference with Sheriff J. Irving Baucus and then find out what he could about this shady camp out in the woods.

—

Already in Albany following up on a lead, Duncan Kaye took the time to check out the camp's owners, brothers Alexander and Henry E. Kramrath, who were also proprietors of a furniture store in Albany. Henry was a forty-one-year-old Albany realtor with deep pockets, and once his name appeared in the papers, he soaked up the attention, protestations notwithstanding. He grumbled and roared. Sex parties at his camp? Women held against their will? Utter nonsense, he contended.

Back home, Henry was a big shot, at least in certain circles. But his taste in friends was dubious, and he was no stranger to the courtroom. In March 1905, he was called on to testify as a defense witness at the murder trial of his close associate Richard E. Preusser, a prominent one-armed stockbroker whose life the *Albany Law Journal* described as riddled with "revolting details" in reviewing the case. Preusser was charged with killing a Boston gambler named Myles McDonnell—himself a murderer—with a double-barreled shotgun after the two men had gotten into a nasty spat early on the morning of June 8, 1904. Immediately after the shooting, he walked two blocks to the Albany cop shop to turn himself in. "I have just killed McDonnell, and I came to give myself up," he told police.

Kramrath had seen Preusser just four days prior to the murder; the *Albany Evening Journal* reported that under cross-examination by the prosecutor, Kramrath "expressed a desire to talk about everything but the matter at hand." District Attorney George Addington "straightened him up with a few stiff interruptions." There was never any doubt that Preusser had murdered McDonnell, but his lawyers peddled an insanity defense, arguing that venereal disease had addled his brain (a defense that Kramrath bolstered by claiming that when he and Preusser had discussed bad checks that a mutual acquaintance was passing around Troy, Preusser's response was "totally at variance with the subject under discussion"). Preusser was found not guilty by reason of insanity but spent only five weeks in the Matteawan State Hospital for the Criminally Insane before the superintendent ordered his release.

Once Kramrath's name surfaced in the Drew investigation, the press savored his theatricality. He bellowed and bawled about how allegations of "improper conduct" at his camp had sullied his reputation. It was great copy! Reporters tittered among themselves: What reputation?

In 1900, Kramrath had earned modest fame locally, as one of just four people in Albany to own an automobile. Two years later he was one of fifteen motorists to set out on a driving expedition for Petersburg, New York, about twenty-eight miles away; just four of them made it to their destination, Kramrath among them. In celebration they feasted at the home of the mother of Kramrath's good friend Chauncey D. Hakes, a prominent motorist and charter member of the Albany Automobile Club who fraternized with Henry Ford, Thomas Edison, Harvey S. Firestone, and James R. Watt, who would be Albany's Republican mayor from 1918 to 1921.

Hotelier Christopher Crape's report of having seen a car fly past his place at the foot of Taborton Mountain with its lights off at two o'clock on a July morning prior to Hazel's death, and then return later with one of its female passengers missing, resurfaced, as investigators pondered how these suspicious campers might have made their way to

Teal's Pond. The detectives had earlier dismissed the clue, after learning that Hazel had been seen walking on Taborton Road the evening of July 7—after the Crape sighting.

O'Brien sought to squelch the rumors, declaring that there were many stories they had looked into and discounted that were never reported to the press, consistent with his vow to keep "innocent" people out of the papers. He said the driver of the mysterious automobile had been identified some time earlier but had no apparent connection to Hazel, so his name would be withheld.

However, O'Brien's plan backfired magnificently, as the press, swarming around as usual, uncovered on its own that the driver was none other than Alexander Kramrath, Henry's younger brother, and co-owner of the infamous Tsatsawassa camp in Alps. Although Alexander's late-night drives were apparently innocent (with respect to any *known* crime, at least), the revelation stoked conjecture around the family name, especially given the Kramraths' connections to powerful members of the Republican Party, an affiliation that O'Brien, Kaye, Powers, and others involved with the case all shared. Henry Kramrath had business connections with a man named Frank P. Dolan. Like Henry, Dolan was prominent in real estate in both Albany and Troy, and also heavily involved with insurance.

Investigators were convinced by now that Hazel had left Troy on Monday, July 6, on an 11:30 a.m. train bound for Albany. Hazel was rumored to have had a social engagement in either Averill Park or Troy on the evening of Monday, July 6, with a man who was a real-estate dealer and an insurance agent. Newspapers reported that "officials do not wish to make known the man's name at the present time."

In the early days of the investigation, the detectives had gotten a tip that an unidentified but "striking" blonde woman had been seen by Sand Lake farmers driving through town with a prominent insurance man. According to stories told to the investigators, this man disappeared after the discovery of Hazel Drew's body, and for nearly a week his whereabouts were unknown. Members of the Troy Maennerchor, a German society of male vocalists, believed they had spotted him in Utica, New York, about one hundred miles northwest of Troy, during the Säengerfest of the Central New York Säengerbund, three days after Hazel's body was discovered. The unidentified man badgered the members of the society with queries about the case and even visited the offices of a Utica newspaper in search of information about it. Investigators were intrigued enough to look into the matter but refused to release the man's name.

Was Frank Dolan that man? He was based in Albany but had connections in Troy: in later years he was a member of the riding club there and co-owned the Troy Theatre, which he was instrumental in building in 1922, almost fifteen years after Hazel's death. Dolan's tentacles stretched into Sand Lake, too: he owned a summer house on Crooked Lake—he named it Camp Killarney—and was friendly enough with the family of Mabel Brown to host a dinner party for her sister Lena on the occasion of her wedding in October 1908.

That was about three months after Mabel Brown—and Minnie Clifford—mounted the witness stand at the Hazel Drew inquest and denied ever having told William Powers that she heard screams coming from the direction of the camp or having been visited by any women who were staying there.

None of these men—Dolan or the Kramrath brothers—was ever publicly identified by the investigators as a suspect in the murder of Hazel Drew. Of the three, only Henry Kramrath testified at the inquest, to defend his "honor."

Which raises the question: Why was O'Brien so eager—more eager than Henry Kramrath, apparently—to keep the brothers out of the papers?

Chapter 9

THE MAMIE KILLION AFFAIR

Every reporter in Upstate New York remembered the name Mamie Killion. Jarvis O'Brien did, too. Of all the major figures in the Hazel Drew murder investigation, he was the only one involved in the Killion affair, one of the most notorious scandals in Troy history.

On the morning of Thursday, July 16, nearing the end of the first week into the Drew investigation, O'Brien was sitting alone in his courthouse office, in a contemplative mood, a collection of newspapers piled high in the middle of his desk, his four-fingered left hand cradling a cup of piping-hot coffee. His attention was drawn to a front-page story in the Albany *Times Union*, headlined: Murderer May Never Be Caught: Troy's Mystery Appears Like Duplicate of Killian Case. O'Brien grimaced; everything about the headline soured him. He peered closer at the article, looking as if he'd just guzzled a shot of crab apple juice. They hadn't even spelled her last name correctly.

~

Mamie Killian was really Mamie Killion, and like Hazel Drew she was a young beauty from Troy whose life had been snuffed out by a murderer, nearly seven years earlier. What made the memory particularly disagreeable for O'Brien—who was serving under DA Wesley O. Howard as assistant district attorney at the time—was that the killer was never publicly identified or apprehended. It was an ice-cold case, and O'Brien would have been very happy to never hear the name Mamie Killion again.

Rumors ran rampant during the Killion investigation that someone connected to the administration of Mayor Daniel Conway was involved in the murder, and newspapers across the country had ripped into city and county officials with abandon, alleging a pervasive cover-up. Clues disappeared. Witnesses were "encouraged" to keep quiet. One, John Lennon, who claimed to have seen a man beating up a woman on the night of the murder in the vicinity where Mamie Killion had last been sighted, simply vanished when the press went looking for him (not unlike at least two different witnesses in the Hazel Drew case). Reporters were shadowed and harassed; one was attacked in a scuffle in front of city hall, in full view of the chief of police, by a cop alleged to have been seen in a saloon with Mamie and another girl on the night of the murder.

The whole case was an unmitigated disaster—a permanent stain on the city of Troy and the Rensselaer County District Attorney's Office, as well as anyone else in the city whose job it was to bring criminals to justice. Not that Troy's reputation for dispensing justice free of political influence was sterling to begin with; after all, this was a city that in 1882 and 1883 had two warring police forces, one (the existing force) backed by Democrats and the other (newly created) by Republicans and independents. The old force refused to surrender its uniforms and equipment or to vacate the precincts; they set up barricades to repel raids by the new force, which had set up its own alternate headquarters in the basement of city hall. This standoff lasted for fourteen months before finally being resolved in court.

Perhaps it was no coincidence that, just decades earlier, a Troy attorney and newspaperman named William L. Marcy, who served as governor of New York State from 1833 to 1838, had coined the phrase "To the victor belong the spoils" and originated the political spoils system (or so legend has it).

Politics, it seemed, ran through the lifeblood of the city.

On Wednesday, September 4, 1901, Mamie Killion, who worked at Tim & Co.'s collar factory in Troy, appeared to vanish from the face of the earth. Nobody seemed to know what happened to her. Friends and family scoured the city in search of her, to no avail.

Three days later, two young men named Frank Snyder and Peter Gregory were out rowing in the Hudson River at seven o'clock in the morning when they came across Mamie's mangled, fully clothed body, partially submerged but clinging to a sandbar near Bath, New York. Her face was embedded in the sand, with one shoulder extended above the surface of the water. The corpse's eyes protruded, and the entire head was swollen. The two men managed to tie a rope around her arm and tow her to a point from where the body could be recovered.

Dr. William Finder performed the autopsy (for some reason, in a barn). Mamie was wearing a white shirtwaist and black skirt. Due to the bloating of her body, a decorative ribbon had become so tightly entwined around the neck that it snapped like a cracker (again, shades of Hazel). The body was free of abrasions except in places where the skin had loosened due to a buildup of gas from decomposition. The tongue and eyes protruded, and much of the skin was missing from the face, which appeared to have been badly scraped by sand.

Mamie Killion was ruled a suicide: death by drowning. Drs. Finder and William L. Allen of Rensselaer both insisted there was no evidence of strangulation. As with Hazel Drew, wounds were present on the back of the head, but Finder insisted that in all likelihood they had occurred *after* Mamie's body hit the water, perhaps from the fall itself or from being struck by the propeller of a boat. There was a puncture, about three and a half inches from the left ear, extending to the skull. Near this was a semicircular wound that had been cut or torn through the tissue, all the way to the bone. The skull wasn't fractured, and there were no dislocations of the vertebrae of the neck, but blood was plentiful.

At the inquest, District Attorney Howard asked Dr. Davidow, who assisted with the autopsy: "How, in your opinion, doctor, were those wounds caused?"

"It is probable that they were inflicted by contact with some object while in the water," Davidow said.

The coroner's inquest—at which O'Brien was present—lasted almost six hours, with nearly forty witnesses called. The plan had been to hold it in the grand-jury room of the county courthouse, but the crowd of spectators was so large that it was moved to the main courtroom. When the inquest concluded, the initial verdict remained unchanged: death by suicide. The investigation into the death of Mamie Killion was officially over.

The press, however, wasn't buying it—not for a second. The inquest was labeled a farce; one reporter for the *New York Herald* wrote that it "so skillfully, or rather so clumsily, whitewashed the affair."

Mamie's family was livid and dismissed the ruling as an absurd miscarriage of justice. The citizens of Troy rallied in their support, demanding an official investigation. Women were particularly indignant. Clergymen sermonized. Thomas Killion, Mamie's brother, gave up his business, devoting all his attention to unmasking his sister's killer.

At an emergency meeting on September 14, the Troy Common Council publicly flayed both the police and the district attorney's office, calling their investigation feeble. A resolution was approved, calling on Mayor Conway to post a reward for the arrest and conviction of the murderer. Conway took his time about it—initially protesting that he had yet to receive the certified minutes of the meeting—but eventually he acquiesced, offering up $500 in the name of the city and $500 on his own.

The Troy Press Company added another $500. Michael Murray of Albany, Mamie's uncle, offered another $200. An anonymous citizen chipped in another $2,500, raising the ante to $4,200. Eventually the total hit $6,200.

The only problem with dangling a reward that rich is that you never could distinguish between who was telling the truth and who was just looking for a score. It was human nature. The same thing would occur in the Hazel Drew case after Rensselaer County posted a $1,000 reward, which would be bolstered by smaller copycats from the newspapers—people started to "remember" things.

In the Killion case, four young men came forth to claim they had found Mamie's hat and picked up a broken soda-water bottle smeared with blood on the dock at the foot of Grand Street. The bottle had been smashed in two. They also claimed to have found a piece of cloth saturated with blood. Unfortunately, these helpful lads had tossed the bottle back into the river and done such a good job at hiding the bloody cloth that even they couldn't find it later when they went back to look.

Another upstanding citizen came forth to claim he had found bloodstains in the vicinity of a drainpipe at the corner of Front and Grand Streets. Mamie had been spotted at that exact corner around midnight, sitting on the steps of Malony's saloon, possibly waiting for a trolley to take her home.

A workman named John "Jack" Lennon claimed to have seen a man striking down a woman answering the description of Mamie Killion in the very early morning hours of Thursday, September 5. Lennon, on his way to work at the time, said he turned down Grand Street on the north side and passed a passageway called Dark Alley, where he spotted two couples standing on the opposite side of the street—that's when he observed the altercation. The second couple stood farther back from the river. The woman who was knocked down got to her feet, and her companion slapped her.

"Don't," she pleaded. "Stop it."

"Her hat fell off," Lennon said. "Her companion did not knock her down with much force, but when she got up he hit her with a pretty hard slap."

Why didn't Lennon step up to protect the girl?

"It wasn't any of my business—this scrap," he said. "If I stopped at all the things I see nights, I'd get my head kicked off."

Lennon admitted that he drank sometimes but insisted he was stone-cold sober that morning. He did concede that it was dark in the alley and difficult to distinguish the features of the people he saw.

John Williams, who worked at a store in that vicinity, said he found Mamie's hat on the pavement, about ten steps from the river and half a block from the corner where Lennon had witnessed the beating. The round, black chip hat—later positively identified as Mamie's by her family—had been crushed and punctured by a man's thumb. Williams laid it aside, thinking the owner had cast it aside just before leaping to her death in the river.

A detective identified in newspaper reports only by the name Butcher told the New York *Evening World* he was absolutely sure of the identity of the killer and would reveal his name in a matter of days.

"I am sure that I will unravel this mystery yet, and that the identity of the man that murdered Mamie Killion will be established," he boasted. "Of course, it would not do for me to give out all of the facts that I have learned, as justice might be defeated. I am convinced that I am on the right track."

Of course.

Butcher did drop some hints, though: the crime had been unintentional, yet he was confident the perpetrator could be tried and convicted of first-degree murder. Two men were involved: one who had never yet been mentioned in connection with the case and one who "has been associated with it, and he knows more than he has been compelled to tell."

Butcher's theory was that Mamie died while "defending her honor." She had struggled with her assailant; he struck her, knocking her down. She tried to scream; he grabbed her around the throat to stifle her cries. But she struggled free and ran toward the river; he followed. She stumbled and started falling into the river. Her assailant reached to grab her but only managed to grasp her hat, which was left in his hand as she plunged to her death. Frightened, the assailant dropped the hat and fled.

Another theory put forward asserted that Mamie had been rendered unconscious by blows to the back of the head, which were meant to subdue rather than kill her (a theory that some floated with regard to Hazel Drew as well). She was then taken to a house to recover but never did—so in an act of desperation her attacker disposed of her body by dumping it in the river.

The pressure intensified until the Troy police finally had to at least pretend they were investigating.

This is when rumors of disreputable behavior started circulating about Mamie. Several saloonkeepers went on record saying Mamie was not an unknown presence in their establishments. The Reverend Hector Hall, pastor of the Seventh Avenue Presbyterian Church, took advantage of the stirred-up frenzy surrounding Mamie's death to deliver a vigorous protest from his pulpit against the authorities for protecting "dives" and gambling establishments in the city—not because it was relevant to the case, but because why not? (The Albany *Times Union*, referencing the case almost seven years later, in the midst of the Hazel Drew investigation, opined that Mamie was a frequenter of places "that girls careful of their reputation would not care to be seen in.")

Mamie's family and friends floated a counternarrative: she was a good girl who died defending her honor.

Detective George Tyler of the Troy police announced that he could definitively place Mamie Killion in Albany on the night of September 4 in the company of a man, whose name he refused to release.

"Yes, I know that Mamie Killion took the 9:30 p.m. boat from Troy to Albany on the night she was last seen alive," he said. "I know that she was accompanied by a man. He is a perfectly respectable man, and he made the trip to Albany for a perfectly legitimate purpose. I will not tell you now who the man is. In good time I will make his identity known."

The trip would have taken about an hour, meaning they disembarked at the Albany pier at roughly 10:30 p.m.

So what happened next? Detective Tyler hadn't figured that part out yet.

As in the Hazel Drew case, theories went forth and multiplied. But nobody could say for sure what had happened to Mamie Killion. Or if they could, nobody wanted to.

⌐

Like nearly everything in Troy, the Mamie Killion murder probe stank of politics. The anonymous citizen who had donated twenty-five hundred dollars to the reward was revealed to be Edward Murphy Jr., who had never been particularly renowned for his bleeding heart. But he was famous for other things. Murphy was a deep-pocketed Troy brewer who, by most accounts, was as crooked as a country lane. He had served as mayor of Troy, a United States senator, and chairman of the New York State Democratic Committee. Those were official titles. His unofficial title was "Boss Murphy," on account of the fact that he lorded over Upstate New York's Democratic machine.

In an example of the ever-shifting political coalitions and factions recurring in Troy politics during this era, Mayor Conway, though a Democrat, had broken with Murphy and won election promising reform, coalescing with a group of independent Democrats and progressive Republicans. Boss Murphy wasn't very happy about that. What better way to pay the turncoat back than by implicating one of his cronies in the murder of Mamie Killion?

During the inquest, it was determined that Mamie had visited her friend Annie Calt at about 5:00 p.m. on September 4, accompanied by another friend, Mary Glynn, a forewoman in the collar-starching department at Tim & Co. who, at thirty-two, was considerably older than Mamie Killion. Annie's husband, Martin J. Calt, was a liquor salesman and a former city alderman with political ties to city hall, a fact that wasn't lost on the newspapers, which played up the connection—clearly suggesting that Mamie and Martin Calt were more than just friends. Calt acknowledged having met Mamie about a year earlier through his wife but said he had never been anywhere alone with her and called the rumors absurd. Still, they persisted.

The three women dined together the night of September 4. Martin Calt arrived home at 7:40, left again, and returned at about 8:00 p.m. with bottles of lager and sarsaparilla, which he and the women proceeded to share; Mamie had a glass of each. At approximately 8:40, she and Mary Glynn departed.

"Well, you can get on the car and ride, but I'm going to walk," Mamie told her friend.

Mary Glynn jumped aboard the trolley car and Mamie bid her farewell for the night, referring to her by her nickname.

"Goodnight, Googey," she said. "Will see you in the morning." And that was the last Mary Glynn ever saw of her friend.

Why didn't Mary Glynn walk with Mamie?

"Why, I had new shoes on, and they hurt!"

But later she confided to her mother that Mamie had acted as if she was going somewhere other than home, intimating that she didn't want Mary to tag along.

Mrs. Calt said she retired for the night at nine thirty. No one else came to the house. Neither she nor her husband left until the following morning. Mrs. Landrigran, who shared their house at 589 River Street, confirmed that account.

"I know he didn't go out that night, for I would have heard him," Landrigran said. "When he went to bed I heard him in his room. He is a heavy man, and his room is over mine. He walks heavily. I was in the doorway until about nine thirty, when I went to bed. I know nobody else came in or went out that night. I haven't talked the case over with the Calts." (Although nobody asked her.)

The following night, Mary Glynn was among those who went out searching for the missing Mamie Killion in all her usual haunts, along with Martin Calt. They visited several bars but never found her.

Lennon at one point was asked if Mary Glynn and Annie and Martin Calt were the three people he had seen with Mamie in the alley in the middle of the night. He couldn't identify either of the women and said Martin Calt might have been one of the men, but he wouldn't say for sure.

Much of the information that surfaced during the investigation was the result of old-fashioned gumshoeing by reporters, the Killion family, and other concerned Trojans who were exasperated by the police's apathy. The *Evening World* spoke for many when it wrote that the coppers were "doing nothing, and the charge is openly made that the reason is that persons close to Mayor Conway, who is running for re-election, are mixed up in the case."

William Killion, another of Mamie's brothers, agreed with the *World*—that is, Police Chief William Coughlin found himself staring down the barrel of Killion's gun, as he threatened to blow Coughlin away. "Unless you find the murderer of my sister, there will be a chief of police buried in a few hours," Killion vowed.

"Your hands are tied by politicians," he told the chief, "but let me tell you that politics can't hide the murder of my sister. My sister's blood is crying for vengeance, and you must do something."

The chief, trying his best not to have a conniption, promised to do all he could.

But what was that?

~

On Sunday, October 6, 1901, the *New York Herald* published an article that triggered apoplectic rage within the confines of Troy's city hall.

Headlined The Girl-Stranglers of Troy: Mamie Killion's Shade Appeals for Vengeance Against the Corrupt Political Wing Said to Be Protecting Her Murderers, the story asserted that Mamie had been strangled to death by "one of the scoundrels who regard the factory women as their prey and who rely on their political friends for immunity.

"It was found that a gang of political ruffians and other dissolute characters running dives and similar low resorts, but prominent in city politics and controlling many votes, were in the habit of enticing girls employed in laundries and shirt factories through acquaintances already on the downward road and familiar with bad men about town," the *Herald* reported. "Their system is to lead the girls astray naturally and gradually, with apparently no object in view except to have a good time with friends. A feature of these 'evenings out' is a quiet trip to Albany on the boat or cars, there to meet acquaintances formerly employed in the Troy factories and well known to these visiting maidens."

Once in Albany, the women were said to be wined, dined, taken to the theater, and then wined some more. Finally, they were promised a tour of the city, but the tour began and ended in Albany's notorious red-light district, "and down the Niagara of night she drifts. If she manages to keep her head and wits and has a strong will, refusing to go over the falls, a clutch at her throat, a gasp and a gurgle, and down into the fearful waters she disappears, to be found in a day or two under the grassy banks of the river, her hair full of sand, her face cut by pebbles of the shore, her eyes starting from their sockets, her tongue lacerated and protruding, and the beautiful creature that was the joy of her family and the pride of friends is proclaimed a suicide at the inquest, controlled by the representatives of that unscrupulous gang having the city by the throat."

The *Herald* claimed this was described to its reporters "by men and women in Troy and Albany who are profoundly moved by the horror of this last crime"—some of them factory girls who had themselves resisted and managed to escape the clutches of their would-be killers. It's "death or consent," one said.

Mamie had indeed taken a boat to Albany with a male companion on the night of September 4, the paper contended. But she had managed to escape and caught a late boat back to Troy. A trolley dropped her off at the corner of Grand and River Streets—this was about a city block from the water—where she waited for a connection to take her to her home, about a mile to the south. It was midnight.

What Mamie didn't know was that her assailant, "hungry for blood, was lying in wait for her," the *Herald* wrote.

> The refreshments that she had had on that fatal night in Albany must have deadened her sense of caution, for she lingered on the street corners near the river with her girl companion until a late hour, not observing the character of the beast awaiting his prey.
>
> At all events, a quarrel was picked with her, and, maintaining her old defiance, she thought she was safe until the half-drunken murderer clutched her throat, thrust his thumb through her hat, forcing her head back against the wall, and when the poor girl was found a few days later four miles below Troy, in peaceful waters, her eyes were bursting from their sockets, and her swollen, bruised tongue was far out of her mouth,

showing that she had gone to her death struggling to the last at the river's brink, her hat pulled out of shape in the fight for life, bearing the marks of the grasp of the ruffian who hurled the girl into the river, battered and mutilated to death.

⌒

So what did all this have to do with Hazel Drew?

Maybe nothing at all. But reporters couldn't help noticing the similarities between the cases. Two pretty young women from Troy found dead, their bodies submerged in water. Both coquettish. Both women were from working-class families and had multiple male admirers somewhat above their allotted station in life. Both died from wounds suffered to the backs of their heads. In both cases hats were left at the scenes of their deaths. Both dead girls had ribbons tightly embedded around their necks. If Dr. Elias Boyce—who had been practicing medicine for five decades—was right, Hazel Drew had been strangled. Could she, too, have been a victim of the "Girl-Strangler"?

Beyond that, Mamie Killion was a reminder of the insidious way in which politics had polluted almost every aspect of life in Troy, including its criminal justice system.

And not the only reminder, for those who recalled the Veiled Murderess, another of Troy's notorious murder cases. In the spring of 1853, two Irish immigrants, Timothy Lanagan and his sister-in-law Catherine Lubee, were poisoned to death inside their grocery store in Troy's Tenth Ward. A motive for the murder was never definitively determined. The prime suspect: a raven-haired, blue-eyed beauty who was the mistress of banker John Cotton Mather, a prominent Democratic politician and the descendant of seventeenth-century Puritan minister Cotton Mather, a notorious witch hunter who authored the controversial book *The Wonders of the Invisible World*, justifying the Salem witch trials.

At the time of the crime, John Mather was on the verge of being indicted on corruption charges in connection with his position as a New York State canal commissioner. The woman, who went under the assumed name of Henrietta Robinson (not to be confused with Henrietta Robertson from the Hazel Drew case), wore a dark veil over her face throughout the trial (and even in her jail cell). Robinson's true identity was rumored—though never proven—to be Charlotte Wood, a wealthy Emma Willard graduate who was married to a British aristocrat, Sir William Francis Augustus Elliot, and whose father, Robert Wood, was reputedly the illegitimate son of Edward, Duke of Kent.

Robinson, defended by Martin I. Townsend, a former Rensselaer County district attorney and a future congressman, was ultimately convicted of the murders and sentenced to death, though her punishment was later commuted to life in prison.

And now, all these years later, Jarvis O'Brien was hoping he didn't have another case like one of these on his hands.

But a newspaper reporter by the name of William M. Clemens was convinced otherwise. And he was going to do everything within his considerable power—the power of the press—to convince the public that Hazel Drew had been mixed up in a salacious entanglement that directly instigated her death.

Chapter 10

The Circus Comes to Town

To the press, Hazel Drew was, in life, a ghost.

She appeared in a newspaper possibly just this once: in the July 2, 1907, edition of the *Troy Times*, her name is listed in a classified advertisement documenting the participation of a number of women in a competition for a "Complimentary Vacation Trip" to Asbury Park, New Jersey, sponsored by Millards, a Troy shoe store. Hazel received only 201 votes, fewer than all but one of the other thirty-two contestants.

In death, Hazel Drew was a superstar.

For three weeks during the summer of 1908, newspapers—not just Troy papers, or even New York State papers, but papers from all across the country—couldn't get enough of the fetching young flaxen-haired woman who had been clubbed to death by an unknown assailant in the densely wooded outskirts of Sand Lake, New York, her corpse indifferently tossed into a secluded body of stagnant water about twenty feet from the nearest roadway.

The press covered the story but also *drove* the story.

Reporters—"gum-shoed hawkshaws," in the parlance of the time—invaded Sand Lake and Troy, hunting down leads, suspects, and clues, hounding anyone who had ever crossed paths with the enigmatic

Hazel Irene Drew. Every tip—legitimate or not—was page-one fodder: Orgies at a summer camp! Females held against their will! Secret lovers! Illegitimate pregnancy!

Separating fact from fancy wasn't easy then and isn't easy now. There's no disputing the fact that copious columns of newsprint were spent sensationalizing the story in order to sell more papers, yet reporters also uncovered crucial suspects and clues that investigators had somehow overlooked.

Early in the investigation, Louis H. Howe of the *Evening Telegram* and John Kelly of the *Evening World*, two New York City papers, were meandering around the scene of the crime when they made an important discovery. Getting nowhere pumping the rubberneckers who had flocked to the pond with questions, Howe and Kelly took a walk around the premises, keeping their eyes glued to the ground in case they happened to stumble upon something that so far had been overlooked.

"Hey, over there," Howe said, pointing to a stone on the bank of the pond.

"Yes, siree," said Kelly.

Crouching together, the journalists admired their find: a pair of gold pince-nez eyeglasses, which had been snapped, and a small silver hatpin.

"What d'ya make of that?" said Howe, pointing to the broken glasses.

"I don't know," said Kelly. "Maybe a struggle?"

"Either that or maybe one of these bumpkins wasn't looking where they were going and stomped on it."

"Be careful," Kelly warned. "Look at that smudge on the lens. A fingerprint?"

It sure looked like it. Howe withdrew his handkerchief, gingerly wrapping both discoveries inside.

"Let's give 'em to the cops," Howe said. "Maybe it'll earn us some goodwill, for a change."

The reporters passed their discoveries on to the detectives; both, it would turn out, had belonged to Hazel. County Detective Duncan Kaye ended up in possession of the glasses and promised to hand-deliver them to the state lab in Albany for fingerprint analysis—still a relatively new practice at the time—but it took him almost two weeks to do so, and any findings were never reported publicly.

The press also played a key role in identifying and speaking with some of Hazel's closest friends, who provided valuable insights into Hazel's day-to-day life that her family members either couldn't, or wouldn't, share. Two of those friends—Mina Jones and Carrie Weaver, both out of town when Hazel was killed—corresponded with local papers, requesting updates on the case.

Whether these and other revelations by reporters were due to sloppy police work or the ingenuity of the press—or both—is debatable, but out-of-town papers didn't really care. They roasted District Attorney Jarvis O'Brien and his investigators relentlessly, demanding arrests every time a new suspect emerged, riling up readers with righteous indignation every day that passed without justice. Newspapers warned that unless somebody was arrested soon, townspeople might take matters into their own hands, even lynching suspects of their own choosing.

Only July 26, the *Troy Northern Budget* wrote:

> Many false rumors have been set afloat by sensational newspapers and the wildest of stories have been print-ed for the sole purpose of exciting the people, creating sensations and to make it appear that the officials of the county and city have been amiss in their duties . . . Those sensational metropolitan papers have sent their most 'brilliant' reporters here, backed by their criminol-ogists, sleuths, photographers and all the parapherna-lia they can command, yet they have failed to find the slightest clew [sic] to the murderer of the girl. Now that

> they have so signally failed in their efforts, and they
> have been given every courtesy and assistance within
> the power of the office of the District Attorney, they try
> to cover up their failure by criticizing the officials of the
> county and city.

During one of his regular morning briefings with reporters, the beleaguered O'Brien urged them all to just simmer down and scolded them for their treatment of three of the more notorious characters in the case: Uncle William Taylor, Aunt Minnie Taylor, and the "dullard" farmhand Frank Smith—which was curious, because O'Brien himself had been casting various aspersions on all three all along.

"Listen up," O'Brien said, launching into one of his famous orations. "Some people have been clamoring for the arrest of William Taylor, the uncle. There is no evidence against him; no motive has been shown for his murdering the girl. Others have been advocating the arrest of Miss Taylor, the aunt. She has answered all of our questions, apparently in an honest manner, and has assured us over and over again that she will do anything possible to fix the responsibility for the crime. Of course, no one suspects her, but some think she knows more about the girl's previous whereabouts than she has told. We have no reason to believe that she does.

"Others have clamored for the arrest of Smith and [Rudy Gundrum], but there is nothing, in a sense of fairness and justice, which would warrant our placing a strain upon their lives by taking them into custody. All is being done that can be done. If others can come to this city, from New York or any other place, and capture the murderer I will be glad to have them do it. We are not looking for glory in this case. All we want is to see the guilty party or parties brought to justice."

The reporters did their best to keep up with him, jotting down every word as expediently as possible, nodding in agreement, all while visions of another page-one story were dancing in their heads. Then they ran off to cover the case exactly as they had been doing all along.

⁓

The turn of the twentieth century was a gilded age for newspapers. Historians refer to it as the era of the popular press, but it was also the age of yellow journalism.

With the Industrial Revolution—most prominently Ottmar Mergenthaler's 1886 invention of the Linotype machine, which enabled printers to set type automatically rather than by hand—newspapers were reinvented, becoming bigger, bolder, and timelier. Advances in communications—the telegraph, telephone, seabed cables—enabled instant newsgathering from faraway locations. Railroads transported reporters to and from the front lines of newsworthy events at unprecedented speeds, simultaneously revolutionizing the speed with which newspapers could be delivered to readers.

Late-nineteenth-century innovations in photography also boosted circulation; news events had been photographed as early as the 1850s, but the pictures had to be reinterpreted with wood engravings before publication for compatibility with the printing presses of the time (this was how Mathew Brady's landmark Civil War work was published in *Harper's Weekly*). On March 4, 1880, the *Daily Graphic* of New York published the first halftone (rather than engraved) reproduction of a news photograph; additional innovations, like the invention of flash powder in 1887, followed. By 1897, halftone photographs could be reproduced on printing presses running at full speed.

Newspaper readership soared, as did the number of papers, from 850 nationally in 1880 to nearly 2,000 in 1900. Weeklies continued to serve smaller, more rural communities, but every major urban center had at least one newspaper of its own; New York City had over a dozen. By 1908, Troy wasn't far behind. Newspapers became a mass-market industry, and profit-obsessed press barons went prowling for readers and advertising dollars in every way they could imagine: a "race to the bottom" critics—of which there are many—have called it.

Stunt reporting was one such innovation, famously exemplified in 1869 when the *New York Herald* dispatched correspondent Henry Morton Stanley as part of a roving commission in the Middle East to track down Dr. David Livingstone, missing in action since his 1866 expedition to Africa in search of the source of the Nile. Stanley did indeed find Livingstone, on October 27, 1871, in Ujiji, near Lake Tanganyika in present-day Tanzania (though whether he actually greeted him with "Dr. Livingstone, I presume?" is subject to debate).

During the so-called partisan press era, or party press era, news editors collected patronage from political parties, either directly or in the form of government printing contracts, in exchange for championing that party's candidates and principles—without ever directly informing readers of their bias. Although the 1830s is often cited as the end of that practice—both for economic reasons and because of the development of higher journalism standards—many American newspapers remained highly partisan into the early years of the twentieth century.

Publisher Joseph Pulitzer, for instance, was prominent in Democratic Party politics. Born in Hungary in 1847, "Joey the Jew"—as he was known in certain circles—immigrated to America at the age of seventeen, and in 1878 he purchased two St. Louis papers, merging them into one, the *St. Louis Post-Dispatch*, making him a wealthy and powerful man.

Five years later, he paid $346,000 for the failing *New York World*, a city daily that was losing $40,000 a year. Within three years, circulation had spiked from 15,000 to 250,000, and the *World* had become the world's most-read paper. Its recipe for success was a seductive blend of idealism and sensationalism: crusades against public corruption, crime stories, vivid headlines, and stunt reporting. In 1889 Elizabeth Jane Cochrane, who wrote under the name Nellie Bly, trotted across the globe on assignment for Pulitzer's *World* to see if she could beat the fictional eighty-day odyssey by Phileas Fogg depicted in the 1873 Jules Verne novel *Around the World in Eighty Days*. (She did, by eight days.)

In 1895, Pulitzer's nemesis, William Randolph Hearst—who had cut his teeth in the newspaper trade in the Wild West of Northern California—purchased a rival New York paper, the *Journal*, and proceeded to raid the entire Sunday staff of the *World*, including cartoonist Richard F. Outcault, author and illustrator of the phenomenally popular *Yellow Kid* comic strip. In response, Pulitzer brought in a replacement cartoonist to continue the strip, so that both papers were publishing a version of *Yellow Kid*, but with different creators and different content.

As the battle for readers intensified, the two papers stooped to new lows of sensationalism—"yellow press," a term coined by Ervin Wardman of the *Evening Press* in reference to the warfare over the *Yellow Kid* comic strip. While it's true that yellow journalism has been blamed for launching wars, the real bread and butter of the yellow journalist was crime, violence, and sex.

In July 1908, Pulitzer's *New York World* dispatched a man by the name of William Montgomery Clemens to Troy, to cover a story that combined elements of all three: the murder of Hazel Drew.

The investigators leading the case would rue the day.

⁓

William Clemens had no use for modesty. Greatness deserved reward, he believed, especially his own. He loved nothing more than dazzling his fellow ink slingers and his readers with tales of derring-do and Holmesian deduction.

At the age of forty-eight, he was still a handsome man, with a full head of black hair parted neatly down the middle and dark, intense eyes that rarely stopped moving.

Born on January 16, 1860, in Paris, Ohio, and educated at Buchtel College (now the University of Akron), Clemens launched his newspaper career at the age of nineteen as a staff writer at the *Pittsburgh Leader*, then went to work for the *Pittsburgh Dispatch*, Cleveland's *Plain Dealer*, the *Los Angeles Tribune*, and the *San Francisco Chronicle*, before finally heading east, where he spent two years—1894 and 1895—at Pulitzer's paper, the *World*.

For the next decade, Clemens kept busy. He served as a correspondent during the Spanish-American War; authored biographies of Benjamin Franklin, John Brown, and Mark Twain; and penned eclectic works of fiction (which, his detractors argued, was an accurate description of his newspaper work as well), including *The Gilded Lady*, an espionage thriller, allegedly based on true events as revealed by a government insider; *The House of the Hundred Doors*, a bizarre collection of short stories united by an antivivisection message, featuring a variety of dogs as the protagonists; and numerous other short stories, in which daring criminal hunters worked through labyrinths of clues and red herrings to bring the true culprits to justice.

His most famous work, *Mark Twain: His Life and Work, A Biographical Sketch*, about Samuel Langhorne Clemens, was published in 1892. Although this is cited as the first of many full-length biographies on the legendary author, the journalist was accused of pulling much of its text from previously published articles and other sources.

William Clemens went around boasting that Twain was an uncle, though he most certainly was not. Many years later, Twain biographer Gary Scharnhorst would uncover a letter from Twain to his *actual* nephew, Samuel Moffett, in which he refers to Clemens as a "singular tapeworm who seems to feed solely upon other people's intestines & who seems to be barren of any other food-supply."

Clemens did, however, have a passing acquaintance with Twain and once approached him about providing a foreword for a book he had written on America's great humorists. He received this droll response from Twain:

Will M. Clemens,
My Dear Friend: Your letter received. God bless your
heart. I would like ever so much to comply with your
request, but I am thrashing away at my new book, and
am afraid that I should not find time to write my own
epitaph, in case I was suddenly called for.
   Wishing you and your book well, believe me.
   Yours truly,
   Samuel L. Clemens.

"Will Clemens" was nonetheless thrilled by Twain's rejection letter, which he published and made reference to throughout his career.

Clemens was thrice married, twice divorced, once by Edna Graves Clemens on grounds of cruelty, possibly having something to do with the time he threatened to shoot her. Or perhaps it was the time he attacked her aboard a Europe-bound steamer for allegedly flirting with another man.

By the time Clemens had returned to the *World* in 1907, a year before the Hazel Drew murder, he was no longer a mere staff reporter but had earned the title, as boldly proclaimed by the paper, of "The World's Expert in Criminology" (or was it "The *World's* Expert in Criminology"?). As an "expert criminologist," Clemens earned an annual salary of $10,000 a year (more than $275,000 adjusted for inflation), according to Edna's petition for "reasonable" alimony—despite having absolutely no background or training in the field.

What was possibly Clemens's greatest claim to fame came in 1904, when he announced to the world that he had, merely as an intellectual exercise, solved the sixty-three-year-old mystery behind the murder of "pretty cigar girl" Mary Cecilia Rogers, an employee at a New York City tobacco shop who had been missing for three days before her corpse was discovered floating in the Hudson River off Castle Point, near Weehawken, New Jersey. The case was the inspiration for Edgar

Allan Poe's short story "The Mystery of Marie Rogêt." Clemens was adamant that Rogers had not in fact been killed by gang members roaming around Elysian Fields in Hoboken, as police asserted, but rather that she and the tall, swarthy mystery man who had accompanied her on that fateful Sunday afternoon were robbed at gunpoint and then murdered in a nearby roadhouse after seeking refuge from a rainstorm.

In January 1908, the *World* reported that Clemens (the "Sherlock Holmes of America") had singlehandedly solved the "great murder mystery" of Harrison, New Jersey—colorfully titled "The Adventure of the Embroidered Jacket"—in which the nude body of Helena Whitmore had been found on Christmas Day 1907 in a swamp, a crime for which her husband, who had been hauling his ashes with a woman from New York City's Tenderloin District, was arrested. "The *World* takes great credit for the work and says that the police authorities admit that it is one of the greatest achievements ever placed to the credit of a newspaper," the paper humbly proclaimed.

Ah, but it wasn't all grandeur and glory: In March 1908—just four months before arriving in Troy—Clemens mistakenly identified an overweight forty-eight-year-old schlump of a machinist named Heinrich Wilhelm Esser of Brooklyn as a German spy, instead of the petty thief he really was. As a result, the *Brooklyn Daily Eagle* and other rival papers mocked Clemens as the "Sherlock Holmes person" and a "private detective seeking fame as a 'criminologist,'" with his "beautiful cards printed from copperplate on which he describes himself as a 'criminal investigator' with offices in London and Paris and headquarters in old New York."

Now, in July 1908, William M. Clemens was bringing his unique brand of criminology and shameless self-promotion to Upstate New York, to solve the murder of Hazel Irene Drew.

Clemens arrived in Troy in the days following the discovery of Hazel's body and quickly proceeded to inveigle his way in with the investigators, touting his dubious, though widely publicized, track record as a master sleuth. Leads and tips had been growing exponentially, and the detectives were in no position to decline an offer of help. By the end of the investigation, District Attorney Jarvis O'Brien would have been very happy if the famed criminologist had never stepped foot in Rensselaer County.

On July 17, Clemens joined Detectives William Powers and Louis Unser in Sand Lake. They spent most of the day reinterviewing Frank Smith, William Taylor, and, after finally tracking him down, Rudy Gundrum. The detectives sweated them hard and combed through every inch of Taylor's property looking for something amiss but came up empty.

Powers also wanted to speak with Dr. Elias Boyce, who had helped conduct Hazel's autopsy, regarding a rumor that the doctor had seen Hazel in Sand Lake on July 7, the presumed night of her murder. Although Boyce could neither confirm nor deny that the girl he had seen walking down the road with a companion that afternoon was actually Hazel, the conversation meandered and at one point turned to the cause of death. Clemens, who had tagged along with the detectives, sniffed controversy, leading to his first sensational headline of the case: **Drew Girl Was Strangled and Then Thrown in Pond: Throttled with Cord**.

"I have eliminated the uncle, Taylor, and the lout, Smith, from any complicity in the murder," he boasted. "I have established the true cause of death as strangulation, the result of a silk lace cord tied tightly about the neck. Dr. Bryce [*sic*], who made the autopsy [. . .], said to me, in the presence of others: 'I witnessed the removal of the body from the water to the bank of the pond . . . The whole appearance of the body indicated strangulation.'"

Hazel wasn't clubbed to death, according to Clemens; she was strangled and died of asphyxiation. Any idiot could see that the blow to the head—so anemic that it hadn't even dislodged the combs from her hair—couldn't have killed her; the real murder weapon was the shirred pink silk ribbon that Boyce had found drawn and knotted so tightly around the throat as to become embedded in her neck.

This directly contradicted the finding of all three doctors present for the autopsy—that Hazel had been killed by a blow to the head. Even Boyce, who suspected the girl had also been strangled, was convinced it was the blow that killed her and that the perpetrator had strangled her afterward simply to make certain she was dead.

As Clemens's speculation about strangulation spread, Dr. Harry Fairweather, speaking on behalf of the investigation and defending the results of the autopsy, responded: "That wild story that was spread about her having been strangled with a corset string is as ridiculous as many of the other stories that have spread about during the week. Her neck was greatly extended and had a corset string been tied about her neck it would have cut the flesh."

Clemens, not one to cede the last word, responded by asserting that the doctors had "made a superficial examination of Hazel's decomposed body," and he went on to cite his great success in solving the Helena Whitmore murder the previous year. In that case, he reminded his readers, a shoddy autopsy had failed to deduce that Whitmore had ever been pregnant (and Clemens had tracked down the child, born fifteen years before, to prove it). "Thus we see what doctors can do when they don't try," he snidely concluded.

Furthermore, Clemens crowed, his tenacious sleuthing had uncovered the real truth about what had happened to Hazel Drew, and it was explosive: Hazel had been "brutally assaulted!" which meant, in the newspaper language of the time, that she had been raped.

The press pounced on the discrepancy between the doctors' findings, and O'Brien found himself on the defensive at his morning briefing, barraged by an onslaught of questions: How confident are you that the autopsy caught everything? What do you think about Dr. Boyce's theory that Hazel was strangled? Are you planning to exhume the body?

By now, O'Brien was ready to take that shirred pink ribbon and wrap it around Clemens's neck himself. Keeping his temper in check, the DA relented and allowed those gathered in his office to examine Hazel's clothes.

"Please take a look, gentlemen."

He spread every article of clothing found on Hazel's body across the floor of his office and then crouched down by the corset cover, pointing to the pink lace ribbon, a quarter of an inch wide, which was interlaced through the top of the cover.

"It has been postulated that the killer had used the cord as a garrote and then tied it into a knot to seal her fate. Please, everyone, take a close look," he scoffed, handing the water-stained corset cover around to the gathered reporters. "If anyone sees any trace of this supposed knot that caused Hazel to draw her last breath, please do draw it to my attention."

The pink ribbon was intact, except where it had been cut by Boyce to remove the corset.

Was O'Brien then insinuating that Boyce—a licensed medical doctor—had erred in his conclusion?

"The protruding tongue and eyes were the result of gasses from the body . . . built up from being in the pond for so long. That's what the doctors tell me. I do know that Dr. Boyce had some differing opinions from the others who participated in the autopsy, but I very sincerely doubt he would state under oath that Hazel Drew was strangled to death. You know not all members of the press are as straightforward with their reporting as the gentlemen present here today," he concluded to a scattering of chuckles.

O'Brien wasn't alone in not being the world's biggest fan of the infamous William Clemens.

Following the impromptu fashion show in O'Brien's office, the July 20 *Evening Telegram* declared, "A story that the girl's corset cover was found ripped open under both arms which would have permitted its being drawn up around her neck, which was used to build a theory that the girl was strangled, was dispelled by an examination of the girl's garments to-day [*sic*]. One arm of the corset cover had been cut underneath the arm by the undertaker in recovering the girl's clothing, but the other arm hole was out at the top. While the garment could have been removed from the body, it could not possibly have been drawn up around the neck."

Clemens wasn't budging. He strode down the steps of the Rensselaer County Courthouse, his anger simmering. But he hadn't traveled ten feet when he abruptly halted, turned, and marched off in the opposite direction, down Second Street, toward W. H. Frear's Cash Bazaar, one of Troy's bustling department stores, where Hazel was known to have purchased her corsets and covers.

Arriving at Frear's, Clemens sought out the saleswoman who typically had waited on Hazel, and after purchasing the same brand and breed of corset cover, he asked the woman to try it on.

"Pardon? You'd like me to do what, sir?" she said.

"Now, bear with me, young lady," Clemens said. "I'd like you to take the corset and put it on yourself. Over your shirtwaist, of course. I can assure you it's for the noblest of reasons."

"Right here in the store, sir?" the saleswoman said, looking around sheepishly.

"Yes, yes, right here. Go ahead, please. No cause to be timid."

The woman hesitated. Clemens was a charming man, eloquent and dapper. It would be quite a story to tell her family at home that night. Everyone was talking about the murder of Hazel Drew, and here was her chance to play a role in it, however small. She did as the newspaperman requested.

"Now, I'd like you to tie it just the way you normally would, with the pink ribbon in the center of your chest, right there in the bosom."

After a moment's hesitation, the saleswoman obliged.

"Wonderful!" said Clemens. "Now, I need you to draw the corset cover up and tie the ribbon under your chin, like just so."

"Oh sir, it cannot be done," she said, blushing. "It catches at the armpit, and the only way to accomplish it would be to tear or rip the garment several inches under each arm."

Clemens tingled with excitement. The doctors—even Boyce— had gotten it wrong! He hurried from the store armed with his next headline.

In this report, Clemens doubled down on the strangulation theory, now blaming Boyce for claiming the corset had been lifted over Hazel's head when her assailant had strangled her to death.

He found an ally in Hazel's friend from Watervliet, Amelia Huntley—she bonded with the reporter over their mutual befuddlement as to why Hazel hadn't been wearing an undershirt when her body was recovered.

"I cannot understand it," Amelia said. "I am positive that Hazel would never dress without wearing such a garment. She had a large bust and her corsets necessarily had to be laced tightly. In this warm weather the perspiration would have rusted her corset steels and ruined the corsets if she had worn them next to the skin. She was the neatest, tidiest girl I ever knew and was over-fastidious in her dress."

Hazel, known to be discriminating when it came to fashion, was "dressed abnormally, unusually, unnatural to Hazel or her habits," according to Clemens. She was wearing three skirts—a medium-weight black cloth skirt, plus two underskirts—in over-ninety-degree weather. Six safety pins had been fastened to her clothing. Surely she must have been undressed and then redressed, presumably by someone with little understanding of female attire.

"Here, then, was actual proof that Hazel Drew was strangled at a time when she was not wearing her shirtwaist," Clemens wrote. "The corset cover could not have been torn and drawn up on the neck, and the red [more commonly described during the investigation as pink] ribbon tied under her chin so tightly as to cause strangulation under and beneath a shirtwaist, the high collar of which encircled the neck of the girl."

Clemens displayed a remarkable gift for uncovering clues that eluded detectives; the problem was he was equally adept at discovering clues that might never have existed, then running eye-grabbing headlines, trumpeting theories based on his dubious finds. It was never easy to establish which was which.

On Wednesday, July 22, Clemens reported that "light is beginning to break in the Hazel Drew case." He had just orchestrated another of his "exclusives," accompanying the investigators to Whitman Court to ask Mary Cary about a story that had surfaced regarding a possible relationship between Hazel and a dentist. As the detectives were talking with the Carys, Clemens wandered around the house, gaining an intimate perspective of where Hazel had last lived and worked. Mary wasn't much help in identifying the dentist, but that didn't stop the famed criminologist from finding his next big story.

Slowly, Clemens descended into the dark, dank basement; though he was not a spiritualistic man, the silence unsettled him. Two weeks earlier, Hazel almost certainly had walked down these same steps, into this same room. Who knows what Clemens was thinking as he navigated the narrow, creaky stairway? Perhaps he sensed the spectral presence of Hazel herself, trapped between this world and the next one, waiting for her killer to be exposed. Maybe he felt a phantom tug at the shoulder of his finely tailored pinstripe suit, or heard a whisper, nudging him this way or that. Or maybe he just got lucky.

Whatever the impulsion, Clemens accomplished exactly what he had set out to do, uncovering a clue that everyone else had overlooked: a hatbox stuffed with photographs, bills, receipts, circulars, even her address book, with the names of sixty friends, some men, some women, that Hazel had left behind, probably expecting them to be incinerated. His haul included letters and postcards written not just *to* Hazel, but also *from* her, thanks to her idiosyncratic practice of writing missives first in pencil, then rewriting them in ink and retaining the original copies. Hazel had only a "slight education," Clemens remarked, and her penmanship was "like that of a country school girl, with little regard for spelling and punctuation and with noticeable lapses in the grammar."

In short: manna from heaven. And what made it even more delicious was that O'Brien's brigade of bungling sleuths had completely missed it.

Clemens hankered to return to his office and start writing, but not quite yet. He still had some poking around to do. In the presence of Mary Cary, he went from closet to closet, finally discovering a ragbag full of Hazel's clothing, which he proceeded to dump on the floor so that he could take a complete inventory. Even Mary Cary was "astonished at its size and the quantity of its contents": skirts, underwear, gloves, stockings, handkerchiefs, shoes, and aprons, all in fine condition and, Clemens posited, discarded by Hazel at the last minute in her haste to skip out on the Carys.

Later that night, Clemens plopped himself down onto his beat-up old black leather swivel chair, fired up a cigarette, and started pecking away at his Royal Standard No. 1 black flatbed typewriter (that damn *E* kept sticking). He would show them! He was, after all, the Sherlock Holmes of America.

Clemens had no intention of holding back. He walloped Hazel right off the bat: "There would never have been such a black wall of mystery in this case if Hazel herself had been less secretive and more frank and honest with her friends and relatives. The fact that she made her young life so secretive has brought about the puzzling problem of her death. She was her own worst enemy."

But he was just getting warmed up: Hazel was a "flirt . . . vain of beauty and clothes." During the past year she had "dropped, one by one, her girl friends and the young boys of her [youth] and began making acquaintances of the more worldly sort. Every time she made a trip to another city she made a new acquaintance."

Julia Drew had said Hazel didn't have a beau; Mary Cary insisted she seldom received letters. Both were wrong, Clemens said—both oblivious to the double life that Hazel had surreptitiously lived.

Clemens next did something that even he considered to be ethically dubious—a violation of the "sacredness" of Hazel's life, as he put it—but necessary as a demonstration of her "flirtations and the sort of men she attracted by her beauty and personality." He revealed in full a letter from one of her admirers:

To my lady of the blond hair: I am taking the great liberty in addressing this letter to you, my lady, but considering what a pleasant time you afforded us I cannot help but express our deepest sympathy for the loss of your glasses. We feel that we were partly to blame, for had we not been so forward in our notions you probably would not have been in our boat. Still I do not wish you to have the impression that we are heartless flirts, even though we have come from the city. We noticed that you were somewhat agitated upon leaving the car, and we have thought it was because he and I have made such a peculiar appearance and as though you were ashamed of us. If we had suspected that we were to meet such charming young ladies we would have dressed accordingly.

I trust that your wrists are not injured, for I couldn't forgive myself if I had caused even the slightest bruise. 'Tis true that I had to use force on some occasions, but I tried not to be rough or rude in my actions. My friend and I have more mental than physical work in our business, and a week's outing in your and your friend's company is worth more than a month in the mountains.

It is very possible that a pretty girl like you has many admirers, and you undoubtedly have a preference among them. I shall always remember the happy scene enacted on Snyder's Lake and dream of my lady of the blond hair. I have sketched your face and shoulders and I cannot get the proper expression of your eyes as they looked to me while you were holding my hands on the beach. I hope you will forgive me for taking possession of your napkin, but I really had to take something as a souvenir.

It seems strange to me that we should both take to you more than to your girlfriends, but somehow you seemed to belong to a higher sphere, and considerably more sensible, modern, and have more pleasing ways. If we send postals we shall expect others in return. "If Knighthood Were in Flower" I should live only for and have fond clinging memories of "my lady of the blond hair" and be faithful unto death, under the names of your "KNIGHT OF THE NAPP KINN AND YOUR ARTIST FRIEND, HARRY."

Clemens leaned back in his chair. On his desk, beside his typewriter, he kept a stack of the day's papers, and atop the stack—always—was a copy of the *Evening World*. Today's front page featured a photo of Hazel Drew. By now the image was seared in his mind. Her thin, angular face, the haunting eyes, the delicate neck, and that striking mound of flaxen hair, crested into her signature pompadour.

Clearly, Hazel had had a mesmerizing effect on men. Her beauty and charm were prodigious. She was an artist's muse. She was "modern"; she belonged to a "higher sphere." She held hands with a man she barely knew in public, and for some indeterminable reason he had felt compelled to be "forceful" with her. Elegant girl that she was, she may have been embarrassed by her fancier's feeble sense of fashion. All of which added up to this for Clemens: Hazel was not the girl her family and friends were portraying her to be to the press, whether they believed what they were saying or not.

On the morning of Friday, July 3, Hazel had received another letter, also discovered by Clemens; this one was written in pencil, in what he described as the handwriting of a man. Within an hour of receiving it, he claimed in a July 22 column, she was carrying articles of clothing from her room to her trunk, which she kept in the cellar of the Cary home.

Here, Clemens argued, was proof that Hazel's departure from the Carys' on July 6 wasn't sudden at all; rather, she had been planning it for at least three full days.

Why? What exactly was she up to?

Clemens believed, based on the evidence at hand, that Hazel intended to flee Troy by train on the afternoon or evening of Monday, July 6, and had left her clothing behind expecting to "replenish her wardrobe at a very early date, necessarily with money furnished by the person whom she expected to accompany her in flight."

Who was that person? Clemens didn't have a theory—yet. But he was convinced that Hazel, at some point during her time in Troy, had been transformed by the city, as symbolized by the missive she had received from Harry, the "Knight of the Napp Kinn."

"This or some similar letter may have been the beginning of bringing Hazel's little narrow world something of the vanities and flattery that men and women know so well in the rapid civilization of city life," he wrote. "She, poor rural innocent, whose beauty was a real danger, soon became the moth before the flame, and fate had marked her for the fire."

～

Clemens's self-promoting account of visiting the Carys, where he unearthed Hazel's hidden possessions, was the final straw for O'Brien—Clemens didn't even mention in his article that he was there accompanying detectives—and the relationship between the two parties effectively came to an end. There would be no more joint site visits or interrogating suspects together.

"The District Attorney caused a $1000 reward to be offered last Friday with the hopes that information would walk in upon him every hour of the day. In this he has been disappointed and to-day [*sic*] realizes that to obtain information he must send his sleuths out and hustle for it," Clemens helpfully suggested in the July 22 edition of the *Thrice-a-Week World*.

A day later, the *World* reported, in an article appearing without a byline, "If the murderer of Hazel Drew escapes the penalties of his atrocious crime, Rensselaer County citizens will have official inactivity to blame. Promptness and thoroughness have been sadly lacking in the effort of Troy's authorities to unravel the mystery." O'Brien was singled out as "over-cautious" for failing to "break at once the obstinate silence of the victim's relatives and friends."

Once Clemens mocked O'Brien as a "$100,000 politician, large, tall, impressive, wears a goatee, strikes military attitudes and smokes cigarettes." O'Brien countered: "I wish I had that $100,000. I never had a goatee and I don't know that I want one. As to cigarettes, I don't use them. A cigar is good enough for me, and I don't smoke them very often."

Recalling the earlier encounter with Clemens in his office, O'Brien claimed that the newspaperman "wanted to sleep with the Drew girl's clothes, but I wouldn't let him. He was permitted to see the clothes and had to ask my stenographer what each article was called."

Another incendiary article appearing in the July 20 edition of the paper—again without a byline—asserted that O'Brien had asked an unnamed correspondent from the *World* to "withhold information he had secured, because . . . publicity might defeat what promises to clear the mystery of this girl's murder. This information was obtained from investigation of Hazel's secret friendships for the past year." The article further stated that false evidence was being manufactured to distract detectives from the real culprit.

A few days later, when a photo of a young man (later identified as F. W. Schlafflin) who matched the description of a person of interest was found among Hazel's possessions, Clemens strongly implied that the floundering investigation was perhaps seeking a quick end to the case: "This description fits exactly the cheap photograph of the unknown man found in Hazel's trunk by the detectives to-day [*sic*]. When they searched the trunk before it was not there, and it looks to me like a plant."

In one of his more embarrassing gaffes, Clemens asserted that the murderer had made off with two of Hazel's precious solid-gold brace-lets—gifts from a since-deceased aunt—that she never went anywhere without.

"To all pawnbrokers: Arrest man who attempts to pawn one or pair of heavy, solid chased gold bracelets, one-half inch wide, with a small, looped chain three inches long attached. These were stolen from the body of Hazel Drew, murdered near Troy, NY, July 7," Clemens led off his July 22 report for the *Thrice-a-Week World*. From his talk with Amelia Huntley, he coaxed, "I have been astonished that the police have been stupid enough to overlook the gold bracelets that Hazel wore. I never saw her where she did not wear one or both of these bracelets."

In fact, neither was missing: Minnie Taylor, Hazel's aunt, had one; the other had been packed away in Hazel's trunk.

⁓

In that same July 22 *Thrice-a-Week* article, Clemens made his boldest assertion to date: Hazel Drew had left the home of John and Adelaide Tupper the previous January to "hide her shame." Translation: Hazel was pregnant. Why else would she have chosen Taborton, of all places, as refuge in the dead of winter, "with the thermometer at twenty below zero and snow drifts everywhere"? Why remain in seclusion for nearly a month? Why, if she was seriously ill, as everyone maintained, was no doctor summoned? Why was no one allowed inside Hazel's room for a full week, except for her sister-in-law, Eva Drew, who nursed her back to health?

Clemens boasted of having confirmation from family members, whom he had interviewed, learning "for the first time the real secret of the Drew [family] attitude of silence and unconcern over Hazel's tragic death." But he never identified his informant, and no family member ever came forward to publicly confirm his version of events.

Never mind that; Clemens had tangible proof as well. During his trip to the Cary house, he had discovered "certain medicines" bearing the imprint of a "quack medical concern in Chicago." (Another article, appearing in the July 23 edition of the *Washington Herald* without a byline, identified the medicine as pink lozenges.) Clemens's implication—though again, never stated outright—was that Hazel had taken the medication to induce a miscarriage.

Such drugs—known at the time as "French female pills"—were indeed readily available by mail, marketed as a way to assist women in maintaining regular menstrual cycles. Sharum's Vegetable Tonic ("It will cure you or Killilea Pharmacy will refund your money."), for instance, was astonishingly touted as a cure for "female weakness" that acted "directly upon the sexual system, toning up the membranes, strengthening the relaxed muscles and invigorating the weakened organs."

But there were other plausible explanations as to why the medication might have been in Hazel's possession that Clemens ignored. For one, Hazel had been nagged by nettlesome eye and head issues and had been treated for related ailments at Troy Hospital. Additionally, letters found in her trunk disclosed that she had been in touch with physicians in Providence, Rhode Island, where Hazel had once visited her friend Mina Jones, about an undisclosed medical condition.

Further, despite the push from the progressive movement, this was still a time when little regulation existed to ensure the efficacy and safety of medicine. The Food and Drug Administration wasn't formed until 1927 (from a reorganization of the Bureau of Chemistry), and it wasn't until 1938, when President Franklin Delano Roosevelt signed the Federal Food, Drug, and Cosmetic Act into law, that the government required a third-party review of new drugs before they were allowed on the market. This act also effectively banned false advertising in the labeling of medications.

But in 1908, mail-order companies had sprung up all across the country espousing "miracle cures" for illnesses of every kind, from S. Andral Kilmer's Swamp-Root (said to cure catarrh of the bladder, rheumatism, and weak kidneys) to Paine's Celery Compound (a "remarkable blood purifier and nerve food") to Anheuser-Busch's 2 percent alcohol Malt-Nutrine ("nourishment for both convalescent mother and nursing child"). None of these patent medicines required prescriptions, and many contained addictive drugs like opium, morphine, and cocaine, which had become so vexing a problem by 1908 that the US Post Office prohibited their distribution by mail.

Clemens, however, wasn't interested in other explanations; here, he said, was further proof of Hazel's duplicity: "There is now no question of the double life that poor Hazel had been living for a year before her death." He'd been hawking that notion for days, but now Clemens had something new to report: a year earlier, he wrote on July 22, Hazel had fallen in love with a married man, and it was this man—this "schooled, worldly villain," as Clemens called him—who, desperate to get rid of her, had taken her life at Teal's Pond on the night of Tuesday, July 7.

～

The *Washington Herald* article datelined Wednesday, July 22, which identified the medicines found in Hazel's room at the Cary house as pink lozenges, had all the bearings of a Clemens story except one: his byline (no name is attached to the article). The piece starts off by posing the question "Was Hazel Drew, a girl of previously unsullied reputation, finally a victim of the wiles of some man as yet unknown, who won her trust and confidence last fall?"

In wondering what Hazel had planned to do next, after quitting her job at the Carys', the reporter mentioned having come across a piece of paper among her torn letters with the name Florence Barker written over and over again, in Hazel's hand: "Florence Barker is not the name of any friend of Hazel's so far as is known. Was it to be her name in this new life she had planned for herself, with all old ties broken and destroyed?"

None of the local papers ever mention the name Florence Barker in connection with the Hazel Drew case. The *Herald* may be the only publication in which this clue was reported, and there was no follow-up story reporting as to whether detectives even pursued this lead, let alone discovered who Florence Barker was.

But it wouldn't have been very hard for them to do so, because Florence Barker was living across the street from Hazel on Whitman Court.

Florence was the wife of William Barker Jr., another of those prominent Trojans in whose orbit Hazel constantly seemed to find herself moving. On the cusp of turning thirty-five at the time of Hazel's death,

Barker held an interest in his father's collar-and-cuff company, the William Barker Company, a midsize outfit with offices in Troy and a factory in Watervliet, across the Hudson River. He was a striking-looking man, with black hair, black eyes, and an intriguing backstory. His mother's ancestors had landed at Plymouth Rock on the *Mayflower*, and the family was prominent in New England. In the 1600s, a William Barker who may have been a distant ancestor was placed on trial for witchcraft.

William Barker Sr., a Republican, had founded the collar-and-cuff company; his son joined the family business after dropping out of school during a holiday recess, at the age of sixteen.

On October 12, 1899, Barker married Florence Herring, of Harrington Park, New Jersey. They had one child, also named William, born on March 25, 1908—about three and a half months before Hazel's murder.

Barker belonged to all the right clubs, traveling in the same circles as Jarvis O'Brien, Thomas Hislop, and Edward Cary, including the Troy Citizens Corps, the Colonial Club, the Chamber of Commerce, the Island Golf Club, the Lametide Fish and Game Club, and the Pafraets Dael Club. (Nearly every prominent man in Troy seemed to be a card-carrying member of this last club.)

The Barkers and the Carys were neighbors, but at some point they also became close friends, vacationing together at the Barkers' camp up in the Adirondacks on Thirteenth Lake years after Hazel died.

So why did Hazel Drew write "Florence Barker" over and over on a slip of paper?

History doesn't say.

～

William Clemens's last word on the death of Hazel Drew was a bylined article appearing on July 24: "To-day's [*sic*] developments have only added additional interest to this interesting case. Tomorrow promises that things may happen worthwhile, and I repeat my prediction of a few days ago that light is breaking." And then, without another word on the case, the whirlwind that was William Clemens abruptly departed from Troy. Although he never solved the mystery behind the murder of Hazel Drew, he apparently found time in the midst of his investigation to crack the infamous Mystery of the Veiled Murderess from 1853, having filed a report with the *St. Louis Post-Dispatch* on July 18 headlined Murderess Who Died in Prison Wife of Noble.

Hazel Drew was the one case that even William Clemens couldn't claim to have solved, but the fires he stoked, exposing Hazel's most guarded, intimate secrets, propelled the narrative of Hazel's double life for the rest of the investigation. And despite his steady stream of half-truths and probable fabrications, did Clemens have a point? Were Hazel's family and friends telling everything they knew? Did they even know everything about Hazel? Did anyone?

Chapter 11

WHEAT FROM THE CHAFF

As the first week of the investigation drew to a close, most of the initial theories and leads had dried up. While Frank Smith and William Taylor were not completely absolved of guilt, they had been subjected to multiple interrogations, and nothing beyond circumstantial evidence connected them to the murder.

"Is there any definite and substantial change in the character of the story of the death of Hazel I. Drew?" a *Troy Record* reporter pressed O'Brien the morning of Friday, July 17.

"There is not," O'Brien admitted.

"Is there any truth in rumor to the effect that someone has made a confession to you?"

Rumors and gossip had been swirling the past few days, but that was a new one.

"Not the slightest."

"Have you decided to swear out a warrant against any person?"

"No. We have no intention of doing that at present."

With the investigation faltering, pressure mounted on O'Brien and his team. Young women who had been boarding for the summer in Sand Lake departed in droves, fearful of becoming the next victim; one farmer who had eight young women boarding at his place saw all of them depart two days after the discovery of Hazel's body.

At the same time, there was renewed speculation in the press that Hazel had taken her own life, despite adamant claims to the contrary by the physicians who had examined the body.

"The suicide possibility gains ground, and the police are willing to admit that they would declare it self-destruction were it not for the declarations of the doctors who were at the autopsy," reported the *Troy Record* on July 17. "Officer Powers and Unser, who have been at the scene day after day, were asked if they did not think suicide could have been possible. County Detective Kaye was asked the same question. The answers were: 'We are not positive; we know nothing of medicine or anatomy.' . . . From the weight the suicide theory has assumed it does not appear improbable that the question of having the body exhumed may be talked over."

The *Record* painted the detectives as not being completely satisfied with the work of the doctors, and Hazel herself as being down on her luck, without funds, a job, or prospects, speculating that she had thrown herself into Teal's Pond in a state of despair.

The physicians who performed the autopsy were unanimous in refuting this claim, with Drs. Elmer Reichard and Harry Fairweather rushing to defend their work. "The autopsy was very thorough and none of the technicalities of the work was hurriedly passed, but every move was slow and deliberate," declared Fairweather, who had taken notes during the procedure. Most importantly, the lack of water in Hazel's lungs was incontrovertible proof that she had not drowned, as would be the expected cause of death if she had killed herself.

And yet the suicide theory would not die.

Three days later, O'Brien was pressed again on how comfortable he was in ruling out suicide, and once again it was the *Troy Record* leading the charge: "If not for the doctors' report would you have ruled out suicide?"

O'Brien confirmed the importance of the autopsy report. Another reporter raised the possibility of errors being made in such examinations. Of course he had heard of such mistakes, but he had full faith in the results of Hazel's autopsy and could not accept the suggestion of suicide.

Most of the press reported that the suicide theory had once again been refuted, but the *Record* continued to stoke the fire in its July 20 edition: "The suicide theory is gaining weight—not that it is being offered to justify a failure of the authorities in detaining someone as the possible murderer, but rather because there have been reasons offered which make it possible that she may have thrown herself into the pond."

Was the *Record* merely emulating the big-city tabloids in pushing a less-than-credible story line to stand out from its peers and sell more copies? Or was something else going on?

The *Troy Record*, one of three major dailies in the city that covered the case, was run at the time by David Banks Plum, who came from an old Troy family and had strong ties to the Republican Party—the same party handling the murder investigation.

Throughout the probe, the *Record* was able to land exclusive interviews with County Detectives Duncan Kaye and William Powers, indicating some sort of relationship that possibly ran deeper behind the scenes. A ruling of suicide or accidental death would shut down this dead-end investigation and allow the detectives to move on from the increasingly flaming seat they found themselves perched on. Was the *Record*, intentionally or not, leading readers to believe what was convenient for the investigation, based on the inside information detectives were feeding it?

The July 17 article promoting the suicide angle reinforced the close relationship between the *Record* and the county detectives: "[A]n official who has been prominent in the investigation, but who requested that he not be quoted because of the fact that some people might be unkind enough to say that the county authorities, unable to find the murderer, are now endeavoring to make it appear that the girl took her own life, last night made this statement: 'I do not think it impossible and perhaps improbable that Hazel Drew committed suicide. This theory of mine is substantiated by the fact that the girl was out of employment, out of money and had few friends. Walking along the dusty road on that hot evening, one of the warmest of the summer, she may have become despondent and drowned herself upon reaching the pond near her uncle's home. The physicians, of course, say that such could not have been the case, but not casting any reflection upon them, I do not think they could determine positively whether the girl met an accidental death, committed suicide, or was murdered from the condition of her body after decomposition has set in to so great an extent.'"

Based on the number of exclusive interviews granted to the *Record* during the investigation, the source behind this leak, which contravened the official stance of the investigation, was almost certainly Kaye or Powers.

Meanwhile, on Monday, July 20, reports emerged about an oak club being found on the banks of Teal's Pond, about twenty feet from the spot where Hazel's body had been dragged to shore. The club, about twenty inches long and weighing nearly four pounds, was half-round and half-flat on one side, partly covered with bark, with a dent that could conceivably have been caused by a hard blow. Dr. Fairweather was particularly enthused over this discovery, jumping to the conclusion that the murder weapon had, in all probability, finally been identified.

"Tomorrow I will make a microscopic examination of the club to see if there are any hair particles in evidence to further substantiate my belief that it was the instrument with which the girl was killed," he said. "If such evidence is not found, the club still must play an important part in the search for the slayer, as it is just such a weapon as would have caused the blood clot found at the base of the victim's brain. Had the wound been inflicted by a stone the scalp would have been lacerated, but this was not the cause. There was merely a bruise, which we did not deem sufficient to have caused death, until the skull was lifted, disclosing the blood clot."

For investigators, this raised a key question: If the oak club was in fact the murder weapon, did the murderer bring it with him or find it in the middle of the woods? If the latter, did that mean the killer hadn't ventured out to the pond intending to murder Hazel, but acted impulsively, perhaps following a dispute?

Despite Fairweather's excitement over the discovery, his "microscopic examination" came to nothing, and the murder weapon was never found. As others in the investigation noted, there was no shortage of clubs, branches, and other bric-a-brac found in the pond and surrounding vicinity. It was like the metaphorical haystack, with no guarantee that the needle was even to be found there.

Facing ongoing attacks in the press regarding the results of the doctors' autopsy—William Clemens also was hitting investigators hard while promoting his strangulation theory—O'Brien was compelled to summon all of the physicians present at the procedure to a conference, with the stated goal of determining if Hazel's body should be exhumed. On the afternoon of Wednesday, July 22, O'Brien convened Drs. Boyce, Reichard, and Fairweather, and Coroner Morris Strope at Reichard's home in Sand Lake; Kaye also attended the meeting, which was held behind closed doors.

When O'Brien emerged from the more than hourlong conference, he proclaimed, "The physicians were unanimous in their opinion that the wound on the back of the girl's head near the base of the skull was in itself sufficient cause for death."

Further, O'Brien said, "the strangulation theory is conclusively eliminated, and there was a unanimity of opinion that the girl was dead before her body entered the water."

According to O'Brien, the physicians reconsidered the issue of whether Hazel had been pregnant at the time of death and once again concluded that she was not.

Whether or not Hazel had been sexually assaulted remained an open question, impossible to resolve due to the decomposition of the body.

O'Brien was adamant that Hazel's body would not be exhumed.

The doctors' report mainly corroborated previously expressed conclusions but is useful in illustrating a few recurring motifs of the case. The press once again was instrumental in steering the narrative of the investigation; the much-ballyhooed doctors' conference was convened largely to refute allegations from reporters—suggestions of sexual activity, the *Record*'s repeated insinuations that Hazel had taken her own life, and Clemens's refusal to back down from his sordid strangulation theory. The conference pulled both O'Brien and his primary lieutenant, Kaye, out to Sand Lake—their automobile broke down twice on the way—essentially wasting a day when their energies could have been devoted elsewhere.

But it is also important to understand that different newspapers had different underlying motivations in this age of yellow press. Big-city tabloids like the *World* and the *Evening Star* favored tawdry, provocative headlines, like the kind William Clemens was so good at providing. The Troy papers *seemed* more objective, but let it never be forgotten that in Troy, politics were pervasive. And the county detectives' apparent cozy relationship with the *Record*, run by their Republican brethren, would surface as an issue again before the investigation concluded.

Although the doctors' conference proved anticlimactic, it didn't deter the press, as the second full week of the investigation kicked off with an array of new headlines—none more tantalizing than the story told by a farmer and his wife who lived in the back hills of Taborton.

On the evening of Tuesday, July 7, William and Elizabeth Hoffay were driving their carriage home from a long day in Troy. The Hoffays had spent the day peddling their homegrown fruits and vegetables in the city; like many in Taborton, they supplemented their income this way, so were accustomed to the arduous fifteen-mile drive each way to and from the city. Bill Hoffay, fifty-four, and his wife, Libbie, forty-six, were sensible, down-to-earth people and knew better than most how grueling the journey was, especially on a broiling midsummer day like this one. Which is why they had waited until the sun was deep into its descent to start their trek home, and were only just setting sight on Crape's Hotel, at the foot of the mountain, as the hour crept past seven.

Passing Crape's, they started the climb up the mountain and soon crossed paths with their next-door neighbors, Henry and Charlotte Rollman, who were heading in the opposite direction.

As the couples approached each other, Charlotte bowed theatrically and shouted ahead, "Hello there! I wouldn't recognize you driving that horse."

Bill Hoffay had left his usual, more reliable black horse back home in favor of his new colt, which he was breaking in.

"Indeed. This is the new foal," Bill said. "First trip back and forth to the city. Not too sure about him yet . . . Keep having to give him breaks along the way. And what about you, Mr. Rollman? Surely you and your lovely young bride are heading the wrong way for this time of day?"

Charlotte smiled at the compliment, while Libbie Hoffay rolled her eyes.

"Wherever could you be heading?" pressed a mock-stern Bill Hoffay.

"Nothing sinister about it, Bill. Just heading into town to run a few errands."

The couples gossiped on for nearly fifteen minutes before the approaching dusk forced them to wrap up their conversations and wish each other a good evening.

Despite feeling the lateness of the hour in their bones, the Hoffays quickened their pace, hoping to make it home to their beds—and their eight children—at a respectable hour. The sun was still planning an early rise in the morning, and as ever, there would be much to get done.

Continuing up the slopes, the couple came across another familiar pair of figures; Libbie was first to make them out.

"Oh no, look. It's that Smith boy. Whatever is he doing with Rudy Gundrum? Those two should not be mixed up together—ever. No good can come of it."

Rudy and Frank were rumbling down the mountain in Gundrum's buggy, a little ways past the Hollow, the grove of chestnut trees that marked an abrupt turn in the road. Just a few minutes earlier, Smith and Gundrum had passed Hazel Drew casually strolling along Taborton Road by herself, in the opposite direction.

"Just keep driving, Bill. It's already so late," said Libbie, smiling and waving at the pair.

"Evening, boys," said Bill Hoffay, pulling over to the right side of the road to give Gundrum a wider berth but barely slowing down.

Gundrum offered a lopsided smile and nodded in return. "Pleasant evening, folks."

The Hoffays continued onward, taking the turn at the Hollow.

"Did you see the expression on that boy's face?" said Libbie, turning to her husband. "Rudy probably has him all liquored up."

Their colt fretted on the road ahead of them.

"Think I'll lighten the load for this young fella one more time 'fore we get home," Bill said, slowing the carriage to a halt and handing the reins to his wife.

With Bill Hoffay now walking ahead of his wife in the rig, the pair trudged onward in the dimming twilight. They passed the road to Will Taylor's place and were walking alongside the fringes of Coon Teal's land when, up ahead, they noticed yet another carriage out on this unusually busy summer evening. Peering ahead, Bill could see this one was different—not one he recognized.

As he approached, Bill couldn't help but be a little envious of the stylish Concord coach that had pulled over to the side of the road by the pond: its yellow gears and tires looked sharp and contrasted boldly against the dark box and seat. And look at that horse! He would gladly trade this colt for that sturdy bay mare; it was brown with tinges of black in its mane and tail. The world-renowned custom-built Concord coaches implied exclusivity and luxury not common to these parts—city folk, likely. Probably tourists from Albany or Troy. The area was flooded with them this time of year.

Definitely time to be getting home.

Libbie was trailing behind her husband in the carriage by some thirty feet at this point, and as she neared the buggy, which had parked by a gate in the fence that bordered the banks of Teal's Pond, she surreptitiously took a long sideways glance at the driver, who was sitting outside the carriage in the raised box seat.

The man had turned away from the road, but he was clearly a stranger. He was in his midtwenties, about five feet six or seven, with sandy-blond hair and a matching mustache. He had a slight build and light complexion and wore a brown straw hat. His attire was nondescript, somewhere between light and dark. The young man was huddled up, tightly gripping the reins of the wagon's sole horse, as if nervous about something.

Nobody seemed to want to make eye contact. Libbie continued her subtle scan of the stranger and his ride. Wait a second. Was there someone in the back of the rig after all? No, surely that's not a person, is it? There is *something* back there. She felt certain of it. But as her husband led their wagon onward, her vantage was lost.

As Libbie's carriage drew nearer, the stranger in the wagon urged his bay mare farther to the side of the road to allow the approaching vehicle more space. As the Hoffays drove past, the farmer and his wife noticed a second figure, across the pond, on the far shore. He was lurking about where Hazel's hat and glasses would later be found.

This second man was somewhat older and of a heavier build than his presumed companion in the wagon. It was hard to make out his features behind the thick foliage, but he was wearing a light-colored checkered shirt, dark trousers, and a straw hat. Libbie stared more openly now, trying to see through the trees and unruly underbrush; the man was gazing intently into the murky pond, probing through the shrubbery scattered on the marshy shore, as if he had lost something. Was he actually wading into the water?

Despite the muggy evening, something caused Libbie to shiver involuntarily. She tapped the reins to the side of the colt to make it hurry along.

Up ahead, Bill glanced back over his shoulder to check on his wife and that fancy runabout. He, too, noticed the second man plodding along deliberately on the narrow path, on the far side of the pond, but dismissed him with a shake of his head.

Damn tourists. Let Old Man Teal get wind of them skulking about looking for bait. They won't be back here in a hurry.

～

The detectives had heard the Hoffays' story about seeing the two enigmatic strangers with their horse and carriage pulled over near Teal's Pond secondhand, earlier in the investigation. But as O'Brien's team had been inundated with tips and rumors of all sorts, the investigators found themselves having to prioritize which leads to focus on. Thus, the Hoffays' tale was left festering on a scrap heap of gossip until the start of the investigation's second full week.

Detectives William Powers and Louis Unser, who had been leading the investigation out in the country, had returned to Troy over the weekend of July 18 for a huddle with O'Brien. That Monday morning, the pair hired a rig in Averill Park and headed back out to the countryside to follow up on some leads that had been left dangling. They spent much of their morning trying to chase down a story told to them by a Taborton hotelkeeper: at eight thirty on the night of Tuesday, July 7, a charcoal burner had come into his hotel in a half-drunken state and loudly exclaimed, "Too bad, too bad, but it had to be done." The man then gulped down four shots of whiskey in rapid succession and disappeared into the summer night. From what the hotelkeeper could recall from the man's incoherent ramblings, he had claimed to have just come from Troy and been up on Taborton Road.

It wasn't much to go on, but the timing did coincide with accounts from Smith, Gundrum, and the others who had seen Hazel on Taborton Road that night. The detectives once again fanned out over the Taborton countryside, speaking with scores of locals, most of whom they had become familiar with by this point; nobody had seen anything, nobody knew anything—a now-familiar refrain.

However, during the course of their morning search, the detectives heard again about the Hoffays' story, and Unser managed to track Bill Hoffay down at a farm owned by his neighbors, the Hoffmans, where he was working.

"Good afternoon, sir. I understand that your name is Hoffay."

Unser had found Hoffay taking a smoke break behind a barn near the back of Hoffman's property.

"Mm-hmm. Bill."

"Mr. Hoffay, do you have a few minutes?"

"Well, I am on my break."

"This won't take long. Thank you for your cooperation," said Unser, seizing the opportunity.

"We heard a story that on the night that it is thought that Hazel Drew was killed . . . You've heard of the Hazel Drew murder?"

"I heard about it."

"We heard a story in town that on that same night—it was Tuesday, the seventh of July—we heard a story that on that night you were out on that road and that you might have seen something."

"I don't remember telling no story to nobody."

"Yeah, well, we hear lots of things," Unser replied, riffling through his notebook. "We talked to a Jacob Sticklemeyer. He said you were at his liquor store in Troy . . . on Congress Street."

Hoffay was scratching his chin when it suddenly dawned on him: he might have said something about that odd pair of strangers they had seen out on the road that night to that clerk.

"Now that you mention it, I suppose I might have mentioned something to that young fella about the whole thing. Once it was all out in the papers and everything."

"Mr. Hoffay, as you say, this story has been in the papers for a week now. I must ask you, if you thought you might have seen something important, something that could help us catch the killer, why hesitate in coming to talk to us?"

Hoffay was momentarily taken aback, staring at Unser as if he was insane.

"Why, detective? Think about that for a moment. If I tell that, one of 'em may see me coming home some night and blow my head off."

Strange, thought Unser. The thought had never even crossed his mind.

~

After fully questioning Bill Hoffay about his account of the two men and the Concord wagon, Unser visited Libbie Hoffay at home; her version of the story was nearly identical to her husband's.

This could be legitimate, Unser thought. He scampered off to look for Powers.

The two detectives spoke again with the Hoffays, to confirm the particulars, and then tracked down Frank Smith, Rudy Gundrum, and the Rollmans, all of whom the Hoffays claimed to have seen and spoken with that night on the road. Yes, they all *now* remembered coming across the Hoffays that evening. Not for the first time, Powers was perplexed at what these people considered relevant information—never mind that he had sat on this lead for a week himself.

Mr. and Mrs. Rollman explained that nobody had asked them about the Hoffays, and they didn't want to drag good people into this kind of thing if they didn't want any part of it. Rudy scratched the back of his head and said it must have slipped his mind. They didn't even bother asking Smith for an explanation.

Regardless of the usual local obstruction, the story seemed reliable, and Detective Powers was off. Leaving Unser in Sand Lake, he returned to Troy and rushed to update Detective Kaye on the situation. They would spend the rest of the night, and into the early morning hours, canvassing the livery stables of Troy, looking for any sign of the Concord wagon and the men who may have hired it out on July 7.

Seemingly, it didn't take long for the detectives to find what they were looking for. Directly across the street from the DA's offices in the Rensselaer County Courthouse, they spoke to a clerk at William T. Shyne's Horse Mart, a Troy livery, who confirmed possession of a wagon and horse identical to those in question. Furthermore, the wagon had been taken out for a ride on the evening of July 7, by a young man with blond hair and a sandy mustache, who was accompanied by a female companion. They returned from their drive at about ten thirty that night.

Kaye turned to his associate. "Good work, Detective Powers. We may have our man."

～

The next day's headlines blasted out the Hoffays' story about the two men and the wagon they had seen near the pond. The *Troy Times* reported, "District Attorney O'Brien said this morning that he considered the story about the mysterious rig the most important development of the day. The officers spent a greater part of the night trying to trace the horse and wagon seen by the Hoffeys [*sic*], but were not successful."

Powers succeeded in locating the alleged driver of the rig and roused him out of bed in the early hours for questioning. However, the *Daily Press* reported the following morning that he had "proved an alibi" and was no longer under suspicion. The man, whose name was initially left out of reports, readily admitted that he had been out to Sand Lake on the night in question but had gone no closer to Teal's Pond than Crape's Hotel, at the foot of Taborton Mountain. What had initially been touted as a vital lead had seemingly become irrelevant overnight. Even more curiously, many of the papers didn't even report on the match at Shyne's.

Two days later, the *Daily Press* finally revealed the name of the man detectives had absolved so quickly: "The hiring of a rig at William T. Shyne's livery has been thoroughly explained. It had nothing to do with the mysterious death of the Drew girl. The facts are that Fred W. Schatzle, embalmer for Undertaker Thomas H. Nealon, telephoned to the livery Monday night, July 6, for a horse and carriage for a friend, William Cushing, the Republican committeeman for the Eleventh Ward. Mr. Cushing and a young woman went driving the following night. They were at Sand Lake, but not in the vicinity of Teal's Pond."

The *Daily Press*—Troy's only Democratic-run major daily—was one of only two known papers, the other being the Albany *Times Union*, to cover the early morning visit the detectives paid to Cushing. Only the *Daily Press* made his name public. The name of his female companion was never disclosed. O'Brien had been vowing to keep people's names out of the press whenever possible, and on this occasion, he did just that.

⌒

There was an unusual energy at the district attorney's offices in the Rensselaer County Courthouse on the morning of Tuesday, July 21. The

Albany *Times Union* reported, "The attitude of District Attorney Jarvis P. O'Brien, as well as the mysterious manner assumed by his detectives, to-day [*sic*] has caused the inference to be gained that the authorities are now on a clue that will lead to the arrest shortly of some one [*sic*] connected with the murder of Hazel Drew."

Early that morning, O'Brien had been closeted in his office for more than an hour with an anonymous young man, after which the DA discreetly escorted him out through a side exit—away from the prying eyes of the now-usual morning gathering of huddled reporters. At one point during the meeting, O'Brien sent for a copy of the Troy city directory, and he later summoned Duncan Kaye to join the discussion. Despite the investigators' best intentions, members of the press did get a look at this new mystery man, albeit from a distance; he was of medium height and had a sandy mustache. But nobody recognized him or could associate him with the case.

When the press got hold of O'Brien about the secret meeting with the stranger, O'Brien admitted that the man he had spoken with that morning was connected to the case but would give no further details and adamantly refused to reveal his identity. There was never any follow-up reporting on this enigmatic interrogation.

The *Times Union* concluded, "On other days the officers have been most willing to tell what they were going to do and where they were going, but to-day [*sic*] they professed to be in ignorance of their movements. After the newspapermen had left the district attorney's office, the detectives and officers were summoned to Mr. O'Brien's office and each left the building singly and in different directions."

It seemed as if here was yet another dramatic twist in the Hazel Drew case. Who was the stranger whose identity O'Brien guarded so closely? And why was the DA so reluctant for him to even be seen? Could a resolution possibly be imminent?

Yet somehow this story was lost among the headlines; it turned out that of the numerous papers reporting on the case, only the *Times Union* even bothered to cover it.

William Clemens, now running his own, parallel investigation into Hazel's murder, also latched onto the story of the Hoffays and on July 22 spoke to William Shyne, the proprietor of the livery at which William Cushing rented the rig to take his lady friend on a ride to Sand Lake on the evening of July 7. Clemens reported that Shyne told him of a curious incident that had occurred on the previous evening:

> On Monday night, July 6, at 7 o'clock a telephone call came asking that a rig be sent at once to Seventh and Congress Streets. Mr. Shyne told the man at the phone that he would have to come to the stable in person. In a few moments a stranger came, gave his name as D. Shaltus, and drove away. He did not return until after midnight. There is no man named Shaltus in Troy and none of the hotels harbored a man of that name on Monday July 6.

The intersection that the caller asked for the livery to be delivered to was less than a block away from 1617 Seventh Street, the address of Joseph Drew, Hazel's brother, and Eva Drew, Joseph's wife, who was also one of Hazel's closest friends; this was the same location where Hazel and Minnie had dropped off their suitcase on Saturday, July 4, before attending the holiday festivities in Rensselaer Park, returning later that day to retrieve it.

Might Hazel have spent the night of Monday, July 6, at the home of her brother and sister-in-law? Joseph and Eva insisted otherwise.

But Joseph did cause a ruckus when, on Tuesday, July 21, he told authorities that Hazel had gone for a ride just hours before her death, with a man who had hired a buggy from one of the livery stables in Troy, and that the young man had returned to Troy alone. Unfortunately, it was never clear from reports what Joseph's source was, or if he was merely repeating information that was already circulating in the wake of the Hoffays' story.

Clemens absconded from Troy soon after this report and so never followed up on the mysterious D. Shaltus, although he seemed to be implying this was the same person who took the carriage out again the following evening. It is interesting to note the similarities between the names Shaltus and Schatzle, and also that Clemens would sometimes gloss over the underlying facts of a story in his rush to create the headline. So perhaps Schatzle and Cushing were in the habit of taking drives out to the country?

The detectives continued their hunt for the phantom carriage, scouring the livery stables of Troy, Albany, and the vicinity of Sand Lake. Except for the initial find at Shyne's, they came up completely empty.

For a variety of reasons, the detectives focused on Albany as the likely source of the mysterious wagon. The road where the Hoffays saw the rig parked led to Glass Lake Road, which was a straight shot there. Additionally, Henrietta Robertson had recently testified that she had seen Hazel heading to board a train for Albany when she bid her farewell at Union Station on the afternoon of July 6.

Also, Detective Kaye had been leading the hunt for an unnamed man in a photo recently unearthed among Hazel's possessions, which led him to the Capital City. (Clemens had suggested the photo was a plant by investigators, to throw reporters off the scent of the real killer.)

The young man in the photo was described as being not more than twenty-one years of age, with a smooth round face topped by heavy, sandy hair. He was well proportioned, with a light complexion and prominent features, though there was nothing particularly striking about his face. The photo seemed to match up with the Hoffays' description of the man in the carriage; the press brazenly agreed, with the *Buffalo Enquirer*'s headline proclaiming, Trunk Contains Picture of Slayer—Mysterious Stranger Who Hired Livery Rig Leaves Photograph Behind.

After finding the Troy photographer who had snapped the picture, Kaye tracked down the young man in Albany on July 23: F. W. Schlafflin, a packer who had met Hazel three years earlier at the skating rink in Rensselaer Park. The two hit it off, and Schlafflin walked Hazel home that night.

"When was the next time you saw her?" asked Kaye.

"Well, let me think. She invited me to call on her again, and I took her up on it. She was really such a sweetheart . . . had a wonderful smile."

Kaye leaned in, sensing a possible romantic entanglement.

"And where did that lead? After you took her up on her invite?"

"Well, she was very particular about which church we went to, so it was always her church in Troy. Hazel appeared to be a lady in every respect, and I always treated her as such."

Schlafflin said their friendship just sort of died out over time, for no particular reason, as young friendships often do. He claimed not to have seen Hazel for two years. He spoke highly of the dead girl but was surprised to know she had a picture of him in her possession.

He shrugged. "I suppose I must have given it to her, though I don't remember doing so."

As their interview wrapped up, Kaye thought Schlafflin seemed more sad about Hazel's murder than anything else.

This guy, he decided, wasn't the killer.

While the prospects of finding the two men and the wagon the Hoffays had seen on July 7 seemed to fade, the Hoffays themselves managed to stay in the headlines with another story that cast suspicion back on Hazel's uncle: Taylor Again in the Foreground, the July 22 *Troy Record*'s headline proclaimed.

After combing the livery stables in Troy, Albany, and the countryside, Detective Powers returned to Taborton to speak to the Hoffays and show them a picture of Hazel; during their initial discussion it had also come up that the Hoffays remembered seeing William Taylor in the village with a girl who seemed to match the description of Hazel just a few weeks earlier. If it was in fact Hazel, it would directly contradict Taylor's long-held stance that he had not seen his niece since her stay at his farmhouse in the winter, when she was recovering from her mystery illness.

Meanwhile, the detectives had also spoken to liveryman John Abel, who recalled driving Hazel and a companion he did not know to the Taylor farmhouse in April—two months after Taylor was claiming to have last seen her. Abel, an energetic young man with fair hair and a boyish face, was a regular outside the Averill Park trolley station, unfailingly dressed in a dark suit, buttoned-up vest, and tweed tailor cap.

He recalled that Hazel had fumbled for her glasses after dropping them inside his rig, and had bargained him down from his usual fare of a dollar to seventy-five cents, saying that was all she had on her. When later asked by a reporter if he could have been mistaken, Abel scowled and spit out the blade of straw he was chewing: "Mistaken? I should say not. I knew Hazel well. I drove her there in April, and that's all there is to it." George Hogeboom, the ticket agent at the Averill Park station where Abel had picked the girls up, corroborated his account; one of the girls wore a blue dress, the other brown.

Detectives Powers and Unser trudged back to the now-familiar Taylor farmhouse to speak with Hazel's cantankerous uncle.

"Good afternoon, Mr. Taylor," began Powers, at the front door.

"What is it now?" Taylor said. He pointedly held his ground, not inviting the pair inside.

"We've been speaking to one of your neighbors, Bill Hoffay, from up the mountain?"

"Yep."

"Told us he remembers seeing you with a girl who looked exactly like your niece. In town. Just a few weeks back."

"Mr. Hoffay was mistaken," Taylor said. He paused, as if expecting that the interview was over. "Is that all for today?"

"No, actually, Mr. Taylor, we also spoke with John Abel, who runs a livery wagon in Averill Park."

"Mm-hmm."

"Mr. Abel says he brought Hazel up to your place last April. He seems to have a pretty good memory, too. Remembers the dress she wore, her glasses, even how much he charged to take her out here. He was kind enough to give her a discount."

"We also spoke with the agent at the station in town," chimed in Unser. "Mr. Hogeboom backs up Abel's story. He says he has also seen you in town with a girl who looks just like Hazel. According to him, it *was* Hazel. This was after February."

"I can't explain that, gentlemen. Whoever they saw, it wasn't me."

Powers and Unser played out their customarily exhausting tête-à-tête with Taylor and left the farm not knowing much more than when they came—this was becoming a frustratingly familiar experience for the pair.

"It's like I keep saying, Lou. Throw these guys in jail overnight, and I bet they come out the next day telling a different story," Powers concluded.

On Thursday July 23, District Attorney O'Brien announced he was finally ready to proceed with an inquest, which would commence on Monday, July 27. For days, O'Brien had been delaying, arguing that the formality of an inquest wouldn't add anything to what he and his detectives had collected from the many witnesses they had already interviewed. He had originally hoped to use an inquest to tighten the noose around the neck of the guilty party, but now, facing mounting pressure from the press and the public, and awash in dead-end leads, he was relying on the inquest merely to bring clarity to the chaos and to hopefully draw out the real story behind the murder of Hazel Drew.

It was less than ideal, but people often spoke about the charmed life of Jarvis O'Brien, and he still had a few tricks up his sleeve. He never felt more confident than he did in a courtroom.

Chapter 12

Inquest

Jarvis O'Brien bristled at the word *failure*. He wasn't used to it and never had an easy time accepting it. But there was no escaping the fact that the investigation into Hazel's murder had been exhausting, exasperating, and, to date, unsuccessful. On Friday, July 17, as the first week of the investigation wrapped up, the *Washington Times* described him as "disheartened and desperate over the absolute loss of tangible evidence" needed to make an arrest. Reports surfaced that he would ask Coroner Morris Strope to convene an inquest the following day. He didn't. He wanted more time, hoping to accumulate enough evidence to build a strong case against a suspect—or at least identify a viable suspect.

It would be ten days later—on Monday, July 27—that O'Brien finally had Strope convene the inquest. Even after all of the delays, the DA was not optimistic about the outcome—perhaps this would be less a grand conclusion to the investigation and more a public demonstration that due diligence had been done. The inquest was planned to run for two days and would be split between Averill Park and Troy, for the convenience of witnesses. This was thoroughly appropriate as Hazel herself had been a product of these two vastly different worlds:

the countryside, where she was born and raised, and the city, where she came of age.

There had been tension between these two groups throughout the investigation: out-of-town investigators and reporters had continually cast aspersions on the reputations of the farmers, lumberjacks, and charcoal burners who lined Taborton Mountain, impugning their intelligence, character, and forthrightness; the Taborton residents closed ranks against these interlopers, convinced they were angling to pin the murder on one of their own.

Just prior to the inquest, on Friday, July 24—as newspapers cried out that the voters of Rensselaer County were clamoring for an arrest and reminded readers that O'Brien was a candidate for reelection in the fall, insinuating that his failure to solve the murder mystery might have been politically driven—the district attorney huddled with his detectives at the county courthouse, reviewing two of his most nettlesome suspects, Frank Smith and William Taylor.

He still wasn't of a mind to arrest either, but their peculiar behavior on the night of the murder and their seeming reluctance to tell all they knew in the days that followed gnawed at him. He couldn't help thinking—as he had throughout the investigation—that he was one rigorous interrogation away from breaking one or both of them, despite repeated failed attempts to do so.

O'Brien was particularly irritated by William Taylor, who had been claiming, since the start of the investigation, that he hadn't seen Hazel since her visit to his farmhouse the previous winter. And yet Taborton farmer William Hoffay, when questioned about the two mysterious men and the carriage he had witnessed at the pond on the night of July 7, recalled seeing Taylor in the company of a young woman whose appearance seemed to match Hazel Drew's in Averill Park just five weeks before. Or was this perhaps just another sighting of Hazel's so-called doppelgänger?

Further, there was that vexing story from livery driver John Abel, who claimed to have driven Hazel and a friend up to the Taylor farmhouse in April. Two people—George Hogeboom, the Averill Park station agent, and the farmhand Frank Smith—had backed him up (though Smith had proven himself notoriously unreliable).

Finally, O'Brien pushed his chair back from his desk and stood up.

"We need to have another go at them," he instructed his detectives.

"Both of them?" asked Detective Duncan Kaye.

"Yup, both of them. Let's have it out once and for all."

That Saturday, July 25, Kaye journeyed out to Taborton Mountain, but neither Smith nor Taylor was home. He tracked them down the following afternoon and interviewed them separately—each session long and punishing, but essentially fruitless. Reporters mobbed O'Brien afterward for his thoughts, and the district attorney admitted that he believed Smith and Taylor to be innocent of any complicity in the murder.

But what of the conflict between Abel and Taylor? Both men were immutable in their versions of events.

In Taylor's defense, Hazel's sister-in-law, Eva Lapp Drew, who had lived at the Taylor farmhouse at the time, told reporters, "John Abel is mistaken about driving Hazel and another girl over to Uncle Taylor's house. How do I know that he is mistaken? Because I was at Uncle Taylor's house at the time. I remember it all quite well. I remember that John Abel drove up to Uncle Taylor's house with his carriage. In it were seated two girls, also my husband, Joe Drew, and Philip, a young man from Troy. One of the girls in Abel's carriage wore glasses. She is Miss Stella Carner of Troy. The carriage held five persons, Stella and Kate Carner, sisters, of Troy, who were to spend the day with me. My husband and Philip were also in the carriage, and with the driver, Mr. Abel, makes five persons. Stella Carner wears glasses and Mr. Abel may now suppose it was Hazel."

Magically, Eva summoned Stella Carner from the next room to vouch for her narrative. "Stella Carner is right here in the house now," Eva said. "I will call her."

"I went out to Uncle Taylor's in March with my sister Kate Carner," she said. "My young man Philip was also expected there that day. Kate, my sister, and myself arrived at the Averill Park depot about two o'clock Sunday afternoon, just before St. Patrick's Day. At the depot we arranged with Mr. Abel to drive us over. We agreed to pay him one dollar. He took us over to the Taylors'. At Crape's Hotel we met Joe Drew and Philip, my friend. Philip and Joe also got in the rig at Crape's and we all drove over to Taylor's."

Eva's testimony wasn't inconsequential, given that she and her husband had vacated the farmhouse soon after this time due to a quarrel with their irascible uncle. It seemed unlikely they would do him any favors, especially by lying to the law. But there was something about this family—the Taylors and the Drews—that distrusted outside intervention; their suspicion and insularity were exasperating.

There were also discrepancies in the details of the two accounts regarding the timing of the visit and how much fare was paid, but investigators attributed this deviance to the passage of time and flawed memories.

Did it even matter if Abel had driven Hazel to the Taylor farmhouse in the spring? Why would anyone lie about it? It seemed like nothing more than another distraction. By this point O'Brien was on the verge of completely eliminating Taylor as a suspect anyway, dismissing him as a taciturn, truculent man with no interest in anything other than his farm—including the possibility of his own niece's body being discovered practically in his backyard.

One down, one to go.

"Take a seat, Frank. How ya been?"

O'Brien sat behind the desk in his office, staring at the gawky country boy who had caused him so much grief over the last two weeks. But could this fool-headed stripling—too young even to grow a proper mustache—have committed murder?

O'Brien took him back over the events of the night of July 7 and the days after, with the boy giving a full account of his activities. It now seemed to O'Brien that the repeated questioning Smith had been subjected to by detectives had finally coalesced his version of events into a more or less consistent narrative that didn't allow much chance for him to have been involved in the murder.

When asked yet again about his neighborhood-wide inquiry into Hazel's whereabouts in the days after passing her on Taborton Road, Frank did dangle a new piece of information: Hazel's little brother, Willie M. Drew, had been staying with a Taborton family named the Sowalskies around the time of the murder.

O'Brien and Kaye, who was also in the room, shared yet another weary glance: Wasn't it a little late in the investigation for such revelations?

When O'Brien moved on to John Abel's story about driving Hazel to the Taylor farm, Smith again sided with the livery driver, insisting that he had seen Hazel in Abel's carriage in April on the way up to Taylor's.

"Now, you know Will Taylor denies Mr. Abel's story completely? Says he is absolutely sure Hazel hadn't been to his place since wintertime."

"He might've said that, but that don't make it so," Frank said.

"Are you saying Mr. Taylor lied to us? Whyever would he do that, Frank?" O'Brien pressed.

"Scared, maybe."

"Scared? Of what?" asked Kaye.

"The way you fellas been marching all over the mountain like you own the place. Maybe he's scared if he says the wrong things, you're gonna lock him up."

The boy seemed rattle-proof; O'Brien had to give him that.

O'Brien felt he had wrung just about every last bit of information he could out of Taylor and Smith. There were still rumors out there that needed looking into. If Willie Drew was really boarding out past the pond with the Sowalskies around that time, maybe Hazel had been going there for a visit? And what about the Concord wagon seen by the Hoffays?

Yet, the case was growing stale, and so many other leads had been investigated fully and turned out to be merely red herrings or dead ends. The district attorney knew he had stalled long enough.

It was time to convene the inquest. Maybe they'd catch a break there.

~

And so at 1:10 p.m. on Monday, July 27, another sweltering day, a throng, comprising close to thirty subpoenaed witnesses and dozens of morbidly curious spectators, crowded into the pavilion at the rear of Travelers Rest and Sand Lake House, more popularly known as Warger's, and the inquest officially began. Warger's was more accustomed to hosting dances, weddings, and occasional political rallies. "It is one where the summer boarders at Averill Park have danced until dawn and wished that daybreak might be deferred. To-day [*sic*] it was a death that threw its shadow over the building that more [often] has vibrated with laughter and song," the *Troy Record* reported.

What a striking scene: summer tourists, mostly women, dressed in merry widow hats and other fashionable articles of clothing, rubbing elbows with the charcoal burners and farmers of Taborton—"uncouth mountaineers," newspapers called them, another illustration of the class distinctions underlying Hazel Drew's day-to-day struggles in life. On display inside the courtroom for all to see as exhibits were the clothing and jewelry she had worn on the night of her murder.

There would be no jury, since Coroner Strope sat as a committing magistrate at inquests in Rensselaer County. O'Brien would handle the questioning. The three physicians who had performed the autopsy—Elias Boyce, Elmer Reichard, and Harry Fairweather—were the first to appear, during the preliminaries, entering their records on the case into the official testimony.

After the preliminaries had ended, the first witnesses were sworn in and called to the stand. Much of the early testimony, from the locals who were present at Teal's Pond on July 11 when Hazel's body was discovered—Lawrence Gruber, George White, Gilbert Miller, George Alberts, Ebenezer Martin, and others—was a rehash of information that had been shared and reshared countless times over the sixteen days since Hazel's body had been dragged from the pond. It wasn't until Strope at last summoned Frank Smith to the stand that the room buzzed with anticipation. The young farmhand had been spectacularly erratic during the course of the investigation; would the district attorney—a man admired throughout the county for his inquisitorial deftness—finally break him?

Smith appeared to be relishing the opportunity. He had arrived early, all spiffed up, coatless and in a soft hat and spick-and-span dress shirt, puffing away on a big black cigar—an absurdly incongruous image of the seventeen-year-old laborer with a wisp of a mustache struggling to assert itself. He was in a voluble mood, jousting with O'Brien for over ninety minutes, parrying the DA's insinuations with confidence and conviction; the repeated interrogations the detectives had subjected him to seemed to have sharpened his ability to answer the questions he had by now heard time and time again.

Smith went over every detail of the night of July 7: flagging down Rudy Gundrum, meeting Hazel on Taborton Road, stopping for drinks at Harris's Hotel, running into the Richmonds at the Averill Park terminus, wagering that he could run to Isaac Wright's pharmacy and back, leaving the village at about midnight that night, returning home on foot along the same route from whence he had come, without encountering anyone. He further recollected happening upon Teal's Pond on July 11 and aiding in the retrieval of Hazel's body. O'Brien jabbed and poked but couldn't seem to shake him.

"How could you possibly have not recognized Hazel's body when you helped recover it from the pond, even though you had seen her dressed in the same clothes in the same vicinity just four days earlier?"

"I wasn't certain enough about the connection at the time to say anything for sure."

"But didn't you tell your parents just the next day that the body was likely Hazel's, even before it was publicly identified?"

"That's right, but I wasn't certain."

O'Brien tried another approach.

"What were you doing traipsing around Taborton in the days after July 7 asking Libbie Sowalskie and others if Hazel Drew had come visiting?"

"She was a pretty girl, and I just was wondering what she was doing up on the mountain."

"Are you sure you saw Hazel and another girl riding in John Abel's rig up to William Taylor's house in April? And that she came to visit you at your house in the presence of your mother and father to listen to the Graphophone?"

"Yes, sir, on that fact, I am."

"I ask you particularly," O'Brien said, "because Taylor said she was not there in April."

"Well, she was," Smith replied. He remained defiant and calm, staring straight ahead at O'Brien as he said it.

226

Following Frank Smith's arduous session, O'Brien breezed through more routine testimony from the others who had been out on Taborton Road that night: Rudy Gundrum, the Rollmans, the Rymillers, and Marie Yeabauer recounted what and whom they had seen and when they had seen it, each painting their own fragmentary picture of the events on the road on the night of the murder. Useful to have on record, but not titillating enough for the summer tourists, who had heard these stories before and were beginning to stifle yawns in the constant humidity.

As William Hoffay was summoned to the stand, the spectators stopped shuffling in their seats. Excited whispers greeted the farmer as he was sworn in; the Hoffays' story of the two men and the carriage near the pond was a relatively recent development, having just emerged over the past week. What had initially been considered a tantalizing lead, however, soon appeared to fizzle out, as William Cushing, the only viable suspect found during the regionwide search of livery stables, had claimed that he had not gone near Teal's Pond that evening. His story about an innocent ride to Sand Lake with an anonymous female companion was cleared by the investigators almost immediately. The desperate search for the carriage the Hoffays saw had otherwise proven fruitless, and the press was openly questioning the credibility of the Hoffays and their story, with the Albany *Times Union* claiming, "Huffay [*sic*] doesn't bear the best of reputations," until the story became lost in the jumble of other leads and headlines being churned out on a daily basis.

Although the hunt for the wagon and the two mystery men had cooled, it was still a dangling thread for O'Brien, who had yet to speak directly with the Hoffays, and he was savoring the opportunity to see what he could pry loose from the Taborton farmers.

O'Brien was originally a country boy himself but had spent the majority of the investigation headquartered in Troy, and he never seemed to connect with the people on the mountain; continually painting Hazel's uncle as a suspicious character and telling the press he knew more than he was admitting to did little to endear the DA to Taylor's neighbors in Taborton. Although O'Brien fancied himself a master interrogator who enjoyed performing on the public stage, the inquest at Averill Park was amounting to a series of frustrations, sometimes even devolving into confrontational exchanges, which is what happened when he chose to challenge the details of William Hoffay's testimony that he had seen a man on the south bank of Teal's Pond on the night of the murder.

"Are you sure it was not a woman?" O'Brien asked.

"Well," Hoffay retorted, "if it was a woman, she had pants on."

"You could tell if it was a woman, could you not?"

"A man would have to be pretty drunk to mistake a man for a woman."

Unbowed, O'Brien pressed on.

"How wide is the pond?" he asked.

"You've been there, haven't you?" Hoffay said.

"Yes."

"You know as much about it as I do."

The exchange elicited chuckles from the onlookers as O'Brien returned to his table, though laughter wasn't what he had been hoping to elicit. The Hoffays had impressed O'Brien with their conviction and the consistency of their story.

Next up were Frank and Frederika Richmond, who worked William Taylor's farm and were the only people to see and talk with both Taylor and Frank Smith on the evening of July 7. Frank Richmond testified that he recalled Frank Smith's father, John, coming to the Taylor farm on Sunday, July 12, the day after the body was found. During this visit, John Smith shared Frank's suspicions that it was Hazel's body that had been taken from the pond. And yet Taylor, who was present for this conversation, never undertook any action to determine if it was in fact Hazel or to inform his sister Julia of what was being said about her daughter. Prior to the inquest, Taylor had denied even being visited by John Smith, let alone hearing rumors about Hazel from him.

William Taylor himself had arrived a full hour before the proceedings were scheduled to begin, dressed sharply in a light fedora and a black suit, with a white shirt and collar and a dark-blue cravat. Unlike Smith, Taylor retreated from the spotlight, sitting alone up front and staring intently at the floor with his feet crossed, a picture of placidity. He spoke to no one, looked at no one. At one point he leaned forward in his seat to scrutinize Hazel's clothes and jewelry but never once betrayed a hint of emotion.

When it was Taylor's turn to take the stand, O'Brien rose wearily from his seat, preparing himself for another round with Hazel's disagreeable uncle. It was almost as if they each knew exactly what the other was going to say before either one had spoken.

Before getting to the events of July 7, O'Brien peppered Taylor with questions about his relationship with his niece.

"How often did Hazel visit your farm?"

"Back when her old man was helping with the place, she'd come out every so often. Not so much since." (The Drew family had lived on the Taylor farm in 1905 and 1906, though Hazel at the time was living and working in Troy.)

According to Taylor, Hazel had been to the farm just four times in total since then: once in the summer of 1906, once in January of '07, once the following summer, and finally last winter, when she was ill.

"What was wrong with her?"

"I didn't ask, and I didn't know. I'm no help around sick people and assumed I would have been told if it were anything serious."

"Is it actually possible that you permitted that girl to remain in your house, sick for three weeks, without asking what was the matter with her, without seeing that she was given medical attention, without so much as asking her sister-in-law whether she had the measles or the smallpox, and without going to her room yourself to see her?"

"Yes," answered Taylor flatly, without offering any further explanation.

O'Brien paused, waiting for the significance of the answer to register.

"That was her last visit? You are sure of that?" he said.

"Yes, I'm sure," Taylor said. "She was not there. Somebody would have seen her."

"John Abel, of Averill Park, says he did see her. He says Hazel was at your house in April and that he took her there. Others back up his claim."

"There's no proof that they did," retorted Taylor.

Next, O'Brien asked Taylor to once again recount his actions on Tuesday, July 7, likely the day of the murder. Taylor responded as he always had: he was in the house all day long, except for about fifteen minutes he spent doing chores in his woodshed. That night he sat on his rocking chair on the porch for a bit smoking his pipe, then retired for the evening at about 9:00 p.m. Most nights, he said, he enjoyed strolling down from his farmhouse to the highway before retiring, but for some reason he couldn't explain he had chosen to forgo the walk that particular night.

He never laid eyes on Hazel that night, he said, and he hadn't heard anything about her supposedly visiting until the following morning, when Frank Richmond mentioned his run-in with Frank Smith the night before.

"I was at home the night she was killed," Taylor said. "I did not see her. I did not go to identify the body because I was told it was decomposed. I knew nothing of the crime."

"When did you hear about a body being found in the pond?" O'Brien asked.

Taylor didn't answer at once, mulling the question over deliberately. Reporters checked their watches as an awkward five minutes passed by.

"Mr. Taylor?" prompted the district attorney.

"What's that?"

"When did you find out—"

"It was as I keep telling you."

"And that was?"

"Come again?"

"Mr. Taylor, I ask you again: When exactly did you hear about Hazel being found in the pond?"

"Eighth of July, most definitely. That was a Wednesday, right?"

"July 8 was a Wednesday, yes."

"Then that's it."

"You are saying you heard about the body on July 8—three days before it was removed from the pond?"

"No, wait just a minute. What are you getting at? I heard about the body being pulled from the pond the next day after it happened."

"So Sunday, July 12?"

"That's what I said."

"Did Frank Smith's father not tell you Sunday his boy had said it was Hazel, and suggest that you go and make the identification?" pressed O'Brien.

Taylor first denied any such conversation had taken place but recanted when presented with the testimony of the Richmonds, who swore that John Smith had come to the Taylor farm and done just that.

"What did you do then?" continued O'Brien.

"I did not do much of anything until that afternoon. That afternoon I went to Averill Park to get shaved but did not ask any questions. I was in the village only a little while."

Once again, O'Brien paused. He wanted everyone in the room to appreciate the import of Taylor's testimony: shortly after hearing that his niece was most likely murdered—just a quarter mile from his house—Taylor had gone for a shave, without even bothering to share the news with his sister that her daughter was dead.

231

"Have you any excuse to offer for not sending word to the girl's relatives that John Smith thought the unidentified body was that of Hazel, even if you did not want to make the identification yourself?"

"None," Taylor replied sullenly.

William Taylor couldn't have come off much worse. The one flicker of humanity that squeezed through came when he remembered teasing and joking with Hazel about a male admirer during one of her visits to the farm. But even then, he cut himself off once O'Brien suggested that jealousy might have been a motive for the murder.

"Taylor proved himself more than ever the heartless old miser that he has been pictured, and was carried time and again over the revolting details without any display of emotion," the *Washington Times* reported.

⌐

The three doctors who had conducted the autopsy—Boyce, Fairweather, and Reichard—testified to close the first day's proceedings, repeating the same message they had been delivering for weeks: Hazel had been murdered; she did not commit suicide. Dr. Boyce continued to dissent from the other doctors by insisting that in all likelihood she been strangled after the blow to the head, which may have contributed secondarily to her death.

"Now, doctor, in your opinion, was this woman dead or alive before thrown into the water?" the district attorney asked him.

"Dead."

"Was the wound on her head inflicted before death?"

"Yes."

"Was it sufficient to cause death?"

"Yes," Boyce said. "The distortion of the face indicated that she may have been strangled, but the decomposition was so great as to make a decision indefinite. The clothes on the body were not disarranged. All of the underclothing was in good condition, and none appeared to be torn or out of place."

"What, in your opinion, was the cause of death?"

"I think the contusion on the back of the head was the cause of death, but it might have been assisted by strangulation."

When the inquest had commenced that morning, the hall had been abuzz with rumors that an eminent surgeon from Troy, previously unconnected to the case, was expected to join Boyce and the other physicians when they testified. This new mystery doctor was said to be of the opinion that, based on the physical evidence and the condition of the body at the time of recovery, it was impossible to accurately determine whether or not Hazel had been murdered. As a result, the press had revived the narrative that Hazel—despondent over a busted love affair and now jobless and in desperate need of money—could reasonably be believed to have taken her own life.

The *World* reported, "District Attorney O'Brien, who has been greatly criticized for failing to make an arrest in the case, has had medical as well as criminal experts on the case. Among the former is Dr. C. B. Herrick, who as a specialist does not agree wholly with the findings of Drs. Fairweather, Bryce [*sic*] and Reichard, who, after performing the autopsy on the body of Hazel Drew declared that the girl had been murdered. Dr. Herrick will be called as a witness at the inquest, and it is expected that he will give testimony to prove Hazel Drew a suicide."

In reality, Dr. Herrick was never subpoenaed or called as a witness.

Who was the enigmatic Dr. Herrick? With so many unanswered questions swirling around the case, this latest mystery figure didn't receive much attention. Only a handful of papers mentioned him, including two of the New York City tabloids: the *World* and the *Telegram*. Notably, when introducing Herrick, the *World* referenced the assistance already provided to the investigation by criminal experts— likely a reference to its own correspondent William Clemens, "The World's Expert in Criminology," who, one might argue—as O'Brien would—was actually more hindrance than help, and who had recently vacated town to solve his next great mystery. Was Herrick another attempt by the *World* to insert itself directly into the investigation?

In addition to being good fodder for the headlines, a sudden revelatory verdict of suicide would make things easier for O'Brien and his detectives, who had so far been stymied in their attempts to find Hazel's murderer. Earlier in the investigation, unnamed inside sources—most likely Detectives Duncan Kaye and William Powers—were casting suspicion on the autopsy findings; O'Brien himself had been quoted as saying that if not for the findings of the autopsy, he would not have eliminated suicide as a possibility. Perhaps not coincidentally, Sheriff Irving Baucus—a Republican, like O'Brien, Powers, and Kaye—had previously shared with the press that he had been tipped off by an informant that suicide might have been the cause of Hazel's death. Any of these law-enforcement officials might have had a reason for bringing in Herrick to create a counternarrative to the official findings; it would have ended the case with a sense of resolution, at least. O'Brien, up for reelection in less than four months, was under fierce pressure from the press to solve the case; ruling it a suicide would have been one way to make it disappear.

～

On Tuesday, July 28, following the first day of the inquest, Julia Drew told reporters she was infuriated by the suggestion that Hazel had taken her own life. "I've thought this matter over, and I am sure Hazel did not commit suicide," she said, nearly raising her usually timid voice. "Why should she? She was happy, and had everything she wanted. If anything had been wrong, she would have come to me. She always did, and I gave her everything she asked, whether it was money or anything else."

Given how little Julia seemed to know about her daughter's life, the comment struck many as further evidence of her extraordinary capacity for self-delusion.

"Then what *do* you think happened to Hazel?" a reporter queried. Her response astounded him.

Julia Drew was convinced she knew exactly what had happened to Hazel: she had been hypnotized, kidnapped, and finally taken out to Teal's Pond, where she was brutally murdered.

"Hazel never went of her own free will to Sand Lake," Julia told the reporter, wiping away a tear. "Some man hypnotized her Monday and kept her in his power until her death. She was taken out there in an automobile or carriage by someone, maybe from Troy. I believe it was someone who was well-to-do, and who had Hazel in his control. He mesmerized my Hazel and she did whatever he asked of her. He took her out there while she was under his influence and murdered her."

She dismissed any suggestion that Hazel had been on her way to visit William Taylor. "If she intended to run out to her uncle's for a few hours, she would never have checked that suitcase, but would have left it with her [aunt] Minnie or myself," she said. "Hazel was careful about money, and she would never have paid to check the bag when she would so easily have gotten it taken care of for nothing."

Further, Julia disputed the conventional wisdom that Hazel had left the Carys' employ suddenly, saying that the last time she saw her daughter, on July 2, Hazel "had told me then that she had trouble with Mrs. Cary about the extra girl Mrs. Cary had in to do the ironing. It's not hard to understand why Hazel didn't tell her aunt Minnie about losing her place. Minnie is a great worrier, and if she knew Hazel was out of work she would have fretted herself to death about it.

"I think Hazel started in right off to look for another place and hoped to find one before she let us know she had left the Carys. I don't know where Hazel would go to look for a place, but I don't think it would be an employment agency, because she tried that. But, mark my words, some rich fellow met Hazel Monday and just hypnotized her and took her out there and killed her."

She was convinced that whomever it was Frank Smith, Rudy Gundrum, and the Rollmans saw on Taborton Road on the night of Tuesday, July 7, it wasn't her daughter.

Asked if she had any specific suspect in mind, Julia slowly shook her head. Nothing could make her waver in her opinion, the *Evening World* reported.

The following day, she denied ever asserting that Hazel had been hypnotized, saying the press had distorted the meaning of her words.

Reporters "came down here and asked me if I knew anything about Hazel being hypnotized," she said. "Why, I said she might have been hypnotized and kidnapped."

More than likely, some less-than-scrupulous reporter had prompted Hazel's mother with questions about a man mesmerizing—a word that could mean either "seducing with charm" or, quite literally, "brain-washing through hypnosis," a practice that was more widely believed in at the time—her daughter, and then printed her response without providing readers with the full context. This was a pattern of behavior by the press throughout the investigation.

But Julia's allegation that her daughter might have been hypnotized and kidnapped, later retracted, may not even have been the oddest development to occur in the background while the inquest was ongoing. Instead, that honor may have belonged to a Taborton farmer by the name of Charles Rankie.

On July 28, Rankie appeared to vanish from the face of the earth, though his wife, Elizabeth—the sister of Rudy Gundrum—didn't report it to authorities until two days later, saying she had no idea where he was, when he left, or why he left.

Rankie had played a minor but crucial role in the Drew investigation, having told Detectives William Powers and Louis Unser: "On two Sundays previous to the murder, I was in the vicinity of the pond and saw this fellow hanging about the water each time. I couldn't get a good look at him, but he seemed to answer the description given by the Hoffays, when they told of seeing the man in the runabout by the roadside and the other, an older man, brushing about in the bushes."

Investigators were particularly intrigued by this because Gilbert Miller, who lived right by Teal's Pond, already had volunteered that he had seen Hazel around the pond more than once during the summer—also on Sundays. Then there was Hazel's friend Lillian Robertson, who had told O'Brien that Hazel frequently visited the farms in Taborton up until a year before, and that Hazel suggested many times that they go to Teal's Pond together.

Rankie's name never appeared on any of the witness lists in either Averill Park or Troy. Why not? Nobody ever explained it. His disappearance was never investigated, though it did catch the eye of O'Brien, who discussed it with his team on July 30, during a break in the Troy portion of the inquest.

Rankie returned home sometime after the inquest had ended. But there was never any public explanation for where he had disappeared to, or why.

～

The inquest session held in Averill Park failed to produce any dramatic revelations, but O'Brien still had leads to pursue, like Frank Smith's revelation—the day before the inquest—that at the time of the murder, Hazel's eleven-year-old brother, Willie, was boarding with Libbie Sowalskie, a sixty-year-old widow, and her thirty-three-year-old son, Tom. The Sowalskies' little mountain farmhouse was located on Bears Head Road, which ran off from Taborton Road, where Hazel was last seen, bordering the eastern edge of Teal's Pond. This late in the game, with the investigation stunted, newspapers were in desperate need of new leads, so this story received maximum exposure, even if many of the underlying facts were garbled in the process. Willie was described as "manly" by the press, which may have led the tabloids to incorrectly report that he was fifteen years old, when in fact he was eleven at the time of his sister's murder. (Subsequent reports misstated his age again, as eight years old.) First Willie, who had started off the summer boarding with William Taylor—but like everyone else couldn't stand living with him any longer—said Hazel had no idea he was boarding with the Sowalskies; then he said she did.

Hazel was said to have an undying love for Willie; he was reportedly the only member of the Drews' immediate family she was close to. Surely she was on her way to visit him on the night of July 7; perhaps she was leaving Troy for good and needed to say goodbye? Maybe she never reached the farm because she was intercepted along the rocky, winding road and lured to Teal's Pond, where the death blow was struck?

First Willie was expecting her, then he wasn't, then he was. "I knew Hazel would never have gone away without telling me goodbye," he said. "I am sure she was on her way to Mrs. Sowalskie's when she started up the road that leads past the pond."

He had talked nonstop about his sister for a week before her death, Libbie Sowalskie said: "When we heard that a girl had been found in the pond . . . and that she wore good clothes, Willie said his sister Hazel wore good clothes too. Then he said: 'If I thought that was my sister I would go jump in the pond and die with her.' He was just wrapped up in his sister."

O'Brien dispatched Detectives Powers and Unser to investigate. At first, they focused on investigating anyone who was camping by the pond that night, since the campgrounds were a mere one hundred feet from the road, and the path from the camp to the pond branched after reaching the top of the dam, with one branch leading directly to the site where Hazel's hat, gloves, and glasses were found on the shore. In fact, the only path free from underbrush to that spot was the one from the campsite. If Hazel had indeed intended to visit Willie that night, and there had been campers at the pond, they would have had every opportunity to commit the crime, O'Brien figured.

But the deeper they probed, the more they focused on Tom Sowalskie, a big, powerfully built man said to be "not quite right mentally," with a "very cruel disposition" he exhibited "towards horses and cows," even reportedly torturing animals on the farm. Willie told the detectives he was "big and naughty."

"I went to Troy on July 6, but I was not away from home that night or the next," Tom told them. "I did not know Hazel Drew's body had been found until the following morning, when Willie, who had been staying at our house, told me he was going to Troy to help look for the murderer."

Libbie and several of their neighbors all confirmed that Tom was home on the night of July 7 and didn't leave the house. However, the detectives also claimed to have been given contrary information by a source never identified—that Tom had left the farmhouse for part of the night and met with Frank Smith, though it was not known if that was before or after Smith met Hazel Drew on the road.

The *Evening World*—which admittedly had a spotty track record about who would appear at the inquest—claimed on July 29 that Tom Sowalskie would be called as a witness when the inquest resumed in Troy, but he never was.

At 1:00 p.m. on Thursday, July 30, the second and final day of the Hazel Drew inquest was called to order in the grand-jury room of the Rensselaer County Courthouse in Troy. Twenty-two additional witnesses were subpoenaed and scheduled to testify, including Hazel's parents, her aunt Minnie Taylor, and her good friend Carrie Weaver, who, O'Brien hoped, would finally have returned from her three-week vacation in Ohio.

By now, Julia Drew had been saddled with a reputation as something of an oddball: she had misstated the age of her daughter, enlisted the aid of a psychic to read the aura around Teal's Pond, and was on the record claiming, without any substantiation, that her daughter had been hypnotized and kidnapped by an unknown wealthy man from Troy. So when, clad in heavy mourning clothes, she took the witness stand—and smiled as she sifted through the various articles of clothing and jewelry Hazel had been wearing when her body was dragged from the pond on July 11—those present, reporters especially, interpreted it as another sign of her emotional instability and general attitude of indifference.

Julia had last seen Hazel alive on July 2, when her daughter paid her a visit at the Drew family home on Fourth Street in Troy, and had had no contact with her since then. Julia recalled that she had loaned her two dollars on that occasion and that Hazel had discussed recent strife at the Carys', but she added that Hazel didn't specifically mention anything about planning to leave her job. In fact, she was taken by surprise when Hazel's trunk arrived at her house from the Carys' on the afternoon of Monday, July 6, but after paying the deliveryman, she propped open the luggage and recognized the belongings as Hazel's.

Hazel hadn't spent much time at home in recent years and rarely confided in members of her family. Julia was unaware of anyone with whom Hazel had problems, and her daughter never mentioned to her that she had been threatened or followed on the street.

After hurling questions at her for over an hour, O'Brien was convinced more than ever before that Julia Drew knew next to nothing about her late daughter's life.

"Mrs. Drew," he said, "can you account in any manner for Hazel going out in July to Averill Park or the vicinity of Teal's Pond?"

"I cannot," Julia replied.

John Drew followed his wife and contributed even less. He, too, professed scant knowledge of Hazel's friends or acquaintances, or what she liked to do in her leisure time. His testimony produced one peculiar moment: while John was recalling that he had last seen Hazel at about 11:00 a.m. on July 4—somewhere uptown, possibly Franklin Square—as she and Minnie Taylor were waiting for a trolley, his sister-in-law, who was sitting diagonally to the right of him in the courthouse, suddenly lost her dejected look, smiled, and shook her head at the witness.

Minnie Taylor, who had provoked so much suspicion and irritation for O'Brien over the course of the investigation, was more complacent than usual on the stand, although she, too, added little that hadn't been said before. Despite being sharply interrogated, she smiled pleasantly throughout. Asked if she and Hazel ever had a room somewhere—implying perhaps that Hazel may have had a secret hideaway where she spent the night of Monday, July 6—Minnie respectfully replied, "No, sir."

Typically she would see Hazel three or so times a week, and since she hadn't heard from her since her impromptu visit to Minnie's place of employment on the morning of July 6, Minnie called on her sister on July 9 to inquire whether Hazel was there; Julia replied that she was not, though her trunk was, leading Minnie to fear that Hazel might have lost her job at the Carys'. But from there, she made no effort to find out where Hazel had gone.

Under oath, Minnie once again insisted that she had no idea as to the nature of Hazel's illness the previous winter, when she recuperated at the Taylor farmhouse, but said that Hazel had complained about her health for some time before that, and that as a result Minnie would sometimes go to the Tupper house to help Hazel with her work. Even after Hazel returned from the Taylor house, Minnie said, she didn't inquire as to what was wrong.

O'Brien was incredulous but also resigned to the fact that no one—not Minnie, not Eva, not Joseph, or anyone—was going to reveal the details of the illness that had befallen Hazel late in December 1907. Yet he firmly suspected that Minnie and Eva knew exactly what it was and were afraid to say.

To reporters, Minnie Taylor was a bloodless old maid who hoarded secrets and knew a lot more than she was letting on; she barked at them, insulted them, and chided them to mind their own business. The press, of course, loathed her back. But even reporters couldn't help commenting on the fact that unlike her sister Julia, Minnie very nearly broke down in sobs while handling Hazel's garments.

꙳

The elusive Carrie Weaver didn't make it back to Troy in time for the inquest, but she issued the following statement from Ohio: "I never saw her in the company of a man all the time I was in Troy, and she told me on more than one occasion that she had no sweetheart. Really, Hazel was a remarkable girl. She could make a dollar go further than any other woman I ever saw. Her salary was only a little more than mine, yet I never could manage to buy as fine hats and as 'swell' costumes as she did, let alone the luncheons at fashionable restaurants and the frequent trips she made out of town. From what Hazel told me she must have had an awfully good time when she went away from home. She said not the slightest attempt was ever made anywhere to offer her an insult. She knew how to take care of herself, but from what our little trips together cost, I know that she must have spent a great deal of money on pleasures of this kind, and for the life of me I don't see how she managed to save enough from her wages."

Harold D. Neach was one of the few surprise witnesses called on the final day of the inquest, momentarily causing somewhat of a stir in the courthouse. Neach was rumored to be one of the people in the car that Chris Crape, proprietor of Crape's Hotel, had seen whizzing past him at 2:00 a.m. with its lights out on its way up Taborton Mountain. The date of that occurrence was disputed throughout the investigation, as Crape couldn't seem to make up his mind, although in the end he seemed to settle on Monday, July 6. Crape maintained all along that the car returned a short time later with one of its occupants—a woman—missing.

Neach, said to be a "popular young resident" of Troy, was a newspaper editor for the *Evening Standard*, and his sudden appearance on the witness list on Thursday, after having at no time been mentioned previously, caused a ruckus among his colleagues in the Fourth Estate. Reporters were chomping at the bit to hear more about Neach's sudden relevance to the case, especially since rumors had floated that the car Crape had seen belonged to Alexander Kramrath, the brother of Henry, with whom he co-owned the camp up past the pond that was rumored to be holding young women against their will and staging wild sex parties.

Due to business obligations, it was arranged for Neach to be one of the final witnesses called, and his actual testimony was given too late to even make it into any known accounts of the inquest's second day. However, even before his testimony, O'Brien contended that Neach had nothing to do with the case; his lost testimony was apparently only a formality.

The inquest was adjourned late on Thursday afternoon. O'Brien packed up his brown leather briefcase and took a familiar seat at the prosecutor's table, where he had scored so many victories over the years. He watched the witnesses and spectators file from the room, until finally he was alone, collecting his thoughts. After nineteen days, the investigation into what the newspapers were calling one of the most mysterious cases ever to occur in Rensselaer County was coming to an end. All that remained now was for the coroner to release his official ruling. O'Brien knew exactly what was coming, and it wasn't the triumphant ending he had been hoping for.

~

On Friday, July 31, Coroner Morris Strope ruled that Hazel Drew came to her death as the result of a blood clot on the brain caused by a blow on the head from some blunt instrument in some manner unknown from some person unknown.

The official verdict read as follows:

> State of New York. Rensselaer County.—Inquisition taken at Averill Park. N.Y., on the 27th day of July and continued at the courthouse in the city of Troy, N.Y. on the 30th day of July 1908, before M. H. Strope, one of the Coroners of said county, upon the body of Hazel Irene Drew, which was found in the pond of Conrad Teal in the town of Sand Lake on the 11th day of July, 1908. From testimony taken on the above dates I find that the said Hazel Irene Drew came to her death from extravasation of blood in the dura mater caused by a blow on the head from some blunt instrument in some manner unknown.
>
> Dated at Troy, N.Y., this 31st day of July, 1908
>
> M. H. Strope, Coroner of Rensselaer County.

Criticism from the press was swift and brutal: the investigation had been sloppy, reactive. O'Brien had appeared indifferent throughout, especially during the inquest. He was overly deferential to witnesses. Detectives had overlooked key clues, discovered only by members of the press. Were investigators cowering under political pressure? This was, after all, Rensselaer County—the possibility couldn't be dismissed. The Mamie Killion investigation—which O'Brien had also been involved in—was a powerful reminder of that.

O'Brien was immediately defensive, insisting that he and his team of investigators had nothing to apologize for. The evidence simply never supported an arrest. They had done everything in their authority and power to bring Hazel's killer to justice, but there were limits as to what they could accomplish without the cooperation of certain witnesses. He would go to his grave believing that some among them—most notably Minnie Taylor—knew more than they were letting on.

A relentless search for Hazel's killer would continue, O'Brien promised, but Detectives Louis Unser and John Lawrenson were relieved from duty in the case and resumed their regular duties in Troy. County Detectives Duncan Kaye and William Powers would continue to pursue leads. Kaye echoed his boss, saying there was plenty of work still to be done.

In fact, there were a plethora of unanswered questions. Where was Hazel going when she left Union Station on Monday, July 6? Where did she spend Monday night and Tuesday morning? Why was she in Taborton on the night of Tuesday, July 7? How did she get there? What was the nature of Hazel's mysterious illness over the previous winter? How did she afford to live so extravagantly? Why did she walk out on the Carys so suddenly? And, of course, who killed Hazel Drew—and why?

District Attorney O'Brien and his team had failed to satisfactorily answer a single one of these questions.

O'Brien told the press that Kaye and Powers would focus on what the July 31 *Evening Telegram* of New York labeled the "most promising clew [*sic*]": locating the two mysterious strangers William and Elizabeth Hoffay had spotted by Teal's Pond on the night of July 7. "Nothing will be left undone to apprehend these men, the authorities say," the paper reported.

It was a nice sentiment, but was it true?

⌐

It would be almost two weeks before the next development in the Hazel Drew case was reported in a newspaper article. It is believed to be the last update the public ever received.

On August 12, it was reported that authorities had uncovered a new suspect and had in their possession letters that proved Hazel expected to marry this young man on a date shortly prior to the tragedy.

"A young man of prominence in the community whose letters show that he knew and loved the girl is under surveillance. This man will be examined by District Attorney Jarvis P. O'Brien, and unless the suspect can establish a satisfactory alibi he will undoubtedly be charged with having dealt the blow that caused the death of his sweetheart," declared the *Scranton-Wilkes Barre Record*. The article claimed that the letters contained evidence proving this new suspect was with Hazel on the night before the tragedy and that there was reason to believe they had planned to meet again the afternoon of July 7, the day she was killed.

Was this accurate reporting? Or more yellow journalism, trying to squeeze a few last dollars from the tragedy? The story wasn't widely reported and could almost have been cobbled together from prior rumors of secret lovers and fiancés. If this mysterious new suspect did exist, he must have "established a satisfactory alibi," because no one was ever arrested for, or charged with, the murder of Hazel Drew. The case faded into the recesses of history.

The mystery of who killed Hazel Drew would remain forever unsolved. Or would it?

Chapter 13

South Troy Against the World

Hazel Drew likely took her last breath the night of July 7 somewhere in the vicinity of the little millpond into which her killer unceremoniously dumped her body. Her rotting corpse went unnoticed for four days until it was finally spotted by the teenage campers and subsequently pulled from the water. By the time Hazel's family had identified the body the morning of Monday, July 13, nearly a week had passed, and the case before District Attorney Jarvis O'Brien and his detectives was already getting cold. Investigators were left with a plethora of seemingly unanswerable questions, beginning with the obvious: Who killed Hazel Drew? As they journeyed deeper into the investigation, they would learn that they first needed to answer another question: Who was Hazel Drew?

It would be impossible to unravel all of the mysteries surrounding Hazel's life and death, but did O'Brien and his team of county detectives and city police do everything in their power to catch Hazel's murderer? Was there an angle that everyone somehow missed? A suspect dismissed prematurely? Was there, like in a hackneyed murder mystery, one vital overlooked piece of evidence that could have helped crack the case?

Incredibly enough, we believe there was.

Strange Days

O'Brien himself had, from the earliest days of the investigation, emphasized the importance of discovering Hazel's whereabouts on the night before her murder. Ultimately, this turned out to be another in a long line of failures, as detectives never came close to establishing Hazel's whereabouts that night. She was alleged to have been seen aboard the steamship *Saratoga*, which sailed from Albany to New York City. DA's officer John Murnane and Troy police detective John Lawrenson spent two days investigating that claim—interviewing everyone they could find by the name of Drew in Troy, Albany, and surrounding neighborhoods—but were unable to dig up any corroborating evidence. Troy investigators were in contact with New York City police commissioner Theodore Alfred Bingham, and even dispatched a photo of Hazel, but the NYPD failed to turn up any evidence that she had stepped foot on their turf on the night of July 6 or the morning of July 7. Further, O'Brien and his team knew Hazel was so low on funds she had had to borrow two dollars from her mother on July 2 to pay for her shirtwaist. Finally, the boat trip to New York City would have taken about ten hours—and Hazel had been spotted the following afternoon in Troy.

The verdict was that whoever had approached the purser about that stateroom, in all probability it wasn't Hazel.

Aurilla E. Horton of Averill Park claimed to have seen a woman who looked like Hazel near the foot of Taborton Mountain on the evening of July 6. Perhaps this was the never publicly identified Sand Lake woman reported to be a near double for Hazel? For whatever reason, investigators lent so little credence to her report that they didn't even summon her to testify at the inquest.

Working backward, detectives knew that Hazel had departed George Harrison's home on Pawling Avenue at about ten thirty on Monday morning, telling her aunt Minnie that she was headed across the Hudson River by trolley to see friends in Watervliet. Yet based

Union Station, in the heart of downtown Troy, was on its third iteration by 1908; the first burned in the "great fire" of 1862, triggered by sparks from a locomotive and gale-force winds. (Courtesy Bob Moore, Sand Lake Town Historian)

Inside majestic Union Station, Hazel's last known stop before her ill-fated trip to Taborton Mountain. (Collection of the Hart Cluett Museum at Historic Rensselaer County, Troy, NY)

THOMAS W. HISLOP.
Esquire. Troy Lodge of Elks.
Marshal of Parade.

Thomas W. Hislop, Hazel's politically ambitious first employer. ("The Troy Elks," *Troy Daily Times*, June 30, 1906, p. 1. Digital reproduction courtesy Troy Public Library)

JOHN H. TUPPER
Republican candidate for Mayor of Troy

Employer number two: John H. Tupper, a wealthy coal merchant and member of the controversial Committee of Public Safety. ("Tupper for Mayor of Troy," *New York Daily Tribune*, New York, NY, October 16, 1897, p. 10. Digital reproduction courtesy Newspapers.com)

Hazel's third and final employer: Edward R. Cary, city engineer and RPI professor. (Courtesy Rensselaer Polytechnic Institute)

The Averill Park trolley station, where a wandering Frank Smith surprised the Richmonds on the night of the murder. (Courtesy Bob Moore, Sand Lake Town Historian)

Detectives turned their attention to Edward Lavoie when a newspaper clipping about him was found among Hazel's possessions. Though he and Hazel had dated years earlier, nothing further was uncovered to incriminate the young Trojan. (Courtesy National Archives and Records Association)

Investigators found the name Florence Barker in Hazel's handwriting at the Carys' house but never pursued the lead, even though Florence and her husband, William, lived next door to Hazel at the dead end of a secluded cul-de-sac while she lived with the Carys. ("Parfaets Dael: A Far-Famed Social Organization," *Troy Daily Times*, May 5, 1906, Arts Section. Digital reproduction courtesy Troy Public Library)

WILLIAM BARKER, JR.,
Secretary Pafraets Dael Club, Troy.

Christopher Crape's spacious hotel and gathering spot was only about a mile from Teal's Pond at the foot of Taborton Mountain. (Courtesy Bob Moore, Sand Lake Town Historian)

WOMAN SAW HAZEL DREW

Latter Was Picking Berries on the Road July 7.

Mrs. Rottman Told Her Husband
Such a Pretty Girl Should Not
Be There Alone.

This headline misidentifies the Rollmans, but the story about the married couple seeing a girl who looked like Hazel picking berries on the evening of July 7 is correct. ("Woman Saw Hazel Drew," *Brooklyn Daily Eagle,* Brooklyn, NY, July 19, 1908, p. 1. Digital reproduction courtesy Newspapers.com)

The picturesque shores of Crooked Lake drew thousands of tourists and campers to Sand Lake every summer. (Courtesy private collection)

SCREAMS IN CAMP AT TEAL'S POND MYSTERY CLEW

Girl's Story of Night Alarm Starts Police on Trail for Hazel Drew's Slayer.

Sensational stories like this one about orgies at the Alps summer camp enthralled the press, whether true or not. ("Screams in Camp at Teal's Pond Mystery Clew," *Evening World*, New York, NY, July 24, 1908, p. 10. Digital reproduction courtesy Newspapers.com)

Employees of Brown's Crooked Lake House, known to be a favorite haunt of Teddy Roosevelt's, were called as witnesses at the inquest. (Courtesy Bob Moore, Sand Lake Town Historian)

The first day of the inquest unfolded at the Travelers Rest hotel (also known as Warger's), where dozens of curious onlookers crammed within its walls. (Courtesy Bob Moore, Sand Lake Town Historian)

Julia Drew's comment that Hazel had been "mesmerized" by a mystery man was reinterpreted to imply that she believed her daughter had been literally brainwashed, an example of the era's practice of yellow journalism. ("Hypnotized and Then Murdered," *Buffalo Commercial*, Buffalo, NY, July 28, 1908, p. 1. Digital reproduction courtesy Newspapers.com)

HAZEL DREW RODE WITH MAN AT NIGHT, IS NEW CLUE IN POND MURDER

District-Attorney Hurries Detectives on Round of Troy Livery Stables After Receiving Letter He Considers Important—Still on Hunt.

(Special to The Evening World.)

TROY, N. Y., July 17.—After a long search in the mountains about Taborton and Glass Lake with the charcoal-burners of the region, two score detectives and newspapermen returned to Troy to-day to hurry out on a possible clue contained in one of five anonymous letters received by District-Attorney O'Brien to-day.

"Hazel Drew met a man at the depot. They drove to Averill Park. He returned the livery wagon after midnight."

The longer the investigation continued, the more Hazel's ample social life was fodder for headlines. ("Hazel Drew Rode with Man at Night, Is New Clue in Pond Murder," *Evening World*, New York, NY, July 17, 1908, p. 12. Digital reproduction courtesy Newspapers.com)

A view of Teal's Pond showing the fenced-off area where the Hoffays spotted two mysterious men and their carriage. (Collection of the Hart Cluett Museum at Historic Rensselaer County, Troy, NY)

Aurilla E. Horton claimed to have seen a girl resembling Hazel from the porch of her store (pictured) at Sliter's Corners at the foot of Taborton Road on Monday night. (Courtesy Bob Moore, Sand Lake Town Historian)

Sand Lake Corners, where Hazel likely began her journey up Taborton Road. (Courtesy Bob Moore, Sand Lake Town Historian)

THE MARCHING REPUBLICANS.
Head of the Parade as it Reached the Corner of Fulton and River Streets.

Three years after Hazel's murder, William Cushing, Thomas Hislop, William Powers, and Duncan Kaye march down the streets of Troy during a Republican rally before attending a clambake in West Sand Lake. ("The Marching Republicans," *Troy Times*, September 1, 1911. Digital reproduction courtesy Troy Public Library)

A portrait of members of the Troy Citizens Corps (a precursor to the National Guard), including Jonathan Tupper (1), Thomas Hislop (2), William Barker (3), and other members of Troy's elite. (Photograph by James H. Lloyd, *A History of Troy Citizens Corps*, Troy, NY: Troy Times Printing House, 1884. Courtesy private collection)

Above: *Fred Schatzle's signature from his World War I draft registration card illustrates how it might have been mistaken for "Shaltus."* (Courtesy National Archives and Records Association, St. Louis, MO); *Right: Under questioning, William Cushing implicated Fred Schatzle as having helped him to secure a carriage to take him to Sand Lake on the night of the murder. Schatzle may have been one of the two men the Hoffays saw near Teal's Pond.* ("Fred W. Schatzle Dies Suddenly at Residence Here," Troy Times Record, October 5, 1944, p. 11. Digital reproduction courtesy Troy Public Library)

FRED W. SCHATZLE DIES SUDDENLY AT RESIDENCE HERE

Had Been Embalmer in City for 44 Years; Funeral Saturday

The scenic twenty-six-mile-long Poestenkill creek originates close to where Hazel was born and ultimately feeds into the Hudson River. (Courtesy private collection)

Hazel's final resting place was originally meant to be Mount Ida Cemetery in Troy before a last-minute change to Brookside in Poestenkill, where she was born. (Photo © 2017 Daniel William McKnight)

Hazel is buried in the family plot with younger brothers Emery and Thomas, who both had died before their second birthdays. (Photo © 2017 Daniel William McKnight)

Record of Deaths in the _Town_ of _Sand Lake_

County of _Rensselaer_   State of New York.

Register No. _271_   Date of Death _About July 6th, 1908_

Full Name of Deceased _Hazel I. Drew_ — _found Sand Lake N.Y._

     body found in lake

Age _20_ years, _9_ months, _____ days.

Single, Married or Widowed _Single_   Color _White_

Occupation _Housework_

Birthplace _East Poestenkill_ (State or Country)

How long in United States if foreign born _____ years _____ months _____ days.

How long resident here _____ years _____ months _____ days.

Father's Name _John Drew_   Father's Birthplace _Vermont_ (State or Country)

Mother's Name _Julia A. Taylor_   Mother's Birthplace _Berlin N.Y._ (State or Country)

Place of Death _Sand Lake_   Last Place of Residence _____

Direct Cause of Death _Death evidently caused by a blow in occipital region_

Duration of Disease _causing extravasation of blood in dura Mater_

Death Reported By _John Drew_

Death Certified by _E. E. Auchers Under of Coroner M.D. Strope Poestenkill N.Y._

Residence of Medical Attendant _Averill Park N.Y._

Place of Burial _Mount Ida Troy N.Y._

By _Larkin Bros._ Undertaker.

Residence of Undertaker _Averill Park N.Y._

Date of Burial _July 14, 1908_

Date of Record _July 14, 1908_

REGISTRAR OF
TOWN OF
SAND LAKE
N Y
VITAL STATISTICS

Hazel Drew's death certificate, certifying that she was killed by a blow to the head (note the incorrect burial place). (Courtesy Bob Moore, Sand Lake Town Historian)

Taborton Road, where Hazel Drew was last seen alive, as it is today. (Photo © 2017 Daniel William McKnight)

A contemporary view of Teal's Pond. (Photo © 2017 Daniel William McKnight)

on the preponderance of evidence at hand—none of her friends in Watervliet admitted to having seen her that day, and she was spotted in Union Station later that morning—it is extremely unlikely that Hazel visited Watervliet on Monday, leaving three possibilities: one, that she lied to Minnie; two, that Minnie lied to detectives; or three, that Hazel did in fact plan to go to Watervliet but changed her mind somewhere along the way.

Given Minnie's history of obstructionism—and Hazel's record of confiding in her aunt—we believe the most likely answer is that Minnie was lying.

But why?

From the early days of the investigation, Minnie had stubbornly refused to divulge the names of certain people with whom she and Hazel were associated. Significantly, this included the two mystery men with whom the pair went for a drive in an automobile on June 21 (although in the end she relented, under the condition that O'Brien keep the names from the press). We know, too, that Minnie was notoriously protective of family secrets. Further, we know that Hazel had been especially excited about visiting Lake George over the July Fourth weekend—to the point of having had a new shirtwaist made for the occasion. But she was dissuaded by Minnie from doing so, purportedly because her aunt didn't like traveling on crowded trains. Yet Minnie apparently had no objections to dealing with the throngs of people who visited Rensselaer Park for the July Fourth celebration, or to riding on a jam-packed trolley car from Troy to Schenectady, where they ultimately spent the weekend.

Could Hazel have been planning to meet someone—most likely a man—in Lake George that weekend? Was she diverted by her aunt, who disapproved of the liaison?

Hazel was next seen on Monday between 11:20 and 11:30 by Henrietta Robertson, who knew Hazel and conversed with her in the waiting area at Union Station. We discount the alleged sighting between

11:00 a.m. and noon on Monday by grocery clerk Lawrence Eagan, who seemed confused about the details and later changed his story. There's no reason, however, to contest the sighting by Henrietta Robertson. If Hazel was being honest with Henrietta, she had by this time—just one hour after leaving her aunt—decided to travel by train "down the river a ways." Asked specifically how far "a ways," Hazel replied New York City. But Hazel was stopping first in Albany—about seven and a half miles south of Troy and one hundred and fifty miles north of New York City—because that was the destination for the only train leaving Union Station at the time Hazel was seen by Henrietta descending into the subway leading to the train tracks (the 11:30 Belt Line).

Possibly, Hazel was merely stopping in Albany en route south to New York, but whatever her intentions, she was back at Union Station in Troy by 1:15 p.m. that same day, placing an order at the Westcott Express Service for her trunk to be picked up from the Cary home and delivered to her parents. Sometime between 1:00 and 2:00 p.m., she was spotted again at the station, this time by Jeanette Marcellus, who also knew Hazel well. Again, no reason to dispute this sighting—the two even chatted, and Jeanette provided a detailed account of their encounter.

The train ride from Troy to Albany took about twenty-five minutes. If the train was on time, Hazel arrived in Albany at 11:55. That gave her thirty-five minutes to catch the 12:30 train back to Troy, arriving at 12:55—the timing of which coincides both with Jeanette Marcellus's sighting and the report from Westcott Express.

Thus, Hazel went all the way south to Albany just to hop on a train back to Troy a mere thirty-five minutes later.

Something happened in Albany. But what?

Either Hazel rendezvoused with someone and it didn't go as planned (or didn't go at all), or she simply changed her plans of her own volition. The fact that she did not place the order at Westcott until *after*

250

returning to Troy suggests that she may have been uncertain of where she was going next, prior to whatever transpired in Albany.

Next logical question: Who was Hazel meeting in Albany?

We know the Kramrath brothers—owners of the purportedly salacious camp in Alps—were based out of Albany, but neither was ever directly connected to Hazel by any evidence or witness accounts. Hazel's known friends and associates from Albany, such as F. W. Schlafflin, the packer Hazel had met while ice-skating in Rensselaer Park, were all investigated, and nothing was found that incriminated them in any way.

Pullman car conductor John Magner's train that day ran through Albany on its way north to Troy. Magner was known to have met with a young woman resembling Hazel in Union Station on multiple occasions, but claimed it was Anna LaBelle, the Frear's department store clerk. Yet credibility wasn't Magner's calling card. He originally denied knowing any young women in Troy, before being caught in that fabrication. He claimed to know only what he had read in the papers about Hazel, even though his name and address in New York City—where Hazel had been heading that Monday, according to Henrietta Robertson—were written on a slip of paper discovered among her possessions. If Minnie Taylor can be believed—and let's face it, she can't—Hazel also shared with her that she was in love with a train conductor from New York.

So there seems to be some—admittedly circumstantial—evidence that Hazel could have been romantically involved with Magner and was meeting him in Albany on Monday. Or maybe she was just obsessed with him, whether he returned the affection or not.

Peter Ross, traveling home to Schenectady from New York City on July 6, claimed that a young woman resembling Hazel had boarded his train a few miles south of Albany and engaged in an "earnest" conversation with a uniformed man matching Magner's description. Both, he said, deboarded at Albany.

Could this have been Magner and Hazel? East Poestenkill resident Mark Marshall, who investigated the Hazel Drew murder along with us, spent a lot of time digging into this, and his conclusion is that it was unlikely. Reports had Ross taking the Number Seven train out of New York; Magner's was the so-called Fast Mail Number Three Line.

Theoretically, Ross could have changed onto Magner's line in Rensselaer, before reaching Albany, and Hazel could have done the same, but why would they? Both could have gone direct to Albany—Ross from New York and Hazel from Troy—without switching at Rensselaer.

Besides, why would Hazel have gone all the way south to Albany to meet Magner when his train was also stopping in Troy? Why not just wait for him at Union Station?

Again, Marshall offers an explanation: Magner worked two different lines; Hazel might not have known which assignment he had drawn that day. Only one passed through Troy, but both stopped in Albany. The one place Hazel was sure to find Magner was in Albany.

Or perhaps she just didn't want to be seen with him in her hometown, where she was easily recognizable.

Let's assume Hazel did in fact go down to Albany to rendezvous with someone—probably a man, possibly Magner.

The *Evening World* speculated at the time that Hazel was meeting her secret lover, hoping to elope with him, but that the man had no interest in marrying her. Instead, he decided to put an end to the relationship—one way or another. Perhaps the two scheduled another rendezvous the following night in secluded Taborton—an ideal place to commit a murder. But these same newspaper reports stated that Hazel's lover was a married man; they seemed to conflate Magner, who was single, with another conductor, Samuel LeRoy, who was married with children. It was ultimately determined LeRoy had no involvement with the Hazel Drew case.

At the end of the day, there was no direct evidence against Magner and no proof that he even knew Hazel; the tabloid press seemed more interested in him as a suspect than the actual investigators did. And yet the scenario of Hazel arranging a quick meeting in Albany—perhaps setting in motion future plans—seems plausible. If this was evidence of some sort of romantic entanglement, then the man she was meeting likely played a role in her demise. If it wasn't John Magner, who was it?

Whatever did happen in Albany, Hazel returns to Troy soon after her brief excursion. Jeanette Marcellus speaks with her at Union Station that same afternoon. Hazel then goes to Westcott Express, also in Union Station, to place the order for her trunk to be picked up from the Cary home. But where is she going to spend the night?

She can't go back to the Carys. She isn't especially close to her mother and father. She can't impose on Minnie, who lives at the George Harrison home.

Two possibilities to consider: If she did in fact travel to Albany to meet with someone, could the two of them have spent the night together in Troy, either in a hotel or at the home of the never-identified person? The hotels in both Troy and Albany were scoured for any sign of Hazel without success, but if the encounter was clandestine—if either Hazel or her companion was trying to hide their identity—the couple surely would have used aliases.

Hazel had another close confidant in Troy, besides Minnie: her sister-in-law Eva Lapp Drew. Although Eva and her husband, Hazel's brother Joseph, would deny having seen Hazel on Monday, their veracity is questionable, given their dubious account of Hazel's stay with them at the William Taylor farm the previous winter while recovering from a mysterious illness. Eva also contested liveryman John Abel's claim that he had driven Hazel to the Taylor farmhouse in April, somewhat miraculously summoning up her friend Stella Carner in support of her account.

Further, the unidentified young couple who visited the Larkin funeral home in an attempt to identify the body on the afternoon of Sunday, July 12, was in all likelihood Eva and Joseph, which raises the possibility that they had last seen Hazel on the night of July 6 or the morning of July 7 and were fearful that something had happened to her in the interim.

Wherever Hazel did spend Monday night, she broke her promise to see her good friend Carrie Weaver off at Union Station as she departed for her vacation in Ohio.

Hazel was next seen between 11:00 a.m. and noon on Tuesday, July 7, three to four blocks from Union Station, by Thomas Carey, who knew Hazel and was certain of the identification. Two to three hours later, she checks her suitcase with Adelbert Atwood at Union Station. Surely Hazel is planning to return to Troy before the night is over, to retrieve her belongings, including her nightclothes and toiletries. (Hazel was said to be particularly fastidious about sleeping in her nightgown.)

For reasons unknown, she next ventures out to Sand Lake, making her way to the slopes of Taborton Mountain. But how did she get there? If Snyders Corner farmer Peter Cipperly's assertions were true, he had spotted Hazel (whom he didn't know but had seen photos of in the papers) with a tall, slim young man, about the same age as her, conversing aboard a southeastern-bound trolley car headed for Averill Park. Cipperly deboarded before the couple; if it was in fact Hazel he had seen, and Averill Park—the last stop on the line—was her destination, she would have arrived at approximately four thirty. Not impossible.

Yet the Cipperly sighting was speculative, and detectives couldn't have been particularly impressed with his testimony as he was called to testify at the inquest.

The Averill Park trolley station was about a mile from the bottom of Taborton Mountain, itself about a mile from the Hollow on Taborton Road, where Hazel was seen later that night. If Hazel did in fact take the trolley out to Averill Park, did she walk two miles to the Hollow in a fancy dress and Cuban heels?

None of the trolley conductors on duty that day remembered seeing Hazel aboard their car, although there were reports that the regular workers were off that day, implying their substitutes wouldn't have recognized her.

None of the livery drivers parked outside the trolley station remembered seeing Hazel, either.

And no one ever admitted to having given Hazel a ride out to Taborton that day.

In summary, either she did take the trolley with her male companion, as described by Peter Cipperly, and then walked up Taborton Road, or she got a ride with someone from Troy to Averill Park—someone who didn't want to be identified. But, regardless of how she got there, she apparently was not alone during the trip. Where, then, had her companion disappeared to when Hazel was later spotted by herself on Taborton Road?

Don't ask O'Brien—he never found out.

Nor did he ever learn the answer to our next question, perhaps the single most consequential mystery other than the identity of her killer: What was Hazel Drew doing in Taborton on July 7? Darkness isn't far off. It's not safe at night. Drunken lumberjacks are traipsing up and down the mountain all throughout the evening. She somehow has to get back to Troy that night, to collect her suitcase.

All sorts of theories were floated; none ever seemed to satisfy investigators.

But what if Hazel had gone out to Taborton on Tuesday by rig with a couple of old friends, who dropped her off on the mountain and then arranged to pick her up later that night? But who wound up murdering her instead?

We believe that's exactly what happened.

The Usual Suspects

Frank Smith and William Taylor were the most prominent suspects throughout the investigation, but at no point were they tied to the crime by anything other than circumstance. Smith was socially awkward, perhaps struggling with some sort of cognitive impairment, and clearly had his eye on Hazel. But whatever motives he might have had for the murder were immaterial—he really didn't have the opportunity to commit the crime. After Smith and Rudy Gundrum passed Hazel on Taborton Road on the night of July 7, the boy was in the company of first Gundrum and then numerous other eyewitnesses in Averill Park—more than a mile away from the pond—until after midnight, when, he said, he finally headed home. It seems extremely improbable that Hazel would have meandered about in the dark on the slopes of Taborton for four hours after being spotted by Smith and Gundrum, in order to give Smith the opportunity to murder her.

William Taylor, on the other hand, had no such alibi. We have only his word that on July 7, after his farmhands, the Richmonds, departed to take Frank Richmond's brother to the Averill Park trolley station, he stayed home alone, whiling away the hours puffing on his pipe as he sat in his rocking chair before retiring for the evening. The Richmonds left the Taylor farm on foot sometime between 8:15 and 8:30, returning home around ten o'clock. Hazel was last seen by Smith and Gundrum in the vicinity of Taylor's farm around seven thirty, allowing for a window of time in which he could have committed the murder and disposed of the body.

From the point that Smith and Gundrum saw Hazel, there are two lanes that branch off from Taborton Road before Teal's Pond: Taylor's Turn (today known as Mosher Road) and Teal's Road. Much of the early suspicion directed at William Taylor was because Hazel was last seen walking directly toward the road that turned off to her uncle's—a theory bolstered by Smith's claims to Frank Richmond that Hazel had said she was on her way there. Smith would later deny hearing her say that, and knowing his less-than-stellar relationship with the truth, he might have merely surmised where she was heading while trying to pry information about her from Frank Richmond.

After combing through every inch of Taylor's property, detectives could not produce a shred of concrete evidence against the man, or even a clear motive. He was consistent, if not overly helpful, when accounting for himself, his actions, and his relationship with his niece. And he was subjected to *many* grueling interrogations over the weeks of the investigation. It's true that Taylor was rumored to have a violent side to his personality, but snapping at workers (a year before Hazel's death, he reportedly had mistreated a young farmhand)—though hardly justifiable—is a far cry from murder. The only other evidence of violence on Taylor's part was directed at himself, when he attempted suicide after his wife's death. Taylor was clearly an unhappy, peculiar man. Yet despite his notorious oddities and quirks, he and Hazel seemed to have a relatively normal relationship: she would come for visits, but not too often; they would talk here and there, but not too much.

Despite the fact that Hazel was seen so close to his farm on July 7, it seems unlikely she was on her way, unannounced and unexpected, to see her uncle that night.

Unless . . .

Her Favorite Brother

Was she going to visit her brother Willie, who was temporarily staying nearby at the Taborton farm of Libbie Sowalskie? Hazel was reportedly closer to Willie than to most of the other members of her family, but it is unclear from statements made by her mother, Julia Drew, and Willie himself, if Hazel even knew Willie was there.

Earlier that summer, Willie had been boarding at the farmhouse of William Taylor, until that situation became unbearable for him, but he later moved on to the Sowalskie farm. If Hazel was under the impression that Willie was still at their uncle's house, was she on her way there to see not William, but Willie? Or, did she in fact know Willie had moved on from the Taylor farm, and was on her way to visit him at the Sowalskies'?

Again, it seems unlikely that Hazel was making an unexpected, unannounced visit to either location, especially that late in the evening. Plus, the Sowalskie farm was another mile or mile and a half beyond the pond. Libbie Sowalskie and Willie both stated clearly that they were not expecting a visit from Hazel. What if Willie wasn't even home? Would she have chanced it by going all the way out to Taborton from Troy? And where would she have been going next, that late in the day, with no visible means of transportation and no known home to return to, having left her job with the Carys?

Secret Rendezvous

At about 7:05 p.m. on July 7, Taborton residents Henry and Charlotte Rollman saw a girl resembling Hazel—and who almost certainly was Hazel—picking raspberries off the side of Taborton Road on their way down the mountain into Averill Park. The Rymillers and Marie Yeabauer, each riding up Taborton Road around the same time, must have been behind Hazel and should have overtaken her at some point near the pond, yet they never laid eyes on her. Hazel was last seen at the Hollow at about 7:30 p.m. by Frank Smith and Rudy Gundrum. Where had Hazel gone?

There are only two possibilities. Hazel could have turned left on the road to her uncle's, although, as discussed, there was no evidence or motive found to support this. Or she could have walked a little farther and then turned right onto Teal's Road, which curls around adjacent to the western shore of Teal's Pond. From there, she could access the western side of the pond by crossing Teal's dam of boulders (possible, but unlikely given her choice of dress and shoes) or gone farther behind the pond via an old logging road, with an open field to one side and a patchy slope on the other side that leads down to the southern banks of the pond, near where her gloves, hat, and glasses were found—the apparent staged suicide.

But why would she have been going to this secluded area—either behind the pond or to the open field bordered by the logging road?

Although Taborton wasn't exactly Hazel's childhood haunt—she was born and spent her early years in East Poestenkill, about ten miles to the north—she had always had family in the area and had spent time there over the past few years when her family was working at the Taylor farm. Gilbert Miller, a Taborton resident, had reportedly spotted her in the vicinity of the pond earlier that summer, and her friend Lillian Robertson volunteered that Hazel had fond memories of the area. Perhaps she had an affinity for a spot somewhere near the pond: a place reminiscent of her childhood where she could temporarily forget the struggles of adulthood.

Perhaps she had chosen to share that spot with someone, and they had planned to meet there that afternoon? If that was the scenario, then whoever showed up to keep their commitment may have been the murderer.

Two Men and a Trojan Horse

William and Elizabeth Hoffay reported seeing two men near Teal's Pond at about eight o'clock that night. The first man they spotted was in the Concord wagon, parked on that same turnoff to Teal's Road. Meanwhile, the second stranger, assuming he had arrived in the same carriage, must already have been on Teal's Road, before making his way to the south banks of the pond, either by crossing the dam or taking the same logging road.

The only innocent explanation suggested for the presence of the two strangers during the investigation was that they might have been hunting for minnows to use as bait. The surrounding area was rife with sportsmen in the summer, and Teal's Pond did in fact have a reputation as a good source of bait. However, according to Conrad Teal, that practice had practically ground to a halt since a state law was passed requiring a license to do so. And besides that, the men, as described by the Hoffays, were in no way dressed for bait hunting—more like city folk out for a pleasant drive: the driver, whom the Hoffays saw more clearly, wore a suit with a high collar and a bow tie. The man wading near the shallows by the south bank wore a smart, checkered shirt, dark trousers, and a straw hat. This second man had to have traversed the patchy, hilly terrain in order to be in the position where he was seen by the Hoffays from Taborton Road. Once he reached the marshy pond banks, one misstep would have found him ankle deep in the mud—not an enticing challenge with darkness fast approaching.

The Hoffays' story was initially greeted with great interest by the detectives, setting off a mad search of all the livery stations in the area for any sign of the Concord wagon. After questioning the Hoffays on the stand at the inquest, DA O'Brien said he considered their story the best remaining lead. There was a good chance, given the timing, that the two men were involved in the murder—and the Hoffays' account resulted in only one possible suspect.

Cushing

This much is undisputed: William J. Cushing took out a Concord wagon from William T. Shyne's livery stable in Troy on the night of Hazel's murder. Upon learning this, County Detective William Powers paid Cushing a visit at his Troy home, roused him from bed in the early hours of Tuesday, July 21, and demanded an explanation for his whereabouts on July 7.

Cushing admitted to not only having rented the rig but also driving it out to Sand Lake with his girlfriend (never publicly identified). However, he insisted they got no farther than the intersection known as Sand Lake's Four Corners at the bottom of Taborton Mountain, about a mile from Teal's Pond. That's a two-hour ride—each way—on what was more or less a driving date. Cushing reported that he returned the rig to Shyne's at about ten thirty that night, which the livery confirmed.

So, what happened next? Investigators immediately absolved him of any involvement in the murder—Cushing's name barely even made the papers.

Who exactly was William Cushing? And why were detectives—and possibly the press—so eager to give him a pass, when Frank Smith, William Taylor, Minnie Taylor, John Magner, Anna LaBelle, and so many others had been scrutinized, interrogated, and generally put through the wringer in the search for Hazel's killer?

Cushing was the oldest of four siblings—two boys and two girls—and was born in 1882 to Irish immigrants Patrick and Ellen. Patrick earned his living as a bottler of a mysterious liquid concoction popular in the nineteenth century known as Hoxsie, named after its proprietor. Its secret ingredients have been lost to time, but it likely consisted of some strange combination of beer, or possibly root beer, mixed with a variety of unknown herbs and extracts, and possibly a bit of fizz. When Patrick passed away in 1897, William became the man of the house at the age of fifteen.

The Cushings moved around a bit but always settled close to the Champlain Canal, which informally divides the city into two halves: North and South Troy. Although the Cushings technically lived a few blocks north of the canal, demographically they belonged to South Troy, which was populated mostly by rugged working-class people—iron-factory workers, railroad men, and small-time merchants addressing the community's day-to-day needs, such as groceries, meats, baked goods, tailoring, and laundering.

In South Troy, husbands would come home tired and dirty after long, exhausting days in the factories and mills. Their wives found work in places like collar factories or as domestic servants (like Hazel), or stayed home to look after their families, or sometimes had to do both. It was a tight-knit, insular neighborhood, wary of outsiders.

It also happened to be the same neighborhood where Hazel Drew spent her formative years and grew up into a beautiful young woman.

William Cushing followed in his father's footsteps, working as a bottler and later a bartender in South Troy. At a young age he showed an interest in politics, which, in Troy, seemed at times to permeate every aspect of life. The Democratic and Republican Parties each wielded extraordinary power, influencing everything from where you worked to how much money you made to whether or not you wound up in jail— or even dead. Everyone had to choose a side, even if those allegiances might change by the next election.

In 1904, at the age of twenty-one, Cushing was named a delegate for the Second Assembly Convention by the Democrats of the Eleventh Ward. Since Cushing was of Irish descent, it is understandable he would gravitate toward the Democratic Party, which built its support largely on the backs of Irish Roman Catholics and other immigrants.

But within a few years, Cushing's loyalties had switched, and he had joined the Republican Party. In 1907, Cushing was selected as a delegate for Troy's Eleventh Ward of the Rensselaer County Republican General Committee. At this time the Republican Party was less entrenched than its Democratic counterpart and offered more opportunity to carve out a meaningful position in the machine's hierarchy—surely, an attractive path to ambitious men seeking advancement, much like Cushing's fellow Irishman Jarvis O'Brien. Cushing was selected to represent the Eleventh Ward once again the following year. Also selected as delegates for the committee that year were Cushing's brother, James, and a fellow by the name of Fred Schatzle—the same man who had reserved the Concord coach that took Cushing out to Sand Lake the night of July 7.

Twenty-nine years old in 1908, Fred Schatzle was four years older than Cushing but was born and raised just a few houses down the street from his friend, in the same South Troy neighborhood, where he also worked as an embalmer. Like Cushing, Schatzle was involved in politics from an early age, working as a Republican election inspector at the age of twenty-three.

His parents, Gerhard and Elizabeth, immigrants from Germany, had three sons: Fred; his older brother, George; and their younger brother, Joseph. The Schatzle boys seemed to have that South Troy edge about them, often finding themselves in less-than-salubrious situations.

In 1908 Fred Schatzle lived and worked at Nealon's Funeral Home, also in South Troy. Less than a year after Hazel's murder, Schatzle was back in the newspapers, having discovered the body of his employer, Thomas H. Nealon, who had been shot twice in the chest in his office at the funeral home. Investigators concocted an elaborate theory in which Nealon had somehow attempted to commit suicide; after failing to finish the job, he apparently staggered over to the phone—it had been found dangling off the hook at the scene of the crime—and, finally, full of remorse, attempted to summon a doctor. Not surprisingly, his family was adamant he had been murdered.

In 1943, many years after Hazel's murder had faded into distant memory, George Schatzle was employed in the government office responsible for gasoline-rationing coupons when he was arrested on a charge of abusing his position to sell and transfer such coupons illegally, a practice known as "tailoring."

At the time of Hazel's murder, Schatzle and his wife, Theresa, owned a summer home in Taborton, which suggests he might very well have had an intimate familiarity with the sometimes rough terrain of that area, including the vicinity surrounding Teal's Pond. Before he had mysteriously disappeared around the time of the inquest, Charles Rankie had told investigators he had seen a man who matched the description of the runabout driver given by the Hoffays. Could this man have been Cushing scouting out the area with Schatzle?

Furthermore, is it possible that Cushing and Schatzle were the two men seen by the Hoffays that night by the pond?

Or, to rephrase the question: Is it possible they were not?

The Hoffays described the man in the carriage as five six or five seven, of slender build, with light hair; Mrs. Hoffay thought he had a sandy mustache. The man wore a cap and had his head turned toward the pond, but they estimated he was young, maybe no older than twenty-five. Although the ages match up, there is unfortunately little known about Cushing's physical appearance. He died young and didn't leave behind a family. The only existing photo that he is known to have appeared in is a dark and blurry crowd shot of a parade at a Republican rally in 1911.

Although the Hoffays told detectives they thought they could identify the man if they saw him again, they were never shown a photograph of Cushing or Schatzle.

Why not?

Perhaps the most critical evidence confirming that Cushing's appearance fits the description of the man seen near the pond by the Hoffays comes from the article detailing Cushing's claim of riding to Sand Lake with a girlfriend. Although he was seemingly exonerated by this alibi, the article also confirmed that Cushing's appearance did indeed match the man seen by the Hoffays.

It is possible that reporters and photographers got a good look at Cushing during the investigation—they just wouldn't have realized the significance of the sighting at the time.

On July 21, the morning after Detectives William Powers and Louis Unser had spoken to the Hoffays about seeing the two strangers and the Concord wagon near the pond, investigators ushered an unknown man into and out of the Rensselaer County Courthouse for an interview with the district attorney. O'Brien and this "mystery man" were closeted in the DA's office for more than an hour. Even after reporters discovered the man covertly exiting via a side door, O'Brien refused to disclose his identity or reveal what he, Detective Kaye, and the stranger had spoken about. Most of the papers covering the case ignored the story, but the Albany *Times Union* reporter who saw the man scurry from O'Brien's offices described him as being "of medium height" and with "a sandy mustache"—echoing Libbie Hoffay's description of the driver of the carriage.

Based on the timing of this meeting, and the context of what was going on in the investigation at this time, it is very likely that the mystery man O'Brien spoke to and shielded from the media was William Cushing. Perhaps Powers—after tracking down Cushing at his home and deciding to absolve him of any responsibility in the murder—reported back to O'Brien, who then met with Cushing separately to sign off on Powers's decision.

Later that morning, O'Brien had Minnie Taylor brought in for what he hoped would be another clandestine session—although the press was having none of that. Reports out of that meeting focused on John Magner, but based on the timing, could O'Brien have also been asking her about William Cushing? There was a story swirling about that Minnie and Hazel had been seen taking rides with two men on June 21 and planned to do so again sometime after July 4. Were those two men Cushing and Schatzle?

Further, Kaye had been dispatched on the evening of July 15 to a saloon located at Congress Street and Sixth Avenue to interview a man identified by the press only as "Linderman [*sic*]," who reportedly could provide him with the names of two men Hazel and Minnie had planned to meet with on July 6, the day before her disappearance. Mark Marshall, our investigator, went thumbing through Troy city directories and was able to identify this man as George Lindermann, a bartender working at John H. Sticklemeyer's saloon at 153 Congress Street.

Both Sticklemeyer and Lindermann had intriguing connections to the investigation. George Lindermann was married to Margaret Teal, the daughter of Conrad Teal, and had lived as a youth in Taborton on the upper end of Walk Road, not far from the Rollmans and the Hoffays. John Sticklemeyer was the brother of Jacob, whose liquor store William Hoffay was in when he mentioned seeing the rig and two men on the night of the murder. Both Sticklemeyers were active in Democratic politics and had been arrested in 1894 for "election engineering."

Sticklemeyer's saloon was just blocks away from the bar where William Cushing worked, owned by a Henry Moss, whose brother Louis worked there as well, and also from the intersection of Congress and Seventh Streets. This was the proposed drop point for a horse and buggy ordered from Shyne's stable by a never-identified man on July 6—the same day Hazel and Minnie were supposedly planning to meet up with two men known to Lindermann. Congress and Seventh was also where Joseph and Eva Drew lived, and on July 21, Joseph had come forward with the claim that Hazel had been riding with a man who had hired a buggy from a livery stable in Troy, and had returned it later alone, the night of her murder. Although the Moss brothers were never publicly identified as suspects, they both lived in this same South Troy neighborhood, on Congress Street, and were clearly part of Cushing's circle of acquaintances.

Isn't it plausible, at the very least, that the two men out driving with Hazel—and with whom Lindermann was acquainted—were Cushing and Schatzle?

The Hoffays had trouble seeing the second stranger, who was obscured by the shrubbery as he crept around the south bank of the pond, where Hazel's gloves and hat would be found four days hence. They did note that he was stouter and older than the driver. We know from Fred Schatzle's World War I and II draft registrations that he had brown eyes, initially brown hair that had grayed by WWII, and a light complexion. He was described as having a medium build in his first registration but was listed as a stouter five feet four inches, 180 pounds by the time of his second. All these physical characteristics check out with what little description the Hoffays were able to provide.

Perhaps most disturbingly, what is the likelihood that Hazel and Cushing (and possibly Schatzle as well)—all from the same neighborhood and all of whom almost certainly knew each other—would somehow wind up at more or less the same place in Taborton at the same time on the same night just by coincidence?

If Cushing and Schatzle were in fact the men spotted by the Hoffays, why did investigators spend so little time looking into these potential suspects before moving on to chase the next red herring?

~

In the years after Hazel's murder, Cushing and Schatzle continued to be active in Republican politics. Just a few weeks after the investigation fizzled out in late July, both men, along with Cushing's brother, James, were elected as delegates from the Eleventh Ward to the Republican County Committee—and, interestingly, they would regularly come into contact with other Republicans who were prominent in the investigation into Hazel's murder.

In 1910, Cushing was once again chosen to represent the Eleventh Ward on the Republican County Committee—this time joined by William Powers, and by Gilbert Miller, who had helped pull Hazel's body from the pond. The secretary of the committee that year was Duncan Kaye. O'Brien's former employer George B. Wellington was elected an at-large member. When the Republicans marched to their state convention in Saratoga Springs that same year, Cushing and Miller were selected as aides to the parade's chief of staff: Thomas Hislop, Hazel's first employer.

Cushing also seemingly reaped the benefits of being a loyal Republican soldier: the year of Hazel's murder, 1908, marked the last time he worked in a saloon; soon after, he was employed as a shipper at a collar-and-cuff factory called Frisbie, Coon & Co. in Troy. Frisbie, Coon & Co. was incorporated that year for the purposes of taking over the operations of a factory on that same site in South Troy that had declared bankruptcy. Notably, among the directors of Frisbie, Coon & Co. was James S. Sherman, yet another Republican—who at that time happened to be the sitting vice president of the United States. In 1914, Frisbie, Coon & Co. itself dissolved, a casualty of another bankruptcy and a cloud of messy charges of fraudulent financial practices.

Although not from a family of note, Cushing had managed to establish relationships with many of the most powerful men of the time in Troy through his involvement in Republican politics. These relationships had also been cultivated during his military service; he served as a sergeant in Company C, Second Regiment of the Troy Citizens Corps—which would morph into the New York National Guard—having enlisted in 1903 as a private. Among those in the Citizens Corps with whom he would have rubbed shoulders, and whose orders he would have followed, were two of Hazel's employers: Major Thomas Hislop and Lieutenant John H. Tupper.

Questions and Possible Answers

If Cushing and Schatzle were in fact responsible for Hazel's murder, four questions emerge, all interrelated:

What was their motive?

Were investigators cognizant of their guilt?

And, if they were, why didn't they arrest them?

Would powerful officials like Jarvis O'Brien, Duncan Kaye, or William Powers have influenced the investigation—and risked their careers—to protect two twenty-something low-level Republican operatives?

There are questions that can never be definitely answered, but we can speculate, based on the evidence accumulated.

One possibility: that Cushing and Schatzle were acting at the bidding of one of Troy's elite. Perhaps Hazel had run afoul of one of her employers—or someone she had met through one of her employers—who decided he wanted "the problem" to simply disappear. For a South Troy girl who had been born and raised in the country, Hazel had managed to gain access to the households of some of the most influential men in Troy. Who knows what gossip and innuendo she was privy to as she scurried about the house attending to her chores, largely unnoticed, while the wealthy and powerful discussed their latest schemes and machinations? She easily could have overheard something she wasn't supposed to. If she tried to turn such information to her advantage, it could have proven fatal.

Or—even more salaciously—perhaps she had become romantically entangled with one of these power brokers, who was married and wanted to end the relationship but was afraid of what Hazel would do or say in her desperation to hang on. All of the doctors present at the autopsy concurred that Hazel was not pregnant at the time of death, but there was no definitive ruling as to whether she had ever been pregnant, and hell-raiser William Clemens and others in the press had speculated that that was the cause of her recuperation at the Taylor farmhouse the winter before she died.

The fact that Hazel was spotted alone on Taborton Road before her death at least once—and likely twice—without any visible means of transportation to wherever she was going next seems to reinforce the notion of a secret rendezvous.

There was a great deal of speculation about this in the press, especially from Clemens, who theorized that Hazel was planning to meet her secret lover at the pond and then elope. Reporters speculated that the lover was a married man who had no intention of leaving his family or jeopardizing his societal status, so his real intention in arranging—or at least consenting to—the tryst was to find a secluded place to "do away" with Hazel. Several names emerged as possible suspects in this scenario, including an unidentified Schenectady man and John Magner, the Pullman car train conductor, but there was never any concrete evidence to implicate any of them.

Men of Power

When Hazel left home to join the household of Thomas Hislop at the age of fourteen in 1902, he was at the peak of his political powers. "Honest Tom," as his boosters sometimes hailed him, had been reelected to his third consecutive term as Troy's city treasurer the year before, and he was contemplating a run for mayor the following year. When Hazel left his service four years later, at the age of eighteen—for reasons never publicly revealed—Hislop was out of public office completely, having lost his mayoral bid and been abandoned by his party as a result of internecine turmoil. He was also on the verge of being embroiled in a major political scandal involving the embezzlement of public funds by his former deputy, Frank Carrington, who was charged and ultimately convicted of the crime only weeks before Hazel's murder, in late May 1908. (Hislop was never charged but was later sued by the city over the missing funds.) And Hislop's troubles didn't begin and end with politics—he seemed to have continual difficulties with his business affairs, with many of his commercial ventures ending in bankruptcy or lawsuits.

After Hazel was shuffled off to work for the Tuppers, she found herself, refreshingly, in a different kind of environment. Leaving her familiar South Troy neighborhood behind, she was now just blocks away from the bustling epicenter of the city—Union Station—as well as the esteemed RPI campus. But she was also within walking distance of the red-light district, home to the brothels of Mame Faye, among others, as well as an excess of seedy bars and gambling clubs.

John H. Tupper, too, had run for mayor of Troy on the Republican ticket and lost, in 1897. His political roots went back to his time as a member of Frank Black's Committee of Public Safety. By the time Hazel came to work for him, he had recently stepped down from running his Black Diamond Coal Company, but he remained active in Troy socially and enjoyed traveling the world, accompanied by his Canadian wife, Adelaide. If the reports are to be believed, the Tuppers—the only family she worked for who didn't have children—were almost like grandparents to Hazel, especially Adelaide, who would bring her back souvenirs from their travels, like the brooch that was found on Hazel's body when it was pulled from Teal's Pond. Still, grandparents or not, they did move quickly to hire a replacement while Hazel was recuperating from her mysterious illness at her uncle's farmhouse in early 1908.

Hazel's final employer, RPI professor Edward Cary, was less distinguished than her previous two. He had twice been appointed Troy's city engineer, but his political ambitions did not seem to extend beyond that. And yet, like Thomas Hislop, he was caught up in a public scandal that occurred around the time Hazel was working for him. Faced with minor accusations of corruption within his department, Cary had been forced to take his name out of consideration for reappointment in October 1907, owing to a law passed in response to the scandal that prohibited city engineers from holding other jobs while in office. This was only a few months before Hazel came to work for the Carys.

There was also one person with at least a tangential connection to the case who was never interviewed—or even identified—by investigators, according to contemporaneous reports.

When detectives visited the Cary residence the night of July 18 accompanied by Clemens, they uncovered a trove of previously overlooked clues in the basement. Most of the attention was focused on the correspondence found in the waste bin, especially after Clemens couldn't help but publish the flirtatious (and somewhat disturbing) letter Hazel had received from Harry, her artist friend from the previous summer.

All but forgotten among these discoveries was a piece of paper with the name Florence Barker on it, signed over and over again, in Hazel's hand. Clemens was baffled, as Florence Barker was not known to be one of Hazel's friends. He speculated that perhaps Hazel was about to forge a new life for herself and adopt Florence Barker as an alias.

But who was Florence Barker? Clemens himself never found out. As far as we know, investigators never even looked.

If they had, they would have discovered Florence Barker living right across the street from Hazel and the Carys in the cul-de-sac at the end of stately Whitman Court.

Florence Barker had been Florence Herring before marrying wealthy Troy industrialist William Barker Jr., in 1899. Thirty-four years old in 1908, William Barker was a bookishly handsome man, of medium build, with black hair, and, according to his draft card, matching black eyes, a rare condition sometimes attributed to excessive melanin or extremely small irises (though oculists maintain that "black eyes" are really just a very dark brown). The Carys and the Barkers became close friends, and it seems likely that the Barkers knew Hazel, given that relationship and the proximity of their homes. *Something* prompted Hazel to write Florence Barker's name over and over on a slip of paper. What was it? The answer is unknown to this day—another in a litany of mysteries involving the life and death of Hazel Drew.

Any of these men could have been motivated to have Hazel killed. None were seriously investigated at the time. All had ties to the Republican Party, and it seems easier to accept that O'Brien and/or certain of his detectives would have been motivated to cover up the activity of Cushing and Schatzle if they had been acting for someone with influence in Troy—especially someone who was active in the party. But it is also conceivable that they were protecting Schatzle and Cushing simply because of secrets about the inner workings of the party that the two young men were privy to.

On the Record

For some reason, certain newspapers also seemed exceedingly protective of Cushing's identity. Earlier in the investigation, the *Troy Record*, run by lifelong Republican David Banks Plum, had distinguished itself from the mob of papers by providing quotes from an anonymous source within the investigation—these comments were at odds with the official stance of the doctors, who had unanimously dismissed suicide as a possibility. The mostly likely source of these comments was either Duncan Kaye or William Powers, or both.

When the story of the Hoffays first broke on Tuesday, July 21, the *Record* rushed in excitedly, along with a majority of the newspapers, to report on "what is considered an important clue."

"This bit of information is considered of great importance by the district attorney's office and every effort is now being put forth to ascertain the identity of the two men," the *Record* reported.

However, less than twenty-four hours later, the tone of the *Record*'s reporting on the new lead completely changed, casting oddly worded, unsubstantiated aspersions upon the validity of the Hoffays' story. "The development of yesterday is not accepted as being final, for the reason that the truth of the narrative is yet to be established," the paper said, adding that "the district attorney and his corps of assistants have worked diligently, and while their efforts have been untiring no direct suspicion rests upon anyone yet mentioned in the investigation. Yesterday's journey of the police who are stationed at Sand Lake revealed only another story and the absolute accuracy of it has yet to be determined."

No reason was stated for the abrupt dismissal of the hot new lead, but the change in reporting happened at the same time that "Detective

Kaye said that they had obtained trace of one wagon seen on the road by the Hoffeys [*sic*], but the occupants when examined proved an alibi."

The next day, the *Record* continued its coverage of the Hoffays but completely sidestepped the relevance of the two men and the carriage they spotted near the pond, instead leading with the headline **Taylor Again in the Foreground: Hoffey [*sic*] Saw Him in Carriage with Young Woman**, picking up on the discrepancy between Taylor's memory of the last time he saw Hazel and the accounts of William Hoffay and livery driver John Abel. Ultimately, the discrepancy between Taylor and his neighbors didn't have much bearing on the case, but it did help to bury the Hoffays' story.

There's Nothing to See Here

If motivated to do so, Detectives Kaye and Powers certainly seemed to have the ability to shape the narrative as reported by the *Record*, especially given the fact that they were all Republican brethren.

Some reports said that it was William Powers who roused Cushing out of bed in the early hours of July 21; others said Duncan Kaye. But it was Duncan Kaye who told the press the man had been looked into and cleared. Kaye was also called into the meeting with the mysterious stranger, likely Cushing, at the courthouse that same morning.

Could Kaye have been pulled into the middle of a deep conspiracy already in progress and chosen to look the other way?

Or, if not Kaye, perhaps Powers?

Although Kaye was O'Brien's chief deputy in the field, he largely operated out of Troy and Albany. Powers, supported by Troy city detective Louis Unser, headed the investigation out in the country and was afforded a great deal of discretion as to which leads he would pursue. Powers and Unser spent most of the investigation in Sand Lake, staying at Crape's Hotel and phoning in regular updates to O'Brien back in Troy.

After the detectives had talked to the Hoffays and followed up with the Rollmans and Gundrum, Powers returned to Troy, leaving Unser behind in the country. Upon learning that the wagon had been rented at Shyne's, he or Kaye—or perhaps both—queried Cushing and quickly cleared him of any wrongdoing, before the day's papers were published. Although the *Evening Telegram* reported that Cushing's story "is being investigated," there is no mention in any report of investigators questioning the woman—never publicly identified—who allegedly accompanied him.

And Powers did his best to discredit the Hoffays' account by telling the *Albany Argus* of July 25 that "little reliance could be placed" on their story of seeing a horse and wagon near Teal's Pond on the night of July 7.

Kaye and Powers were trusted by O'Brien. Both had connections to the local Republican papers, enabling them to influence the public narrative as needed. Both likely knew who Cushing was before they went to his house that night, from their involvement in street-level Troy politics. Two years after the Drew case, Cushing and Powers were selected to represent Troy's Eighth and Eleventh Wards, respectively, for the Rensselaer County Republican General Committee; the committee's secretary that year was Duncan Kaye.

Politics aside, there was another connection among Cushing, Schatzle, and Powers: geography. Powers was born and raised in the same small South Troy neighborhood, clustered around the Poesten Kill creek, that Cushing and Schatzle hailed from. Additionally, in 1902, Eva Lapp—Hazel's cousin and close friend, and in two years' time her sister-in-law, upon marrying Joseph Drew—worked as a domestic servant in this same neighborhood, at 292 Fourth Street, the house next door to the Cushings.

And one other person central to this case also had ties to that neighborhood, having spent her formative years there: Hazel Drew herself.

Between 1901 and 1908, the Drews spent about five years living in South Troy. Initially, they stayed at 217 Fourth Street and then moved to nearby 246 Second, before departing to stay with William Taylor in Sand Lake for a few years. The Drews returned to the city in 1907, settling a few blocks away, at 400 Fourth Street. Hazel, only sixteen at the time, didn't move with her parents back to Sand Lake, staying in the city by herself while living with, and working for, the Hislops, at 360 Third Street, which she had done since the tender age of fourteen. Despite growing up in the country, Hazel ended up spending the entirety of her teenage years in that close-knit South Troy neighborhood.

Powers, Cushing, and Schatzle were all older than Hazel, but not by much. When Hazel turned eighteen in her last year at the Hislops', Powers was twenty-five, Cushing twenty-three, and Schatzle twenty-seven. Additionally, they had siblings close to Hazel in age: Schatzle had an older and younger brother who still lived at home in 1906; Cushing's brother, James, was in his early twenties, and his sisters, Delia and Mary, were each a few years younger and older than Hazel, respectively. With the knowledge that Hazel spent her teenage years in such close proximity to this gang, coupled with her outgoing and sociable nature, it seems more than reasonable to conclude that she knew these men, and they her.

We spoke to eminent historians, with decades of accumulated local knowledge, having been born and raised in Troy, and discussed the little neighborhood in South Troy that Hazel was from. We specifically asked if it was likely that Hazel had known Cushing, Schatzle, and Powers based on where they all lived and grew up. Rensselaer County historian Kathy Sheehan replied, "Absolutely, absolutely, absolutely true. That's true, and that was true until probably twenty years ago." Don Rittner, who has authored more than twenty books on Troy and its surrounding area agreed: "They definitely knew each other. Troy is a bunch of neighborhoods and these neighborhoods . . . they could be up to six blocks, ya know? So you knew everybody within a six-block radius."

In the years following the Hazel Drew murder case, William Powers would continue to have great success in Rensselaer County politics. Even before the Drew investigation, he had proven to be more ambitious than the average county detective. In 1905, at the age of twenty-four, he founded a social/political activist group, still active in 1908, imaginatively titled the William P. Powers Association. Powers even purchased a building on the northwest corner of Washington and Hill Streets for his headquarters. The actual raison d'être of the William P. Powers Association's existence is hard to find, but its name gives us a clue as to whom it was meant to benefit.

In addition to his career as county detective, Powers was at various points in his life a lawyer, public notary, and parole officer before retiring. In 1914, he was elected sheriff of Rensselaer County on the Republican ticket, campaigning as a moral crusader ready to clean up the filthy streets with an ardor reminiscent of the old days, when the spirit of the American Protective Association had infested Troy. After promising on the campaign trail to eliminate the evil sins of gambling in all its forms, Powers was true to his word—he went after not only the pool halls and saloons in downtown Troy but also church picnics and community groups over their raffles.

Final Ruling

Here's one possible solution to the question of what happened to Hazel Drew the night of her murder, which we believe to be quite credible.

What if Hazel didn't take the trolley out to Averill Park, but got a lift from Cushing and Schatzle? We know she was fond of taking rides for leisure and that just two weeks earlier, on June 21, she and Minnie Taylor had been out in a carriage with two men, never identified. She had reportedly planned another trip with the same two men after July 4. This would explain not only how she got to Taborton, but also how she planned to return to Troy that night.

Remember that on Monday, July 6, a man had called Shyne's livery asking that a rig be sent to Seventh and Congress Streets; Shyne replied that the livery didn't deliver carriages, and the man would have to come in to rent it himself, which he did the following day, returning after midnight. Again, the salient fact here is that the intersection of Seventh and Congress Streets is one block away from 1617 Seventh Street—the home of Joseph and Eva Lapp Drew—and also near both Cushing's saloon and the bar that employed George Lindermann.

Mark Marshall, who lives in Poestenkill, informs us that there's a back road that would have taken Hazel, Cushing, and Schatzle up around the Hollow on Taborton Road by way of Oak Hill Road, enabling them to bypass Sand Lake's Four Corners at the bottom of the mountain, where they might have been more easily spotted. This would explain why the Rollmans, Smith, Gundrum, and others never saw the rig on their way up or down the mountain. It would also explain why nobody ever came forward admitting to giving Hazel a ride out to Taborton. Marshall believes Cushing and Schatzle dropped Hazel off on the road and then went on to a tavern, arranging to pick her up at Teal's Pond on the way back to Troy.

The answer to the mystery of what Hazel Drew was doing on Taborton Mountain near dusk on Tuesday, July 7, 1908, might be that she was out joyriding with Cushing and Schatzle and asked to be dropped off near Teal's Pond because—as she told her friend Lillian Robertson—it was a place of solace for her.

What happened next? Sometime after seven thirty, Cushing and Schatzle met Hazel at the pond—and bludgeoned her to death. The murder weapon: perhaps, as Marshall suggests, a blackjack, a short, easily concealable strap filled with lead. Blackjacks were commonly used at the time to bust up bar fights, meaning that bartender William Cushing would have had easy access to one. Saps, as they were known, were specifically designed to deliver concussive blows without lacerating the skull—precisely the type of blow that killed Hazel Drew.

Why kill her? Maybe there was some political secret behind it. Or maybe, as Marshall believes, it wasn't premeditated. They had an argument. Or they were drunk, and Hazel resisted their advances.

Whatever the reason, they had to act quickly to cover up the crime, so they dumped the body into the pond and were disturbed by the Hoffays just as they were doing so.

And so, after five years of intensive research and deliberation, we have concluded that Hazel Drew was likely murdered on the night of July 7 by William Cushing and Fred Schatzle, both of whom she had known for years. Cushing and Schatzle were protected from justice by William Powers and possibly his fellow detective Duncan Kaye. The fact that the two detectives apparently worked so earnestly to solve the crime for much of the investigation is the most damning evidence against them, considering how they treated William Cushing and Fred Schatzle once it was discovered they might have been involved.

Judgment on District Attorney Jarvis O'Brien's complicity is more complex. It can be argued that he was overwhelmed by the circus-like atmosphere of the case, inflamed by the media. There is no doubt O'Brien was politically ambitious, with deep connections to his Republican brethren; given his role in leading the investigation, there is certainly the possibility that he might have been involved in the cover-up. At the very least, he placed too much trust in those close to him, allowing his deputies excessive discretion; he didn't even personally interview the Hoffays—who possessed possibly the most important clue in the entire investigation—until the inquest.

By then, it was too late.

When Hazel Drew met her tragic end that fateful July night at Teal's Pond, she left behind innumerable unanswered questions—many of which still linger, so many years after her death.

This is one possible solution—our solution, based on all the evidence accumulated: interviews, research, conversations, and multiple memorable trips to Sand Lake and Troy.

After spending so much time in her world, perhaps we even started to understand a little bit about who Hazel Drew was: a complex young woman, dynamic, sociable, industrious, adventurous, and—perhaps most defining of all—mysterious.

We hope that her spirit now rests in peace.

Epilogue

The investigation into Hazel Drew's murder exposed many of the people she touched and impacted, from all walks of life, during her brief time on earth. And while Hazel's story came to a sad end in early July of 1908, for everyone else, life continued inexorably onward, if in sometimes surprising directions.

The Investigators
District Attorney Jarvis P. O'Brien

In the fall of 1908, a few months after the investigation into Hazel Drew's murder came to a close, Jarvis O'Brien was defeated at the polls by fellow Republican Abbott Jones. Jones had been spurned by Republican Party leaders, who instead backed O'Brien's failed bid to secure a third term. While typical intraparty battles led to O'Brien's ouster (Jones's coalition of voters included rogue Republicans and rival Democrats), the lingering shadow of Hazel's killer escaping justice also likely played a part in his downfall.

After his loss to Jones, O'Brien receded from public life and focused on his career as the regional legal representative for the Boston and Maine Railroad. He maintained residences in his hometown of Fort Edward, where he raised and auctioned off cattle, and his adopted home of Troy. O'Brien attempted a political comeback only once, in 1926, running as a Republican for county judge. He suffered defeat one last time, at the hands of Judge James F. Brearton.

O'Brien died in Troy at the age of seventy-two, leaving behind his widow, Jessie, after nearly twenty-eight years of marriage. The O'Briens had no children.

County Detective Duncan C. Kaye

O'Brien's top lieutenant, Duncan Kaye, was also soon out of a job at the DA's office following his boss's defeat at the polls. Unlike O'Brien, Kaye, who was a loyal party man but never ran for public office himself, continued to thrive in Rensselaer County politics. He helped party bosses organize the rank and file and filled a variety of key positions within the party, including Republican state committee member and secretary of the Rensselaer County Republican Committee.

Kaye was rewarded for his loyalty with a series of jobs in state government, including positions at the Prison Department, the Department of Purchase, the Department of Fiscal Supervision, and the Department of Standards and Purchase.

Kaye lived in Troy with his wife, Louise, until he passed away in 1943. They had three sons.

County Detective William P. Powers

Like Duncan Kaye, William Powers only seemed to flourish in the wake of the unsolved Drew murder. In fact, he and Kaye remained close in the years that followed, both serving in a variety of leadership roles in Rensselaer County politics.

Unlike Kaye, Powers did seek public office and was elected as sheriff of Rensselaer County in 1914.

There is evidence that Powers's ambitions transcended Rensselaer County, as in the waning days of World War I he traveled throughout

Europe to assist in the war-relief efforts of the Knights of Columbus. His later travels included a visit to Cuba, for reasons unknown.

County Detective John H. Murnane

John Murnane remained in Troy and secured work as a bookkeeper and a clerk in the county courthouse. He died at the age of eighty-eight in 1950.

Troy City Detective Louis Unser

Louis Unser had come to Troy from Germany as a teenager and remained in his adopted home for the entirety of his ensuing life. He retired from the police force in 1923, in his early fifties, and passed away nineteen years later. Unser was a passionate gardener, and his displays won many awards at flower shows.

Troy City Detective John W. Lawrenson

John Lawrenson would go on to have a long and illustrious career in law enforcement, with involvement in many high-profile cases, before retiring at the age of seventy-three in 1935. Less than a year later, Lawrenson was involved in one final criminal case of note, in which, in a reversal of roles, he was the victim. While taking a walk on the streets of Troy with his son, Lawrenson was attacked by a "crazed" man who police suspected may have been on drugs. Michael Franco, a career criminal who was due in federal court that day on charges of peddling narcotics, sent a barrage of gunfire from a .38-caliber Colt the Lawrensons' way before taking his own life with a final bullet. No clear motive was established, although investigators suspected Franco may have been seeking revenge for Detective Lawrenson having arrested him multiple times in the past. Lawrenson was hit three times, once each in his thigh, wrist, and abdomen, but survived, calmly telling police at the hospital, "That was just a fellow taking pop shots at me."

Lawrenson died in 1941 at the age of seventy-eight.

Dr. Elias B. Boyce

In 1909, at the age of seventy-one, Elias Boyce, who had long been active in the Rensselaer County Republican Party, was elected Rensselaer County coroner, succeeding Morris Strope, who had presided over the Drew inquest. Nearly a year after his election, Boyce passed away, and Strope was reappointed to fill out his term.

Dr. Elmer E. Reichard

Elmer Reichard continued his country practice before retiring in 1929 with thirty-nine years of active service in Sand Lake. He passed away at his home in Glass Lake in 1941 at the age of seventy-four.

Dr. Harry O. Fairweather

In April 1909, less than a year after the inquest into Hazel Drew's murder, Harry Fairweather, while on a call as a volunteer fireman, was at the top of an extension ladder when it abruptly snapped, throwing him thirty feet to the sidewalk below. The fall fractured his skull and caused internal injuries, which resulted in his death at a hospital two days later. Fairweather left behind his wife, Rosella, whom he had married two years prior. He was only thirty-four years old.

William M. Clemens

After his abrupt departure from Troy, self-described world-famous criminologist William Clemens continued writing about fictional and nonfictional crimes (sometimes evoking a little of each in the same story). He also authored numerous biographies and was noted for contributing greatly to the then-nascent study of genealogy. Clemens died in 1931 of a heart attack at the age of seventy-one. His obituary incorrectly described him as Mark Twain's nephew.

The Drews

Hazel's family had more than its share of struggles before her tragic demise, and its fortunes didn't improve greatly afterward. John Drew continued to struggle to find meaningful employment, and as a result the household remained financially and emotionally unstable. A few years after the murder, the family moved back in with William Taylor in Sand Lake, less than a mile from where Hazel's body was found. Apparently, harsh economic realities forced John Drew and William Taylor to get over whatever bad blood existed between them. Their reconciliation was short-lived, however, and the Drews soon returned to Troy, to a new home on Hill Street.

John Drew died at the age of fifty-nine in 1914, leaving the widowed Julia A. Drew and their three younger children in desperate straits. A few months following John's death, Hazel's youngest sister, Emma, sixteen years old at the time, had to be tracked down by police after running away from the House of Shelter, a charity establishment whose purpose was "reclaiming and reforming women who had strayed from the path of virtue and were living in vice."

Hazel's older brother, Joseph H. Drew, remained in Troy at his bakery for a few years before leaving the city to embark on a long career in the railroad industry. He was widowed in 1930 when Eva Lapp Drew, his wife and Hazel's close confidant, passed away in her forties. By the time Joseph died in 1959 at the age of seventy-two, he had returned to Troy.

Willie M. Drew found employment with the city of Troy's Public Works Department, and in 1944 he severely injured himself in a tree-cutting accident, forcing him to retire. Willie died in 1956, leaving behind his widow, Mary.

Hazel's sister Carrie, who had married a local man named Charles J. Selleys, died in a one-car accident in Schodack, New York, at the age of seventy-three.

Emma Drew Houser, the last of the line, died in 1978 at the age of seventy-nine, the same age her mother, Julia, was when she passed away in 1941.

Both of Hazel's parents are buried in the same Barberville cemetery as Hazel.

The Taylors
Minnie Taylor

The life of Hazel's aunt took a dramatic turn a little more than a year after her niece's murder when the forty-one-year-old Minnie Taylor, portrayed by the press during the investigation as something of an old maid, married Edward J. Filieau, a widower from Connecticut. Minnie would outlive her husband by fifteen years and reportedly spent much of that time in a continuous cycle of visiting relatives who dreaded her extensive stays.

William Taylor

Like his younger sister Minnie, William Taylor defied the odds and found love in later years, convincing Julia C. Miller to marry him in 1911. The couple later moved to Troy, where William found work as a caretaker. After Julia died, Taylor moved in with his sister Julia, and Carrie and Willie Drew. He died in 1934 at the age of eighty-one.

The Employers
Thomas W. Hislop

Thomas Hislop's political career effectively came to an end following his failed independent bid for mayor of Troy in 1905. Hislop would inveigle his way back in with Republican Party leadership and remained active in politics, but never again ran for public office. The closest "Honest Tom" ever came to being entrusted with public funds again was as a treasurer for the Masons.

Hislop also remained active in the National Guard, rising to the rank of colonel. Although he was a veteran of the Spanish-American War, most of his subsequent accomplishments seemed to involve organizing and presiding over parades and other ceremonial exercises.

John H. Tupper

John H. Tupper had already retired by the time Hazel lived with and worked for him, and soon thereafter he would move to New York City. Tupper spent his golden years traveling all over the US and Europe with Adelaide, his Canadian wife of more than fifty years, who survived him when he passed away in 1919 at the age of seventy-six.

Edward R. Cary

Following the scandals and accusations that led to his early exit as Troy's city engineer in 1908, Professor Edward Cary avoided the political spotlight and focused on his academic career, although he would continue to be awarded an occasional side job as inspector or arbiter for the city or county over the years.

Cary retired from Rensselaer Polytechnic Institute in 1936 as the head of the Department of Geodesy and Railroad Engineering, after spending forty-eight years on the faculty of the university he had graduated from. Years later, RPI named a student dormitory Cary Hall in his memory, and it is still in use today.

Edward and Mary's daughter, Helen, who was eleven years old when Hazel lived with the Carys, passed away in 1986, just short of her ninetieth birthday.

The Locals
Rudy Gundrum

Rudy Gundrum continued his hard-living ways until passing away at the age of sixty-six in 1942. By then, his wife, Carrie, had tired of his shenanigans and left him—an uncommon occurrence at the time. Rudy had at least eleven children that we know of, and many of his descendants reside in the area of Sand Lake to this day.

Frank Smith

Frank Smith remained in the Sand Lake area, continuing to find work as a farmhand and doing odd jobs, although he did move down the mountain from Taborton to Averill Park. He died in 1970.

Mystery Men
Edward Lavoie

In 1917, Edward Lavoie enlisted in the American Volunteer Motor Ambulance Corps, an organization founded by noted archaeologist Richard Norton during World War I to assist with the movement of Allied casualties from war-torn battlefields to the safety of French hospitals. A surprising number of future literary giants also were drawn to Norton's organization and others like it, including E. E. Cummings, Ernest Hemingway, and Dashiell Hammett. The army took over the administration of these ambulance-support organizations when the US entered the war in April 1917, and Cummings and many of his fellow artists balked at the idea of joining the military, as did twice-enlisted former soldier Lavoie, who left the corps and returned to the US in May 1917.

Lavoie married Theresa Yeager in 1920 and found work as a salesman in New York City, where the Lavoies raised their children, Joseph and Joan. He died at the age of seventy-four in Long Beach, California, in 1955.

John Magner

John Magner, another of the men who figured in the story of Hazel Drew's murder investigation and whose role was never firmly established, took an opposite path from Lavoie, leaving behind his career as a railway conductor and joining the New York City Police Department as a patrolman in 1910.

The Killers (???)
William Cushing

In the years after Hazel's murder, William Cushing continued to thrive within the Rensselaer County Republican machine. In 1912 Cushing was rewarded by the party for his years of loyalty with a cozy job working out of city hall and was appointed truancy officer for Troy's public school system.

He was also apparently friendly with Troy city police, appearing as a witness during the murder trial of Nicola Cunsoli, who had shot and killed Officer Michael McMahon on the streets of Troy in July of 1910. Cushing testified that after rushing to McMahon's side, the dying officer told him, "Cush, don't let him get away; he's a stranger, you'll know him." Detective John Lawrenson, one of O'Brien's men on the Drew case, was another witness at the trial.

Cushing remained active in the Troy Citizens Corps. He was a candidate for promotion to lieutenant when he died suddenly in 1913 from heart complications. He was thirty-one years old.

Fred Schatzle

In 1934, tragedy struck Fred Schatzle and his family after a kitchen fire in their apartment grew out of control in the middle of the night. Schatzle was woken by the smell of smoke and was able to help his wife and daughter escape the blaze. However, when he tried to make it to his son William's bedroom, he was driven back by the flames and forced to flee the building. Afterward, firemen discovered William's body, but he was unable to be revived.

Fred Schatzle died at the age of sixty-six in 1944.

~

There's one name conspicuously missing here, and that of course is Hazel Drew. Unlike the cast of characters who orbited around her in life or in death, Hazel never had a future—at least not literally. But she has endured in her own way—first as a cautionary tale about the dangers of walking through the foreboding woods of Taborton on dark summer nights, as told by a woman to her young grandson, and then as the inspiration for the celebrated television show that boy would grow up to create—more than eighty years after her death.

Occasionally, during our investigation, people would say to us, "Can't you just leave the poor girl alone?"

But *shouldn't* Hazel be remembered? "Pity me not," the ghost of Hamlet's father says to him, "but lend thy serious hearing to what I shall unfold." Hazel was a strong, vibrant, determined woman from a troubled family; she left home as a teenager to forge a new life for herself. By every indication, she refused to surrender to the darkness in her world. She embraced life with passion and never stopped dreaming of a brighter future—until those dreams were snatched from her on that sultry summer night of July 7, 1908.

Justice was never served. Nobody ever paid the price for her death. Authorities failed—at least publicly—to resolve every significant mystery that surfaced during the investigation. Hazel was just a poor country girl from a farm in Poestenkill, and life—for everyone else—went on. Many of the people who failed her lived long, prosperous lives, while Hazel's story faded from memory.

If not for Mark Frost and *Twin Peaks*, Hazel Drew might very well have remained forgotten.

Happily, she wasn't.

This has been Hazel's story. Remember her.

AUTHORS' NOTE

Over the course of the more than five years it took us to research and write this book, one of our primary objectives has been not only to highlight the inherent intrigue and drama in this story but to present the details and events that occurred as accurately as possible. This is a work of creative nonfiction; the facts of the case are presented as they happened, and while at certain intervals we imagined interior thoughts and conversations that might have taken place—often using actual quotes from papers as inspiration, but contextualizing them within scenes to enhance the immediacy—these are all based strictly on actual developments.

In addition to speaking with locals, descendants of persons involved with the case, historians, and other experts, we extensively reviewed any historical records and documents we could find. This included census records, military records, birth/wedding/death records, court cases, city directories, and, most importantly, newspaper records.

In fact, the abundance of newspaper stories covering the investigation led to an unexpected obstacle in getting at the truth of the story (and the crime). At first, each discovery of an original account of the same events from a completely different perspective was a blessing, adding valuable details and theories. However, the more we dug in, the more gaps and inconsistencies we encountered. It soon became obvious that human error and bias had crept into the reporting of the time, muddying the waters—and proving that what is past is present.

And so we had to review, assess, and distinguish reliable sources from unreliable ones. Local papers from Troy and Albany, and even reports from nearby Boston, we soon learned, were, for the most part, credible sources. The four Troy papers somewhat resembled the four gospels, with the same core events given different color and emphasis in each retelling, although strong consideration also had to be given to which political party the paper was aligned with, as this could shift the narrative dramatically.

Papers such as the *New York Times* and *Washington Post*, which are still published to this day, presented the relatively objective and generally high-quality reporting you would expect to see in their modern equivalents. Meanwhile, the tabloids from New York City, led by the sensationalist William Clemens, had to be taken with a grain of salt, although they definitely poked into areas other papers ignored, for one reason or another.

Regarding Clemens's favorite launching pad, the *World*, readers should also note that any variations on the title found cited in the text reflect only the particular edition of the same newspaper (e.g., *Evening World* or *Thrice-a-Week World*), and perhaps Pulitzer's goal of monopolizing the industry.

The peculiarities of the daily reporting on the case also played a key role in uncovering what we believe to have been a conspiracy between members of the press and detectives investigating the murder. In this time when newspapers were truly exploding onto the scene, there was pressure to beat rival papers to the next big headline, and many papers put out two editions daily for just that reason.

As we combed through hundreds and hundreds of articles, we would occasionally encounter an apparent ramification of this rush to print: certain articles would seem disjointed, as if written at different points in the day, with almost two sets of facts. An article would definitively state that detectives had looked all night to locate Rudy Gundrum but could find no trace of him, with expectations that the hunt would resume early the next morning. Meanwhile, a quote from Gundrum would show up a few paragraphs later. It seemed that in a rush to get the story out, and to include the most up-to-date details, copyediting was not always a priority.

While there are many other equally banal examples of the kinds of research and sifting of patchy historical records, mixing and matching, and working through baffling inconsistencies that accompany a project like this, such detail would likely not be of the greatest interest to our readers. However, this particular quirk is extremely relevant when looking at the story of the Hoffays' wagon sighting as reported in the July 21 *Troy Record*. The dramatic authorial shift in tone from optimism to pessimism, which must have occurred within a very short period of time, and without any associated evidence, is telling. The context of the article tells us the tonal change must have occurred around the time Powers and Kaye spoke with Cushing—essentially, the origins of the cover-up.

One significant omission in every newspaper's coverage—the role and treatment of women—was a reflection of society at large in the early 1900s, over a decade before ratification of the Nineteenth Amendment. Except in rare cases, women were not in the military and didn't hold public office. They frequently were not even listed in city directories—Hazel's name, for instance, never appeared in Troy's. Newspapers would often refer only to the husband's name when discussing a couple. The net result for us was that it was a lot easier to dig into possible motivations for someone like John Tupper, a retired union-busting coal baron, former Republican candidate for mayor, and captain in the Troy Citizens Corps, than it was to speculate about Adelaide Tupper, his wife, who we know was from Canada and gifted Hazel a pin, but very little else, for example.

We believe that the extensive amount of research undertaken has given Hazel's story the veracity it deserves. In fact, a by-product of this deep dive into early-twentieth-century media studies may have played a part in exposing the Fourth Estate's role in allowing her killers to go free.

ACKNOWLEDGMENTS

First and foremost, thanks to Mark Frost for sowing the seed that became this book, in addition to sharing his memories with us and contributing the foreword.

It nearly did take a village to research and write *Murder at Teal's Pond*, considering all the assistance we received from residents of Sand Lake and surroundings. We owe the deepest, deepest debts of gratitude especially to Sand Lake town historian Bob Moore and to Mark Marshall, whose awe-inspiring digging led to many of the revelations and theories you just read about. The construct of the book made it impossible to thank them in context, but their contributions cannot be overstated.

Many others who live in Sand Lake or trace their roots there were also incredibly generous with their time and insights. We would like to single out Roger Michael, Pat Wright, Ralph Timber, Priscilla Smith, Chuck Smyth, Mary French, Clare Radz, David Ernest, David Gundrum, Ed Gundrum, Kenny and Betty Teal, Donnie Budesheim, Candy Budesheim, Dave Marion, Fred Hoffay, and Robert Ernest.

A very, very special thanks to lifelong Taborton resident John Walsh, who passed away during the research and writing of this book, for sharing his unique thoughts and insights. RIP, John.

We were fortunate to connect with a roster of town historians who couldn't have been more knowledgeable, patient, and generous: Don Rittner, Kathy Sheehan, and Michael Barrett.

Jack Casey never failed to hop on a call to answer our questions about political corruption in turn-of-the-twentieth-century Troy, which was so mind-blowing that you could write a book about it, which Jack did (*The Trial of Bat Shea*).

Thanks to everyone at the Troy Public Library, the Richard G. Folsom Library at Rensselaer Polytechnic Institute (including Jenifer Monger), and the Hart Cluett Museum (especially Elsa Prigozy), all of whom helped us learn things we didn't know about a time we never *really* lived in, although at times it felt like we did, given our immersion.

Thanks to Kathleen Fleming for editorial guidance and to Jeremy Einbinder for research assistance.

Special thanks to Liz "Beth" Givens for all the pro bono legal advice.

Miscellaneous thanks to the following: S. Victor Fleischer and Ian McCullough of the University of Akron, Chad Habecker, Melissa Martin of the Mark Twain Project at the University of California, Berkeley, Susan Mullen Kalafut of the Rensselaer County District Attorney's Office, Rensselaer County clerk Frank J. Merola and his entire office (hat tips to Theresa Russman and Rebecca Clarkson), Ken Mueller, Gary Scharnhorst, Michael Schudson of Columbia University, Dr. Scott D. Swank of the National Museum of Dentistry, Terri Dunworth, James Fallon, Jack Fallon, and Ron Hughes.

In 2008, directors Penny Lane and Annmarie Lanesey made a documentary about Mame Faye titled *Sittin' on a Million*, the title being a phrase Faye reportedly used when recruiting prostitutes, which was a terrifically valuable resource for us; Penny also graciously shared her time and insights by phone.

Scott Ryan of *The Blue Rose* and Zachary Pincus-Roth of the *Washington Post* believed in this story from the start, and for that we are grateful to both of them. Janet and Jason Jarnagin followed us all the way to Washington, DC, to hear us talk about Hazel Drew when this book was in its nascency.

There are certain people for whom the words *thank you* seem woefully insufficient, whose support and encouragement have meant the world to us and kept us going through the *very* long process of researching and writing this book: our agent, Mitch Hoffman; Ken Siman and Benjamin Alfonsi of Metabook; Liz Pearsons, who acquired *Murder at Teal's Pond*, and Anne Brewer, who helped edit the book; Emily Freidenrich, our photo editor; Laura Berrett, production editor; Abby Bass, fact-checker; Lindsey Alexander, copyeditor; and the entire team at Thomas & Mercer. Thanks also to Jane Klain for the introduction to Metabook.

Last but certainly not least, we thank our families for all their love and support: Mariam, Alex, and Scout for David, and Mark cites his parents, Mary Anne and Joseph; Tara and Reggie; and extra thanks to Felix and Greta for their dutiful filing and research.

SELECTED BIBLIOGRAPHY

Books

Baatz, Simon. *The Girl on the Velvet Swing: Sex, Murder, and Madness at the Dawn of the Twentieth Century.* New York: Mulholland Books/ Little, Brown and Company, 2018.

Carpenter, Madolyn V. *Reviews and Reminiscences: A Brief History of the Town of Sand Lake.* Sand Lake, NY: Sand Lake Historical Society, 1979.

Casey, Jack. *The Trial of Bat Shea: A Novel.* Troy, NY: Diamond Rock, 2011.

Crunden, Robert M. *Ministers of Reform: The Progressives' Achievement in American Civilization, 1889–1920.* Champaign, IL: University of Illinois Press, 1982.

French, Mary D., and Robert J. Lilly. *Images of America: Sand Lake.* Charleston, SC: Arcadia, 2001.

French, Mary D., and Andrew St. J. Mace. *Images of America: Sand Lake Revisited.* Charleston, SC: Arcadia, 2007.

McDermid, Val. *Forensics: What Bugs, Burns, Prints, DNA, and More Tell Us about Crime*. New York: Grove, 2015.

Poestenkill Historical Society with Linda Sagendorf. *Images of America: Poestenkill*. Charleston, SC: Arcadia, 2008.

Rittner, Don. *A Century Perspective 1903–2003: History of the Troy Police Benevolent and Protective Association, Inc.* Troy, NY: Don Rittner, 2003.

Rittner, Don. *Images of America: Troy.* Charleston, SC: Arcadia, 1998.

Rittner, Don. *Images of America: Troy Revisited.* Charleston, SC: Arcadia, 2013.

Rittner, Don. *Legendary Locals of Troy.* Charleston, SC: Arcadia, 2011.

Rittner, Don. *Then & Now: Troy.* Charleston, SC: Arcadia, 2007.

Rittner, Don. *Troy: A Collar City History.* Charleston, SC: Arcadia, 2002.

Selzer, Richard. *Down from Troy: A Doctor Comes of Age.* East Lansing, MI: Michigan State University Press, 2001.

Stashower, Daniel. *Beautiful Cigar Girl: Mary Rogers, Edgar Allan Poe, and the Invention of Murder.* New York: Berkley, 2006.

Thompson, Harold W. *Body, Boots & Britches: Folktales, Ballads and Speech from Country New York.* 1939. Reprint, Syracuse, NY: Syracuse University Press by arrangement with J. B. Lippincott Company, 1967.

Video/Film

The Roosevelts: An Intimate History. Directed by Ken Burns; written by Geoffrey C. Ward; produced by Burns, Paul Barnes, and Pam Tubridy Baucom. Florentine Films/PBS, 2014.

Sittin' on a Million. Directed, written, and produced by Penny Lane and Annmarie Lanesey. With support from the Experimental Television Center and the LEF Moving Image Fund. WMHT Albany, 2008.

Newspapers

The authors also relied extensively on contemporaneous reports from the following newspapers:

Akron Beacon Journal (Akron, Ohio)

Albany Argus (Albany, New York)

Albany Evening Journal (Albany, New York)

Auburn Semi-Weekly Journal (Auburn, New York)

Baltimore Sun (Baltimore, Maryland)

Binghamton Press and Leader (Binghamton, New York)

The Boston Globe (Boston, Massachusetts)

Brooklyn Daily Eagle (Brooklyn, New York)

Buffalo Courier (Buffalo, New York)

The Buffalo Enquirer (Buffalo, New York)

The Buffalo Times (Buffalo, New York)

The Columbia Republican (Hudson, New York)

The Evening Journal (Wilmington, Delaware)

The Evening Star (Washington, DC)

The Evening Telegram (Albany, New York)

The Evening World (New York, New York)

Leavenworth Times (Leavenworth, Kansas)

Los Angeles Tribune (Los Angeles, California)

The Marion Star (Marion, Ohio)

New-York Daily Tribune (New York, New York)

New York Evening Telegram (New York, New York)

The New York Herald (New York, New York)

The New York Times (New York, New York)

New-York Tribune (New York, New York)

Northern Budget (Troy, New York)

Pittsburgh Dispatch (Pittsburgh, Pennsylvania)

Pittsburgh Leader (Pittsburgh, Pennsylvania)

Raleigh Times (Raleigh, North Carolina)

San Francisco Chronicle (San Francisco, California)

Schenectady Gazette (Schenectady, New York)

Scranton-Wilkes Barre Record (Wilkes-Barre, Pennsylvania)

St. Louis Post-Dispatch (St. Louis, Missouri)

The Sun (New York, New York)

Syracuse Herald (Syracuse, New York)

Syracuse Journal (Syracuse, New York)

Thrice-a-Week World (New York, New York)

The Times Record (Troy, New York)

Times Union (Albany, New York)

Troy Daily Press (Troy, New York)

Troy Record (Troy, New York)

Troy Times (Troy, New York)

The Washington Herald (Washington, DC)

The Washington Post (Washington, DC)

Washington Times (Washington, DC)

The World (New York, New York)

INDEX

Index

Index

ABOUT THE AUTHORS

David Bushman, a longtime TV curator at the Paley Center for Media, is the author of *Conversations with Mark Frost: "Twin Peaks," "Hill Street Blues," and the Education of a Writer* and coauthor of *Twin Peaks FAQ* and *Buffy the Vampire Slayer FAQ*. He is an adjunct professor of communication arts at Ramapo College of New Jersey, as well as a former TV editor at *Variety* and program director at TV Land. David lives in New York City with his wife and two daughters.

Mark T. Givens works as a consultant for the federal government and is the creator and host of the *Twin Peaks*–centric podcast *Deer Meadow Radio* (www.deermeadowradio.libsyn.com). He lives a sometimes strange and wonderful life with his wife and three children in Washington, DC, where he is currently brainstorming concepts for his next book.